ANDRÉ THE GIANT

ANDRÉ THE

POCKET BOOKS

New York   London   Toronto   Sydney

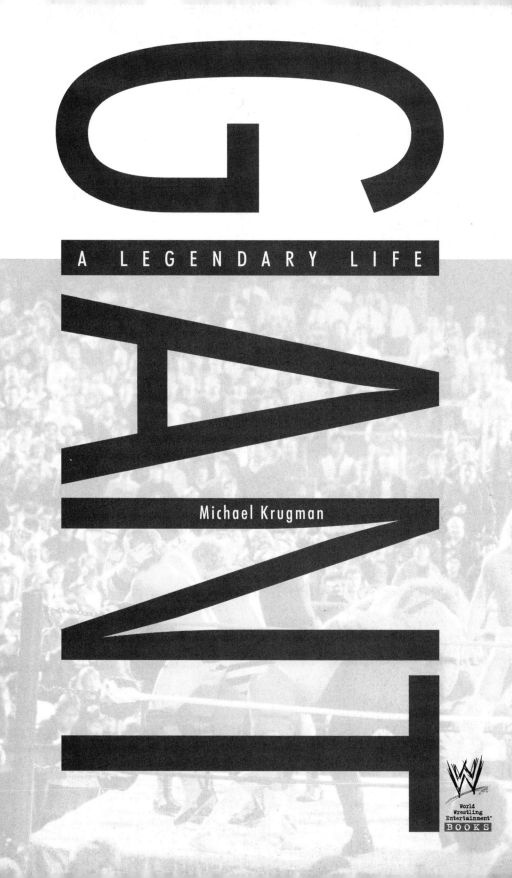

G

A LEGENDARY LIFE

ANT

Michael Krugman

World Wrestling Entertainment BOOKS

Pocket Books
A Division of Simon & Schuster, Inc.
1230 Avenue of the Americas
New York, NY 10020

This book is a publication of Pocket Books, a division of
Simon & Schuster, Inc., under exclusive license from
World Wrestling Entertainment, Inc.

Photo on page 163 Courtesy of the McMahon family.
Photos on pages vi–59, 342 Courtesy of *Pro Wrestling Illustrated*
Photographs.
All other photos Copyright © 2009 World Wrestling Entertainment,
Inc. All Rights Reserved.

First Pocket Books trade paperback edition January 2009

POCKET and colophon are registered trademarks of
Simon & Schuster, Inc.

For information about special discounts for bulk purchases,
please contact Simon & Schuster Special Sales at 1-800-456-6798
or business@simonandschuster.com.

Designed by Richard Oriolo

Visit us on the World Wide Web
http://www.simonsays.com
http://www.wwe.com

Manufactured in the United States of America

10 9 8 7 6 5 4 3 2 1

ISBN-13: 978-1-4165-4112-7
ISBN-10:   1-4165-4112-8

For my father,

a Giant in his own right . . .

Boss.

I'm very happy, traveling all over the world. I'm very happy to see all those people, all different people, and all different country. And lots of promoter, wrestling promoter, and lots of fans around to see me, and that's why I'm proud. I just want to make everybody happy.

—ANDRÉ THE GIANT

He was "the Eighth Wonder of the World," the biggest attraction in the history of professional wrestling. At seven-foot-four, 450 pounds, André the Giant was a living, breathing legend, the kind of make-believe figure usually encountered only in fairy tales. ■ For two decades, André Rene Rousimoff towered over the professional wrestling stage like a colossus, winning over fans of all ages with his humble manner, boundless charm, and fearsome charisma in the ring. An exceptional performer whose very presence was enough to get the crowd on its feet, the French-born Gargantua became one of the most recognizable athletes in all the world, second only to Muhammad Ali. In an age when wrestling stars were ghettoized from the mainstream, André crossed over to become a transcendent cultural phenomenon, with acting roles that are now considered classics by a generation.

While he was a very public figure, André was in many ways a very private man. The Giant was largely trapped in a world he never made, separated from even those closest to him by a language barrier, by his physical stature, and by his worldwide celebrity.

Outside of the spotlight, this astounding athlete struggled for years with his myriad difficulties caused by his size and his stardom. Worse, André fought a constant war with crippling pain caused both by his profession and by the disease that made him who he was. Taken together, these things served to mask rather than accentuate André's true persona.

For André, life and wrestling were one and the same. The stories he told in the ring, the excitement he created in his cheering fans, these were what counted.

What follows is a life history of his World Wrestling Federation career, collecting landmark matches and unforgettable bouts, a series of snapshots from a life overflowing with memorable moments. Offering commentary and perspective is an array of witnesses, including some of the people closest to André. Most often, the tale is told by the tape—move-by-move renderings of some of André's most significant battles.

The story they tell is of a truly unique man, a larger-than-life legend whose gift for entertaining audiences was his greatest strength.

ANDRÉ THE GIANT

André's father, Boris Rousimoff, migrated to France from Bulgaria

in 1934. A fellow farmworker—who had himself emigrated from

Poland—introduced Boris to his sister, Marianne, and in 1938,

the two married. A small, sturdy woman with the figure of a fire

hydrant and wild frizzy hair, she quickly presented Boris with

children, beginning with Antoine and Hélène. ■ The family

struggled as World War II wreaked havoc on the European continent, but somehow, they managed to survive. André Rene was born on May 19, 1946, followed shortly thereafter by Mauricette and Jacques.

A hale and hearty man over six feet, Boris built his family a home in Molien, a bucolic farming village approximately forty miles outside Paris. It was just a small farm, but it was fertile and productive enough to feed the Rousimoffs.

Known as Dédé from his little sister Mauricette's mispronunciation of his name, André was a handsome boy, baby-faced and charming. But as he got older, he kept growing and growing, his jaw and forehead becoming distorted in appearance. Though it was clear that there was something unusual about the boy, his condition went undiagnosed by the country doctors.

André was sent to school in nearby Ussy-sur-Marne. Having grown up on the farm, with only his family for companionship, André loved going to school, especially the social aspect of being around people. Many years later, during production of *The Princess Bride,* André would tell stories of how the Nobel Prize–winning playwright Samuel Beckett used to pick him up when he would hitchhike to school.

Circumstances forced him to abandon his education at the age of eleven, at which time he joined his father and brother at work on the farm. As he entered his teens, André was well over six feet tall, with the physical appearance of a fully grown man. He was strong and athletic and, like all French boys, loved playing soccer. At the age of eighteen, André made the acquaintance of a local wrestling promoter who saw *beaucoup* francs in the oversize young man. He introduced André to the art of *le catch,* and the young athlete soon began wrestling around Paris and its environs. He adopted the ring name of "Geant Ferre"—after a mythical French giant à la Paul Bunyan—which soon became "Jean Ferre."

In 1966, André was befriended by Frank Valois, a Montreal-born wrestler and promoter. Valois became André's most trusted adviser and business manager, finding his charge work wrestling throughout Europe, including Germany and England. It was around the same time that André first met British wrestler and future World Wrestling Federation commentator Lord Alfred Hayes. Years later, Hayes would recall his first encounter with André and the friendship that blossomed between the two men in a witty and touching essay published in the official company publication.

BOUND FOR GLORY . . .

by Lord Alfred Hayes

Although England and France have produced many, many fine wrestlers, one country holds the honor for having given birth to the most incredible wrestler the world has ever seen. This country, of course, is France, and the tremendous understatement I have just made when I refer to an incredible wrestler is specifically bound to André the Giant. When one talks about André the Giant, one also talks of not just the greatest professional wrestler of all time, but also the greatest professional athlete that has ever lived. I wonder if we will ever see the likes of such a person in professional athletics again.

I had made my wrestling headquarters in the comfy district of Place Blanche, which lies within the shadow of the hill of Montmartre. One day before departing for a wrestling engagement at a town near LeMans racecourse, the French wrestling promoter, Maurice Duran, phoned me and asked if I would pick up a young wrestler who would be waiting for me at the Porte-de-Versaille, one of the Gates of Paris. My response was of course, I would be delighted to. In those days as indeed now, I enjoyed impressing upon young rookies how to mind their manners and become decent people without swollen heads. Here was my chance to really give this young French wrestler an earful of my "puritanical moralizing."

With this pleasant thought in mind, I proceeded to the rendezvous where I would pick up this young lad. Imagine my surprise upon reaching my destination and discovering a raw-boned seventeen-year-old French youth who stood almost seven feet tall and grinned at me in the most disarming manner. He spoke no English, which may have been a blessing had I not spoken French. Upon discovering that I could speak French, he immediately began to lecture me! He would gesticulate with each sentence, almost causing a major disaster with practically every turn of the wheel. His booming laughter came from deep down in his stomach and filled my small European car with such decibels of noise, I really thought my eardrums would burst! It suddenly dawned on me this "boy" was not ordinary, either mentally or physically.

Eyeing him slyly, I inquired if he knew who his opponent would be that evening. "I know his name," he replied. "His name is Jacques Ducrez."

"But do you know anything about this man?" I persisted.

"No," he said, "I do not," and quite honestly, he did not seem to care.

"Jacques Ducrez," I said, "is probably the cruelest wrestler in the whole of France. He is a black-hearted man who knows no mercy and will coldly strike you down. He will probably take a mere kid like you and finish your wrestling career with one hold."

Naturally I expected such a young person to at least show some apprehension. However, André looked at me, laughed, and then with a wink of one of his bright eyes said, "You are amusing me, please continue."

From that moment on I had the feeling I was chauffeuring a young athlete who was definitely destined for fame, and whose mother country, France, was certainly not big enough to contain his irresistible spirit to say nothing of his huge dimensions.

Many people talk about the miracle of André the Giant, some few people, myself fortunate to be amongst them, have had the luck to be close to his development, and yet this miracle that is André definitely seems to have an almost fairy(tale)-like quality to me. I say almost because it is a positive fact that André the Giant does exist. Watching him the other evening destroy two men with a single blow, one knows his existence is indelibly printed into the annals of professional wrestling.

Born in Grenoble, his father a French mountaineer and his mother coming from a noble Bulgarian family, his childhood environment equipped him adequately for the strenuous life of the professional wrestler. . . . His reputation as a fair and just wrestler is without blemish. His massive size and strength have already made him legendary and here indeed is the perfect example of a "hero" who has become a legend in his own lifetime.

When André travels to countries where one might think he would go in trepidation, it is the other way around. When André is touring

MICHAEL KRUGMAN

Japan, top wrestlers suddenly find time for vacationing or perhaps visiting Mama.

One might ask, is it possible that here in André the Giant is an invincible wrestler. An improbable task for anybody to overcome his advantage in weight, strength, size and skill. I would have to answer this is probably a correct assumption. However, Lady Luck has not always been the companion of our towering superman. It has always been difficult for André to obtain world championships, and one can understand the reason why.

Many shrewd critics of wrestling still expect this giant warrior to eventually realize that one horizon which until this moment has escaped him. For myself, I can now sit back in relief, comparative safety, and observe with much pleasure André's forays into the ranks of professional wrestling. Good luck to you André, may you achieve that happiness and pride that only a world championship can give its holder. You are truly a man admired by men. You are an example for every sportsperson to follow. I am proud to be considered your friend.

In 1969, André ventured off the European continent to wrestle in New Zealand under the name Monster Eiffel Tower. The following year saw his Japanese debut, wrestling for Isao Yoshihara's International Wrestling Enterprises (the country's number two promotion behind Japan Pro Wrestling Association). Billed as Monster Rousimoff, André wrestled as both a singles competitor as well as in a tag team with European wrestler Michael Nador. The partnership was instantly successful: on January 18, 1970, Monster Rousimoff & Michael Nador defeated Thunder Sugiyama & Great Kusatsu in Fukoka, Japan, to win IWE World Tag Team Championships.

While he was wrestling in Japan, a doctor informed André that his unusual size was the result of acromegaly, a rare hormonal disorder caused by a benign tumor of the pituitary gland. The tumor spurs overproduction of growth hormones, leading to an altered facial appearance and enlargement of the hands and feet. If the tumor develops before bone growth is completed in adolescence, the result will be gigantism.

Unfortunately for André, the discovery of his acromegaly came too late to prevent many of its symptoms. Worse yet, André was advised that acromegaly sufferers were generally lucky to reach forty. He told no one about the diagnosis, and those friends closest to him believe that it was the knowledge of his shortened lifespan that drove André to indulge freely in his many appetites.

André was not the first wrestler to suffer from acromegaly. Maurice Tillet—the French Angel—was a star in the early days of professional wrestling. He developed acromegaly in his twenties, and as a result, his whole body was disfigured. Seeking a new identity to fit his chronic disfigurement, Tillet headed to America, where he was dubbed the "freak ogre of the ring."

So too did André head to North America—in his case, to French-speaking Quebec and the Montreal-based promotion Grand Prix Wrestling. Known as "the Eighth Wonder of the World," he quickly made a name for himself based on his size, his cheerful personality, and his surprising agility in the ring (especially his ability to do dropkicks).

The seven-foot-tall André, billed as Jean Ferre, became an in-demand attraction throughout the territory. He was usually booked in three-on-two matches alongside Grand Prix's Eduardo Carpentier, or in Handicap matches against two unlucky opponents. As a singles wrestler, he went toe-to-toe with some of the era's biggest heels, including Killer Kowalski and Butcher Vachon.

André also continued to wrestle in Japan. Competing as Giant Rousimoff, André won IWE's Third World Series tournament, defeating such legends of the sport as Karl Gotch and Billy Robinson.

His remarkable appearance and unique charisma quickly made André a top star. He was named 1971's Rookie of the Year by *Wrestling Yearbook 1972,* a publication affiliated with the popular *Inside Wrestling* and *The Wrestler.*

In 1972, *Le Geant* Jean Ferre entered his first high-profile program, feuding with one of wrestling's top big men, the six-foot-nine Mormon Giant, Don Leo Jonathan. The two behemoths battled frequently, culminating on May 31, 1972, in "The Match of the Century" at Montreal Forum. The "Battle of the Giants"—André's first main event—set Canada's indoor wrestling attendance and gate record with more than 20,000 fans in the Forum. In the finish, André was DQed after he lost his temper and wrapped his enormous hands around Jonathan's throat. The rest of the locker room ran into the ring to stop him, but André threw them all aside. The match defined André's gimmick for years to come—he's a sweet guy, but if you get him mad, nothing can stop him.

DON MURACO: "Don Leo Jonathan was about six foot six inches, 320. He was a giant of a man in his own right. Could do nip-ups, tight-rope walk on the top rope. He was a 220-pound worker in a 325-pound body. I'm sure he had a lot to do with André's progression as far as working."

Also in 1972 André ventured more and more into the United States, wrestling as a special attraction on a number of American Wrestling Association cards. But after three years in Montreal, the novelty had begun to wear off. André had taken on all of the territory's biggest wrestlers and beaten them all. Moreover, the thrill of seeing a wrestler of such dramatic size had been burned out by overexposure.

Frank Valois still believed that André had a brilliant career ahead of him. To try and revive the young wrestler's profile, he reached out to a man whose booking expertise was considered the best in the business—Vincent J. McMahon of World Wide Wrestling Federation.

Choking the life out of Killer Kowalski.

2

The World Wide Wrestling Federation had its roots in the Capital

Wrestling Corporation, the New York–based promotion founded by

Toots Mondt and McMahon's father, Roderick "Jess" McMahon.

Vincent J. McMahon joined Mondt as promoter in 1953, and thanks

to its northeastern base and McMahon's shrewd booking skills,

the company became a dominant force in the National Wrestling

Association—the umbrella organization that ruled over the many independent wrestling promotions operating in various territories across the country.

Ten years later, McMahon and Mondt formed World Wide Wrestling Federation after a dispute with the NWA. The new promotion—which spanned the territory between Maine and Washington, D.C.—grew into a powerhouse over the next decade, with such stars as Bruno Sammartino, Pedro Morales, Superstar Billy Graham, and Gorilla Monsoon.

McMahon was introduced to the man-mountain who would be his greatest success by Frank Valois, who was concerned that André had already run out of credible opponents in the Montreal territory. In 1973 the New York promoter took charge of Jean Ferre's career, beginning by giving him the name by which he would be known around the world: André the Giant.

McMahon also modified André's gimmick, suggesting he cloak his natural athleticism and instead allow his sheer bulk and remarkable size to do the work for him. André need simply loom large as an unstoppable, immovable colossus, allowing his opponents to do the majority of the in-ring work before finally being crushed by the monster.

VINCE K. MCMAHON: "André was doing dropkicks when he was up there in Montreal. Even though he could, why let him do dropkicks? He was very agile, very quick. I wouldn't say he had a lot of speed, but God he was quick."

On March 26, 1973, André the Giant made his World Wide Wrestling Federation debut, defeating Buddy Wolfe at Madison Square Garden.

The Giant was an out-of-the-box phenomenon, and every wrestling promotion in North America began clamoring for an appearance. McMahon sent André on the road to do one-night stands in every territory associated with WWWF, including the NWA and AWA. For the next ten years, André worked nearly nonstop, touring the world countless times.

By keeping André on the move, never spending too long in any territory, McMahon ensured that the extraordinary novelty of the Giant would not be worn away by prolonged exposure.

VINCE MCMAHON: "My dad booked André all over the world. It was almost a separate part of his book—how many weeks he was going to be here, how many

weeks he was going to be there. André knew he was being booked for the right reasons, but he also knew my dad had some political reasons too. He didn't have a problem with that, and if he did, then he would say something to my dad. When he did, he wouldn't say, 'This guy is a thief' or anything. 'I didn't have a good time there last time.' And my dad knew exactly what he meant."

JERRY LAWLER: "You had to book André the Giant through World Wide Wrestling Federation. You could call Vince Sr. and ask for André for three days or a week or whatever. To get him, you'd have to guarantee André a certain amount and you had to pay the company an extra booking fee."

JACK BRISCO: "I was World's Champion and Vince had just started André touring the country, so in just about every territory in the whole country, when they would have big shows, he and I would headline. I never wrestled him—he would be with somebody else, I'd be wrestling their local star. But he and I, we had top billing on the big shows all over the country for around three years."

HOWARD FINKEL: "Next to the person who was the NWA champion, I would suggest André was the most sought-after person that was out there. No, he *was* the most sought after, forget about the NWA champion. Everybody wanted André."

André's run through the various territories saw him shattering box office records everywhere he went. Billed as seven-foot-four, 420 pounds, the Giant was promoted with a gimmicky photo showing him carrying two women wrestlers on each outstretched arm. Announcers would sit while interviewing André, or have him stand on a box, to further exaggerate his enormous height.

As a rule, André was kept away from the top heels so as not to damage their draw in the territory. Rather, he was usually booked in Battle Royals or in Handicap matches that pitted him against Valois—who'd call the match in the ring—and a local wrestler who would take the majority of the bumps.

HOWARD FINKEL: "You had to find the perfect use for André. If you had André for a week, you'd better book him right. You'd better know how to use him, because if you don't know how to book him in your territory, then there's no need to farm him out there again. It's just going to be a waste of your time as well as our time."

JACK BRISCO: "We were in Houston, Texas, when I was World's Champion, they were having a two-ring Battle Royal, so they had like thirty guys there. In the old days, we had to get there an hour before the matches started. The matches started at eight, and we had to be there at seven. I walked in, André had a cooler full of beer and a couple of bottles of wine. He drank that whole cooler full of beer and all three of those bottles of wine before the matches, and it didn't faze him a bit.

"Then the thirty-man Battle Royal started. We all got in the ring; I could see him eyeballing me, and I knew he was gonna do something crazy to me. As soon as the bell rang, he ran across the ring and grabbed me. He picked me up over his head and just ran across the ring and threw me from the middle of the one ring and into the middle of the next ring.

"I landed and I bounced about three times. I laid there for a minute and thought, 'Do my legs move? Yeah. Do my arms move? Yeah. Well, I guess I could try to stand up.' All the boys just stopped and looked to see if I was gonna get up. I finally got up and everybody started wrestling again. It was kinda scary, though. Talk about a helpless feeling."

Part of André's job as a star was to go from territory to territory putting local people over in order to keep the money rolling in long after he had moved on. The wrestler George Gray—better known as One Man Gang—recalls how the Giant helped elevate him while he was coming up in the Mid-South ranks.

ONE MAN GANG: "I had the other idea, that he was coming in as a babyface enforcer to straighten out the big heel. But it was totally opposite. He'd come in and sell for the whole match. And of course you're gonna put André the Giant over in the end, but other than that he gave the heel the whole match.

"What amazed me about it was that he would actually make the time to take me to the side and try to wise me up to it. After that, I'd go out there, we'd do the big André spots, like where you'd try to reach around him and he'd do that ass thing where he bumped you off, things like that. But when it was time for me to take over, he'd give me a little 'Okay, boss, it's time' and I'd move out of the corner and he'd hit the turnbuckle or something like that. I'd take over on him, it'd be my match the whole way to the finish. He'd always do his little spot where I'd give him some shots and he'd tie himself up in the ropes.

"The main thing, he wanted you to just stay on him tight. He didn't want you to give him any breathing room. Then when it was time for his comeback, he got his little comeback in. Usually he'd give you a big boot and maybe the big splash or something like that. If it was a pinfall, then we'd get on outta there. But more often than not we went to a countout or a disqualification."

JERRY LAWLER: "André knew Jerry Jarrett and I owned the Memphis territory, so when he came in, he was basically working for us, although he wound up working with me in the matches. He was always very respectful and he would call me 'boss,' a term he used for people he liked. He'd greet me, 'Hey, boss.' He was real easygoing. He'd let you do anything you wanted in a match. Other than beat him. If he liked you, he would sell like crazy and he could make you look like a million dollars. You had to work to get him off his feet, but once you did, man, it looked good. You could choke him, pull his hair, punch, kick, everything. He would stay down and sell until it was time for the big comeback.

"But if he didn't like you, he'd make you look like crap, and there wasn't anything anyone could do about it. It was all about strength, and he had that in spades."

André parted ways with Frank Valois in 1974, and McMahon Sr. named one of his closest advisers to serve as André's manager, accompanying the Giant on the road and supervising his booking from territory to territory. Arnold Skaaland had returned home from World War II a hero and began competing as a professional wrestler. Known as "the Golden Boy," he was quick and tough enough to earn multiple shots at the NWA World Heavyweight Championship, though he never truly became a top-of-the-card star.

TIM WHITE: "Arnie was a legend. He was an ex-marine, he was in Carson's Raiders, he took a grenade in China. He was a tough bastard. If there was a guy acting up over in another territory, they'd send Skaaland in, he'd stretch the shit out of the guy and that'd be it. There'd be no more screwing around."

As a shareholder in Capital Wrestling, Skaaland was one of Vince McMahon Sr.'s most trusted associates. He consulted on all aspects of the business, from booking to decisions to overseeing the nightly box office take.

In addition to running WWWF shows in his hometown of Westchester, New York, Skaaland was a major figure at ringside, managing two of the World Wrestling Federation's greatest champions, Bruno Sammartino and Bob Backlund.

It was in his capacity as Backlund's manager that Skaaland entered the

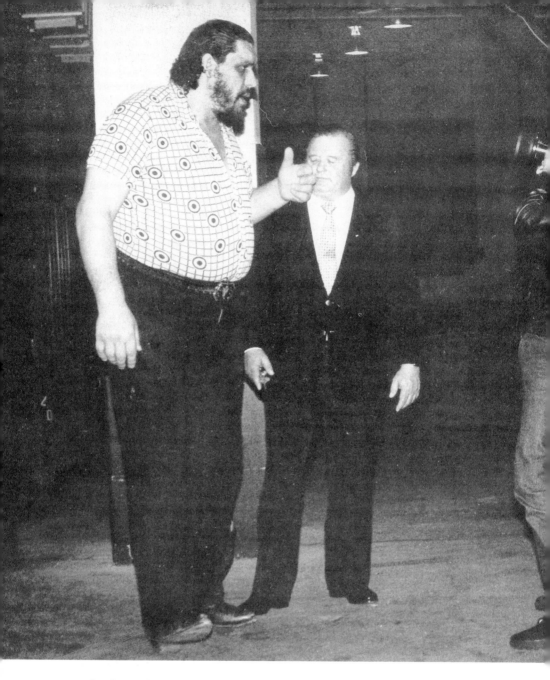

annals of wrestling history's most memorable moments. In December 1983, Backlund accepted a challenge from the Iron Sheik despite having recently suffered a neck injury. When the Iron Sheik caught Backlund in his Camel Clutch, Skaaland threw in the towel—literally—to protect his wrestler's neck from further harm, costing his charge the championship.

MICHAEL KRUGMAN

André & Arnold Skaaland go
before the TV cameras, 1982.

Skaaland and André made a perfect pair. The two bonded over their
mutual interests—wrestling, drinking, and playing cards. Skaaland became
André's dearest companion, the two spending their time on the road together by closing bars nightly and engaging in a seemingly endless game
of cribbage.

TIM WHITE: *"Arnie and André traveled together everywhere, representing the McMahons. When André went to Japan, Arnie would go with him to Japan. If André went to Mexico, they'd go together. André probably wouldn't have gone unless Arnie was with him."*

VINCE McMAHON: *"André and Arnie loved the business. They had a good time doing what they did, not just in the ring but in life. They had a good time traveling up and down the highways, having a drink, closing down bars, and just laughing all the time."*

TIM WHITE: *"Arnie used to say, 'People ask, doesn't the job wear you out? Job? We don't have a job. We're on vacation, brother.'"*

André and Skaaland traveled constantly, often flying halfway around the world to get from one show to the next. The busy schedule did have its upside—the 1974 *Guinness Book of World Records* listed André as "the Highest Paid Wrestler in the World," with official earnings of $400,000.

His drawing power was such that the Washington Redskins offered André a tryout, which he declined, knowing he had greater earning potential as a wrestler. He is said to have asked for the same $400,000 he was pocketing as a wrestler—more than the NFL paid at the time.

VINCE McMAHON: *"It was really just publicity, and everybody went along with it. There were some guys who had no idea that we were just having fun, that thought, 'Oh my God, can you imagine what this guy would do? André would be like half of the line.'*

"André had no intention of trying out for football. He was making too much money in wrestling. I don't know what they could've paid him, especially as a lineman. The linemen were really low on the totem pole. But that notwithstanding, it was really just a publicity stunt anyhow."

With his frizzed-out mane and enormous presence, André was instantly recognizable and immediately iconic. He began receiving mainstream attention, rare for a wrestler in the 1970s. He appeared on *The Tonight Show* (with guest host Joey Bishop) and *The Merv Griffin Show,* and was featured in such magazines as *People* and *Sports Illustrated.*

It was inevitable that Hollywood would come a-calling. In early 1976 André made his acting debut on the hugely popular sci-fi series *The Six*

Million Dollar Man. When the show decided to capitalize on the craze surrounding Sasquatch sightings, the creative team knew there was really only one man who could realistically portray the eight-foot-tall forest creature.

"Obviously we needed a big guy to do it," recalls writer/director Kenneth Johnson. "We looked around at who could've filled those shoes, and there weren't too many other seven-and-a-half-foot-tall guys around."

Johnson—who later created such classic shows as *The Bionic Woman, V,* and *The Incredible Hulk*—remembers André as being both reticent and respectful while filming the episodes.

"He was a very shy, sweet guy. It was probably one of the first film things that he had ever done, so he was completely bewildered about the whole process. But he was also very, very friendly and anxious to please. When I met him at the trailer on the set and walked him out, there was a bit of a look of a frightened puppy in his eyes, which is amusing when you think of the mass that the guy represents. I mean, not only was he a foreigner, not only did he not speak the language, but he was seven-and-a-half feet tall and built like two or three file cabinets.

"I took pains to introduce him to all the cast and the crew people. You get stared at a lot when you're that kind of guy, and I had a conversation with the cast and crew ahead of time to encourage them to be friendly and outgoing and make him as comfortable as he possibly could be, since it was his virgin effort in the film business."

Hidden under prosthetic makeup and a fur-covered bodysuit, André battled seven-figure cyborg Steve Austin in a memorable fight scene that took advantage of the Giant's grappling skills. While he might have yet lacked confidence as an actor, André was more than comfortable engaging in staged fisticuffs with actor Lee Majors.

KENNETH JOHNSON: "We worked through all of the choreography of the fights because Lee was our big star and we wanted to make sure that he wasn't going to get hurt by this four-hundred-pound behemoth. Lee is sort of a terse guy anyway, doesn't say a whole lot. They nodded and smiled a lot. Lee also recognized that it was André's first gig and was anxious to try to make him look as good as he could."

Years later, *Entertainment Weekly* named the episode the number 100 Television Moment of the 1970s in their "Fab 400: The Best of Pop Culture": "Depending on who you ask, it's either one of the scariest or campiest of TV moments: Steve Austin (Lee Majors)—the bionic hero of ABC's *The Six Million Dollar Man*—duking it out with a hairy beast known as the Sasquatch (7'4" grappler André the Giant). As millions of kids watched in horror, Sasquatch treated their favorite cyborg like a rag doll. 'That's the episode everybody always brings up,' laughs Majors, who ultimately won the fight. 'Maybe because the ugly fella was so big, you couldn't forget him.'"

KENNETH JOHNSON: *"Later on, when we did 'The Return of Bigfoot,' we of course went to André first, but he was making more money on the wrestling circuit than all of us put together, so he couldn't carve out the time we needed for him."*

In June 1976, André was a central player in another pop cultural milestone moment, the infamous "Boxer vs. Wrestler" debacle between Muhammad Ali and wrestling legend—and founder of New Japan Pro Wrestling—Antonio Inoki for "the World Martial Arts Championship." While that match was taking place in Japan, half a world away, in New York's Shea Stadium, André had his own mixed match—the Giant represented wrestling in a raucous brawl with boxer Chuck Wepner.

The main event had its genesis in some trademark Ali egotism. The champ was at the peak of his international fame after the legendary "Thrilla in Manila," his third and most brutal bout with Joe Frazier. Having absorbed an incredible amount of damage in that classic fight—"as close to death as you can get in the ring," according to Ali's physician, Ferdie "the Fight Doctor" Pacheco—Ali spent the first part of 1976 taking on low-ranked unknowns. Attending a party in April 1975, the champ was introduced to Japan Amateur Wrestling Association president Ichiro Yada. "Isn't there any Oriental fighter to challenge me?" Ali asked. "I'll give him a million dollars if he wins."

Ali's joking remarks made it into the Japanese press, spurring Inoki to pursue a match between the two icons. Ali eventually accepted, with his handlers and promoter Bob Arum all thinking the match would be a piece of cake. After all, professional wrestling is fake, right?

Inoki had other ideas. His New Japan Pro Wrestling was founded upon an innovative blend of pure wrestling technique—or *puroresu*—and mixed martial arts, or "strong style professional wrestling." To him, the Ali match was a chance to prove once and for all that professional wrestling was among the greatest of all martial arts.

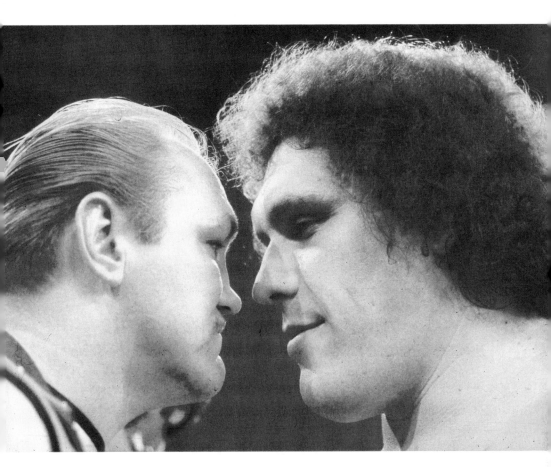

Face-to-face with Chuck Wepner.

What's more, Inoki had long desired fame in the United States, one of the rare goals that had eluded him over the course of an extraordinary career that included a record-setting four NWA International Tag Team titles with the great Giant Baba, the NWA Texas Heavyweight Championship, the NWA United National Championship, the NWA North American Tag Team Championship (with Seiji Sakaguchi), and a controversial victory over World Wrestling Federation Champion Bob Backlund.

Ali, with "Classy" Freddie Blassie acting as his manager (as arranged by Vince McMahon Sr.), arrived in Japan on June 16 amid worldwide attention. At their first meeting, he unleashed some of his inimitable verbal warfare. Inoki, in a move that foreshadowed the bout's result, presented the champ with a crutch.

In Blassie's memoir, Hisashi Shinma explained how Ali was enticed into the match. "We did it by offering him $6 million—more money than any boxer had ever received."

Ali and Blassie sold the hell out of the match, working talk shows across America. The champ joined his longtime friendly nemesis Howard Cosell on ABC's *Wide World of Sports,* where he squashed a couple of AWA jobbers, followed by a more serious match with Buddy Wolfe. The match was stopped due to Wolfe's bleeding, prompting his manager Bobby Heenan to come rushing into the ring to complain. The champ nailed the Brain with a massive punch, sending Heenan down to the canvas.

A week before the match, Ali appeared at a WWWF event in Philadelphia. He stood at ringside during Gorilla Monsoon's match with Baron Mikel Scicluna. After Monsoon threw the Baron over the ropes, Ali pulled off his shoes and climbed into the ring. As he danced about, floating like the proverbial butterfly, Gorilla picked him up, put him on his shoulders, and executed a humiliating airplane spin on the Greatest.

Meanwhile, Inoki did his part to create buzz for the upcoming event. He defeated two-time Olympic gold medalist in judo Willem Ruska in a worked match, landing three back suplexes to demonstrate how wrestling could take out an opponent from another martial art.

On June 25, 1976, Inoki and Ali finally met in the ring of Tokyo's Budokan Hall. Though the rules had been announced months prior to the match, new striking-only rules were stipulated just two days before the event. Apparently Ali and his people had been doing some scouting, and upon seeing Inoki in action, needed cover to protect the champ from being humiliated on the mat. There would be no suplexes, no headbutts or knees or open-handed slaps. Most significantly, there were to be no kicks above the waist. Perhaps the most disastrous of the new rules was one that restricted Inoki from throwing kicks unless one knee was on the canvas. The new rules served to constrain both athletes, thus setting up the disappointing match that followed.

The bell rang and Inoki hit the mat, spending 2:46 of the first round on the canvas, throwing kicks as Ali deftly danced around the ring. Though few kicks connected, by Round 3, an open cut had appeared on Ali's left knee. Then, in Round 8, Ali's trainer, Angelo Dundee, insisted that Inoki tape up his laces, claiming the tips were cutting the champ's leg.

Over the course of fifteen long rounds, Ali threw a mere six punches, as Inoki maintained a defensive posture throughout. Prevented by the rules from using his grappling strength and acumen, Inoki spent most of his time on the mat, throwing kick after kick at the boxer's legs.

The match was ultimately called a draw, though had Inoki not lost points for a karate kick and accidental knee to Ali's groin in the thirteenth round, he'd have won.

At the time, the only losers were the fans, many of whom had shelled out significant money to witness an overhyped fiasco of the highest order. Sadly, the match is said to have began the decline of Ali's career. The open cuts on his leg became so badly infected that amputation was considered a possibility. Moreover, the stream of stiff kicks caused the formation of two potentially life-threatening blood clots in his agile legs. Though he continued to fight for five more years, Ali never scored another knockout. His mobility and punching power were never the same.

The Ali vs. Inoki match was shown as the "main event" at wrestling cards around the world, including 150 closed-circuit locations across America. Each territory featured its own undercard, with WWWF offering a championship match between Bruno Sammartino and challenger Stan Hansen. In Chicago, fans saw AWA World Heavyweight Champion Nick Bockwinkel taking on Verne Gagne, while the NWA put on a show at the Houston Coliseum featuring Terry Funk in a title defense against Rocky Johnson.

The WWWF also presented an additional "Boxer vs. Wrestler" match, pitting André against heavyweight challenger Chuck Wepner. A New Jersey club fighter known as the Bayonne Bleeder, Wepner had been plucked from obscurity the year before to take on Muhammad Ali. The match ended up going fifteen rounds, and while Ali was the eventual winner, Wepner gained such notoriety that he inspired Sylvester Stallone's immortal creation Rocky Balboa.

The match—held before a crowd of 32,000 at New York's Shea Stadium—began with Wepner spending the first two rounds taunting André. Though he was six-foot-five, 230 pounds, Wepner still appeared tiny next to the Giant. He circled the bemused André, throwing a few jabs, which André largely ignored. A showman to his core, he knew how easy it would be to finish Wepner off and opted to give the fans a few rounds.

But in Round 3, Wepner connected, hitting André square in the face. The punch got André's attention. He snorted and hit Wepner with a reverse atomic drop and a headbutt, then lifted the big boxer like a child and tossed

Post-match melee.

him over the top rope. Wepner bounced off the apron and then fell to the infield, where he was counted out.

"Look, boss," André told writer Terry Todd in his seminal *Sports Illustrated* piece. "The boxer-wrestler business is almost a joke. After all, a man may hit me a couple of times, but if I cut the ring off and close in, what can he do after I put my hands on him? The boxer has no chance, since he can't even wrestle in a clinch because of his gloves."

In the moments following the bell, a brawl began between Wepner's crew and World Wide Wrestling Federation officials—including André's cornerman, Gorilla Monsoon. Wepner got back in the ring and went after André, nailing him with a big right that left the Giant stunned. André shook it off, then grabbed hold of Wepner. Fortunately, handlers were able to split them apart before it got seriously ugly.

Despite its lack of technical majesty, the match only served to increase André's growing legend. In 1977 he was named *Pro Wrestling Illustrated*'s "Most Popular Wrestler." He was without doubt the biggest draw in wrestling—literally and figuratively—and as such was in constant demand. Promoters around the world hungered for André to visit their territory and put over the top heel. André battled night after night with a rogue's gallery that included Ric Flair, Nick Bockwinkel, Abdullah the Butcher, Ken Patera, Blackjack Mulligan, and NWA World Champion Harley Race.

Along the way he fought countless Battle Royals and Handicap matches, not to mention his innumerable singles bouts. André even took on Gorilla Monsoon in a WWWF event at Roberto Clemente Stadium in Puerto Rico. There was a catch, however—the two gigantic babyfaces were pitted in a boxing match, refereed by Jersey Joe Walcott. Though André won with a third-round KO, the match marked a historic moment for Monsoon, making him the only man to ever box André and wrestle Muhammad Ali.

Among André's most successful programs was his long-running feud with the groundbreaking Ernie Ladd. Known as "the Big Cat," Ladd was a four-time AFL All-Star defensive tackle who appeared in three AFL championship games, winning titles in 1963 with the San Diego Chargers and in 1967 with the Kansas City Chiefs. During the off-season, the six-foot-nine, 315-pound Ladd began wrestling in the Los Angeles territory and soon became reviled as one of the sport's great heels. His arrogant interviews and controversial use of a taped thumb as a weapon made him a hated figure throughout the territories, which in turn made him the ideal foil for the hugely popular André. The two wrestled regularly across the country in matches promoted as "Battles of the Giants," with the babyface André threatening to depose Ladd from whichever championship he was holding at the time.

"The reason André the Dummy wants me so bad is because I beat him in Los Angeles," growled Ladd in a 1978 interview with NWA Tri-State Wrestling's Reeser Bowden.

He goes around telling people he's never been beat, which is a *lie*. We were in a couple of Battle Royals, for two or three years André the Giant never lost a Battle Royal, but I decided to enter some of the Battle Royals that André the Dummy was in, and I beat that dummy several times in Battle Royals. Now, he feels that he could really hurt me if he could get a shot at the North American title and take my belt, well André the Dummy, you got a shot! The only shot you gonna get, right in your mouth! Your big mouth!

Now, I beat you on several occasions and I will beat you again. And if you stand in my face and call me a liar, I'll slap your face

Sending Ernie Ladd into the ropes.

real good in the general public! Goin' round, tellin' people that you've never been beat before. I want you in the squared circle worse than you wanna get in the squared circle! I will slap your face and whup your fanny real good! For all my fans, anytime, anywhere, Big Boy! Don't call me out, 'cause I am the true champion! Oh! I just get so sick down inside, it make me wanna throw up just thinkin' about how bad I would like to slap your face! I would slap your face in the presence of your parents, let alone in the presence of all the fans, and pin you again, dummy!

ERNIE LADD: *"André was great box office, massive box office. Massive man. Learned how to make money. Good student of Vince McMahon's. What made him special, he learned that he could probably control an audience and bring them back again. Many people could draw an audience for the first time and then never get them back to the arena. He could draw them over and over. He was a good guy. He was moody now and then. But most of all he was a good guy."*

Late in 1978 André won rare championship gold as one half of two tag teams. First, he teamed with Ron Miller to defeat Butch Brannigan & Ox Baker and win NWA Australian Tag Team titles. Unfortunately, the promotion closed later that month, vacating the title through 1982.

Then, on Christmas Day, André paired with the American Dream, Dusty Rhodes, in a ten-team NWA Tri-State United States Tag Team Championship tournament at the Mid-South SuperDome Extravaganza in New Orleans. With amateur-and-professional wrestling legend Danny Hodge as referee, André & Dusty defeated Stan Hansen & Ernie Ladd in the final round to win the titles. But when André was unable to make the first championship defense, he was replaced by Don "The Spoiler" Jardine, and the team quickly dropped the titles.

HOWARD FINKEL: *"He didn't need a title. There are wrestlers here who need titles to really ascend to the top. Because of the novelty that André was, he didn't need a championship belt around his waist."*

3

Those who knew him remember André as a man who didn't see
gray when it came to his relationships with other wrestlers—
"Boss," as he was known, either liked you or he didn't, and
heaven help those who were not in good favor. ■ Among those
who earned the Giant's loathing was future Hall of Famer Ivan
"Polish Power" Putski. Wrestling one night in Providence, Rhode

Island, André teamed with Putski and a young Ted DiBiase in a Six Man Tag against the Valiant Brothers, Jimmy, Johnny, and Jerry.

In the locker room, André explained to DiBiase how the match would go. "André was like, this guy doesn't care about anybody else, he has no real respect for the business, and he's a loser," the Million Dollar Man remembered in his 2008 autobiography. "He said, 'Hey, boss. Tonight, you tag me. You tag nobody else.' I said, 'Okay.' Throughout the entire match, André made sure that I never tagged Putski. Brother, he made that guy stand on the apron all night. I'd go over there, Putski would reach out to tag me, and André would just throw that great big, long arm in front of me and take the tag. André had a way of proving his point."

HOWARD FINKEL: "If André didn't like you, make no mistake about it, he would tell you. And if he didn't like you, he didn't want to be around you. At the same time, André was all business. And you don't have to like somebody to do business with them."

JACK BRISCO: "With people he didn't know, he enjoyed being a little intimidating. But to his friends, you couldn't ask for a better friend or a nicer man. He was an amazing man. The people he didn't like, they knew he didn't like 'em.

"The Iron Sheik, André didn't like him for some reason. I don't know why, but over the years I saw them wrestle several times, in different parts of the country, and André was just unmerciful on the Iron Sheik. He'd just beat the poor guy about half to death."

BLACKJACK LANZA: "If you were genuine, he liked you. If you were phony, he didn't have time for you."

TED DIBIASE: "If André didn't like you, he'd just flat-out tell you. He'd say, 'Get out of the dressing room, go dress somewhere else. I don't care where, just get out of here.' There was no in-between with him. He'd keep his distance till he figured you out. I'll tell you this about the man, you couldn't get much by him. He had great intuition. No matter what you'd see on the exterior, André knew how to call a spade a spade."

VINCE McMAHON: "We had this guy by the name of Uncle Elmer in the company. Elmer was a big man, but not a giant. Almost seven feet tall, big potbelly, skinny little arms. Never trained a day in his life. Elmer sold fake Rolex watches to the boys and

With Ivan Putski.

to the public. He had his briefcase he'd carry around, he'd open that briefcase up and sell fake Rolexes.

"Anyway, André didn't like him. He'd been in the ring a couple times with André, and André roughed him up a little bit. So Elmer went to Bobby Heenan and said, 'Bobby, I don't think the Giant likes me.'

"Bobby says, 'Whatever makes you think that?'

" 'He told me so.' "

In 1980 Vince Sr. paired off André with a bodybuilding newcomer who instantly became his big, blond bête noire.

Inspired by Superstar Billy Graham and Dusty Rhodes, Hulk Hogan—born Terry Bollea—had learned his craft from famed wrestler/trainer Hiro Matsuda before entering the Championship Wrestling from Florida ring in 1977. He worked around the Southeast under such monikers as Terry Boulder and Sterling Golden, drawing well enough to earn a shot at the prestigious NWA World Heavyweight Championship.

> **HULK HOGAN:** "When I first got into the business, in my mind I thought I could get as big as André. I wasn't stupid—I knew I could never be seven-foot-four. I just thought that in the wrestling business I could be so big, people would just believe everything. Like, even if you beat André, nobody would really believe it, he was so big.
>
> "So that was my goal, to be the biggest, strongest I could be and hopefully be more impressive than André. And along with that came my verbiage, and that was a direct threat to André."

In late 1979, Hogan was introduced to Vince McMahon Sr., who gave him his new nom de guerre and teamed him with manager "Classy" Freddie Blassie. The pairing instantly established Hogan as a heel to be reckoned with. A master of crowd antagonism and heel psychology, Blassie's management style drew intense heat from the fans. He would assist Hogan by slipping a "foreign object" into the Hulkster's elbow pad—in plain sight of the crowd, of course, though somehow not in view of his opponent or the referee.

With Blassie waving his trademark cane by his side, Hogan marched through the World Wide Wrestling Federation's babyface roster, defeating such stars as Tito Santana, Dominic DeNucci, Ivan Putski, and then-champion Bob Backlund.

> **HULK HOGAN:** "When I first came to New York, I was the bad guy. Fred Blassie was my manager, and 'cause I was 330 pounds, it was believable that I could give André a run for his money."

In March 1980 McMahon Sr. matched his rising new star with his greatest attraction. André took an immediate dislike to Hogan. Freddie Blassie, in his 2003 memoir *Listen, You Pencil Neck Geeks*, tells of a match between the

MICHAEL KRUGMAN

Giant and Hulk Hogan where "André got it in his head that Hogan wasn't hustling enough.

"Trapping Hogan in a full nelson and clamping on the pressure, André growled in that deep distorted voice of his, 'Work, Hulk, work.'"

André's antipathy to Hogan had no small effect on the junior wrestler's nerves. The very thought of working a match with the Giant filled Hogan with virtually uncontrollable terror, causing him to get physically sick with fear as he approached the arena.

HULK HOGAN: "There was some rough going between me and him. He'd get me in the ring and just tan my hide. I'd be on the way to the building knowing I had to wrestle him and I would pull the car over and vomit, I was so scared. Then after taking several beatings within an inch of my life, which I never thought I would survive, he finally gained respect for me."

On August 2, 1980, McMahon Sr. sent André and Hogan to wrestle for Bill Watts at one of his annual Mid-South SuperDome Extravaganzas in New Orleans. Watts booked Hogan to lose to one of his biggest names, the great Wahoo McDaniel, but the young Hulkster had been advised by McMahon not to lose his match so as to appear more of a threat to André in their bout later in the card.

According to Hogan, Watts was infuriated by Hulk's refusal to job to his champion. He proceeded to tell André not only how the younger wrestler wouldn't job to McDaniel, he was also refusing to go down against the Giant—despite the fact that putting André over was his sole reasoning for opposing Watts.

Nevertheless, André was not about to give this newcomer the benefit of the doubt. When the two finally stepped into the ring together, the Giant made plain his displeasure by "damn near killing" Hogan. "He messed up my shoulder," Hulk said, "screwed my neck up and suplexed me on my head."

The Giant's open hostility toward Hogan persisted even as the two wrestlers ventured halfway around the world to work together in New Japan. Traveling the country together, André continued to torment the younger wrestler, sitting in the back of the bus so he could bounce his empty beer cans off the back of Hulk's head.

Rather than backing down, Hulk accepted his hazing as a rite of passage. He opted to show fealty to the biggest star in the business by taking the abuse with a grain of salt while also going out of his way to run errands and lend André a hand whenever possible.

Despite the Giant's antagonistic behavior, Hogan was able to see André's discomfort in the world, how the adoration of millions was more than countered by the slings and arrows thrown at him by nonwrestling fans who would jeer and gawk and generally treat the Giant as no more than a freak of nature. Hulk grasped how the Giant, whose strength and size inspired awe in the audience and fear in his opponents, was in many ways quite powerless. This huge man was unable to enjoy such simple taken-for-granted amenities as a comfortable chair or a bed that would come close to fitting his massive frame.

"I saw how hard it was for him to get around, big as he was," Hogan recalls. "I just wanted to help him as much as I could."

Early one morning while wrestling together in Tokyo, Hogan learned that it was in fact André's birthday. Thinking fast, he called a restaurateur friend and arranged for the purchase of a case of Pouilly-Fuissé, one of the Giant's favorite French wines.

Returning to the bus, he found André in his usual seat in the back. "Hey, where you been, boss?"

All assembled sang "Happy Birthday" as Hogan presented the Giant with his gift. Though it was only 7:30 AM, André broke into the case and opened one of his dozen bottles of wine.

Two and a half hours later, the Giant kicked Hogan's chair. "Piss stop," he muttered, sending Hogan up to the driver to arrange for a bathroom break.

"Don't tell me you drank that whole bottle of wine already," Hogan said.

"I didn't drink one bottle," André replied. "I drank all of them."

Despite starting his day by drinking a case of wine before noon, the Giant wasn't fazed, wrestling his match that night, as Hogan remembers, "like he'd been drinking nothing but water."

Impressed by Hogan's work ethic and tenacity, the Giant gradually grew to respect the younger athlete. He put Hogan over during a local TV interview in advance of a match at Philadelphia's Spectrum.

"For the first time, I'm gonna have a tough match, I know that," the Giant said. "That guy, he never lost a match. But I never lost a match either.

That guy, he's in the wrestling I think three or four years. I know he gets some good matches, he beats lots of guys. He never wrestled against a big guy before, so I know I gotta . . . my way, because I wrestled big guys before, when I first come in USA, for me it was the first time I wrestled against some big guys, like Killer Kowalski, Don Leo Jonathan, Ernie Ladd. And that time, they gave me a real tough time. But I still beat 'em. And now, this guy comes, he's the biggest after me, he's the biggest guy in the wrestling.

"There are good wrestlers," André continued. "I wrestle against Inoki, Sakaguchi, and other really good ones. Sakaguchi used to be the Japanese champion in judo, he was in the Olympics, and was really good. Antonio Inoki, they are really good wrestlers too, but they don't give me a hard time like I'm gonna have tonight.

"That guy, he have everything to win, because if he beat me tonight, he gonna be the first one who defeat the Giant."

July 26, 1980: Spectrum, Philadelphia, PA

ANDRÉ VS. HULK HOGAN IN "A SPECIAL BONUS MATCH"

Hulk Hogan enters in a gold lamé cape and white tights, preening and posing like the classic superior heel. André follows, stepping over the ropes as he stares down Hogan, who backs off.

They lock up, and André backs Hogan against the ropes. As Hogan hits the top rope, he spreads his arms, challenging referee Dick Worley to break André's hold. Hogan stands up straight and faces André, who grabs him in a headlock. The Giant pulls on the Hulk's hair and readies a right, but Hogan begs off, again making the ref do his job. He complains about the flagrant hair-pulling. They lock up and André catches Hogan from behind and wishbones him, butting his head between the spread shoulders. Hogan makes for the ropes, and André slaps him between the shoulders before breaking.

Side headlock from Hogan as commentator Kal Rudman discusses how many eggs André has for breakfast (that'd be sixteen). André throws Hogan into the ropes and again prepares a right, but Hogan catches the top rope and begs off into the corner, waving a

Big bearhug. Gorilla Monsoon is at right.

"no-no" finger at André. The ref actually explains to André not to use closed fists, only the palm.

Hogan attacks with a kick to the midsection, doubling André over for a few forearm shots to the back. Hulk stays on offense, attempting to slam the Giant, only to injure his lower back in trying the pickup. André takes the advantage and lands a big suplex on Hogan. Both men are downed from the impact, but André rolls over and helps himself upright with a hand around Hulk's throat. He drops a shoulder, but Hogan rolls out and quickly covers André, who throws him off at the one-count.

Hogan gets up and puts the boots to André before leaning in to choke him out. The ref breaks it up. Hogan pulls André up by his hair, hitting him with forearm smashes to the back of the neck. Hogan wraps his arms around André in a bearhug and tries to lift him, to little avail. The crowd chants "André! André!" until the Giant breaks the hold with a headbutt. Hogan goes immediately to another bearhug, but pushes the Giant into the corner, forcing Worley to break it up.

A forearm across André's face leads to a whip across to the other corner. Hogan lunges in and wraps his hands around André's throat. He alternately chokes and punches as Worley counts, finally going for another bearhug. He pushes André off into the ropes, but the Giant catches hold and raises a boot to Hogan's gut.

Hulk goes flying and comes up on one knee, setting André up for a kneelift that sends Hogan to the ropes. André picks him up, chops him twice, and then slams him to the canvas. He lifts Hulk upright and whips him into the corner for a running shoulderblock. He whips him to the other side and goes for another shoulderblock. This time, Hogan pulls Worley in between them and the ref takes the shot from André. Worley collapses in the corner as Hogan escapes to the outside. At last Worley recovers enough to call for the bell at 7:23. Hogan parades around with a raised fist and wounded look, indicating his victory. Meanwhile, André helps Worley to his feet.

Ring announcer Gary Capetta declares the match a DQ and awards it to André as Hogan fumes outside. André challenges him to come back in, but Hogan refuses. André calls for the ring mic and says, "You know what? I think you're talking too much and you not do anything, so come in that ring, I'm gonna show you what."

The crowd cheers, and Hogan goes up the aisle.

André and Hogan battled before their biggest crowd on August 9, 1980, at the World Wide Wrestling Federation supercard *Showdown at Shea*. The event—the third ever wrestling card presented at the Flushing, New York, Shea Stadium—was headlined by a Steel Cage match between WWWF Heavyweight Champion Bruno Sammartino and Larry Zbysko.

In the weeks leading up to the match, Blassie promised interviewer Vince McMahon that André would fall "like a big oak tree. . . . That will be the first time that he will go down in defeat, I guarantee ya, that prophecy will come true."

"There's no doubt that, Hulk Hogan, should you defeat André the Giant, you will be, literally and figuratively, the biggest man in professional wrestling," McMahon suggested to the charismatic challenger.

"Without a doubt, Vince McMahon, I already am the biggest man in professional wrestling today," Hogan agreed. "André the Giant is a freak of nature. I am the only true athlete. I will remain undefeated, André the Giant. It was only a matter of time before the newspapers, the public, the whole world, brought you out of your hiding place and now you're gonna face me, one-on-one, ha-ha. Breaking bones, scarring faces, and remaining undefeated is my goal."

"Hulk's hammer!" Blassie barked at the interview's conclusion, foreshadowing the events to come.

Hogan remembers the day of the match as a bit of a nightmare, including getting lost on the way to Shea and winding up at LaGuardia Airport. But when he finally stepped into the ring with André, the Giant's wide grin reassured him that everything was under control. "It gave me comfort to know I was in the ring with someone who knew what he was doing," Hogan recalled later in his memoir.

A live crowd of 36,295 were in attendance for the *Showdown,* and while Bruno might have been the top-billed star, the match people were most excited for was André vs. the flaxen-haired upstart.

SHOWDOWN *AT SHEA*
ANDRÉ VS. HULK HOGAN (W/FREDDIE BLASSIE)

Blassie escorts Hogan—resplendent in gold lamé cape—across the field to a shower of boos. They get into the ring, where Hogan is immediately greeted by André.

Vince McMahon is the ring announcer. "From Venice Beach, California, tipping the scales just this morning at 349 pounds, Hulk Hogan!"

He spreads his arms and the cape, as if to catch all the boos. The timekeeper rings the bell to restore order.

"From Grenoble, France, weighing 487 pounds, the Eighth Wonder of the World, André the Giant!"

André stands tall and strong, his hair long and bushy, his fists held high. They meet in the middle of the ring to be checked out by referee Gilberto Roman. Hogan—wearing an elbow pad—confers with Blassie before allowing himself to undergo a cursory search.

The bell rings. André and Hogan circle each other, then stare each other down. The ref reminds them that it's okay to wrestle, but they just stand still, gazing into each other's eyes. They lock up, and André shoves Hogan into the corner. He comes out and they lock up again. Hogan catches André in a headlock, pulling him forward. André simply stands up straight, lifting Hogan off the mat. He maintains the hold until André throws him into the ropes. Hogan comes off, and they collide.

Splashing down on Hogan,
Showdown at Shea.

They lock up again, and this time it's André who takes control with a headlock. Smiling, he squeezes Hogan's head. Hogan powers the Giant off and into the ropes. André tackles, but they both remain standing. André has a huge grin, enjoying the hunt. Hogan leans over to confer with Blassie.

André catches Hogan's wrists and headbutts between his shoulders. The Giant smiles widely as Hogan shakes his head, begging for mercy. A second headbutt gets the crowd cheering wildly. Pulling Hogan's arms behind his back, André puts a big boot between the shoulders and stretches Hulk out. After a battle of strength, Hogan reverses the hold only to have it reversed on him, winding up where he started. He backs André into the corner, then turns and starts swinging. André responds with a big right that sends Hogan reeling. André chases him to the opposite corner and headbutts him, leaving him hanging on the ropes for support.

Hogan gets his arms around André's waist in a bearhug. The crowd is chanting the Giant's name. Hogan squeezes, his hands locked at André's lower back. André is grimacing in pain, though not putting much effort into breaking the hold. As the bearhug continues, you can see André and Hulk calling spots. Finally André raises his massive head and butts himself free, dropping Hogan to the mat.

Hulk rolls out and is consoled with a pat on the back from Blassie. Hulk goes up the wooden steps to the apron, only to be caught by André, who suplexes him over the ropes. He goes for the splash, but Hogan rolls away in time. Both men are down, and referee Roman begins counting. The wrestlers rise, with Hogan getting to his feet fast enough to put a boot to André's head. Elbow to the back of the neck is followed by a series of rights. André catches Hogan, scoops him up, and slams him to the mat. Unfortunately, one of Hogan's yellow boots clips the ref as André lifts him up, knocking the ref silly. André goes over and tends to Roman, his back to the fallen Hogan.

Hogan puts a knee into André's back, kicks him while he's down, and then scoops him up for a bodyslam of his own. He covers, but the ref is still down and André tosses him off. They rise, face off, and André lifts and slams Hogan once more. André hits the big splash and covers just as a replacement ref runs into the ring. Hogan kicks out, but the ref counts three.

The crowd cheers, and André basks in the glow, his arms raised and his fists pumping. Meanwhile, Hogan and Blassie are up to no good. André returns to the still-down Roman. Hogan comes from behind and nails the Giant with a newly loaded elbow pad. Hogan whips André into the ropes and catches him with a loaded Hogan Hammer lariat. André goes down flat. As all eyes turn to the Giant, Hogan slips the foreign object out of the pad and into his tights. The bell rings. Hulk comes down onto the field and raises his arms in triumph. Shea boos as he leaves.

A stretcher is brought out for André, but he sits up and waves the trainers away. Vince returns and takes the mic. "Ladies and gentlemen, the time, 7 minutes and 48 seconds. The winner, André the Giant."

André stands up and shows the blood covering his face as he accepts his victory.

Bodyslamming André was something that had rarely been seen in the United States. And while it was the Giant who scored the victory, busting André open marked a milestone moment in Hogan's career. McMahon Sr. knew that the fans would take a wrestler far more seriously after he'd taken the Giant down. Leaving him in a pool of his own blood meant surefire money in the bank for their next matchup.

August 20, 1980: Fieldhouse, Hamburg, PA

"The Incredible" Hulk Hogan, entering with Blassie, draws plenty of heat. Blassie taunts André—475 pounds—with his cane during the introductions. They lock up and do battle until André powers Hogan into the corner. Hulk is unamused, and confers with Blassie before locking up again. Hogan shoves André in the opposite corner, and the Giant responds with a boot to the midsection that sends his back toward the ropes. Fists clenched, they stare each other down. André gets a headlock on Hogan, who throws him off into the ropes and hits

Boot to the back,
Showdown at Shea.

a clothesline into André's belly. Hogan hits a pair of forearms to André's shoulders, then scoops him up for a bodyslam.

"Look at that," Vince McMahon marvels. "I can't believe that!"

Hogan drops a knee, then lifts André up. The Giant punches out and pays back the bodyslam. He whips Hogan into the ropes and a big boot. He attempts a splash, but Hogan rolls out and chats with Blassie. The Classy One slips a foreign object into Hulk's elbow pad.

Hogan gets back in the ring and takes two headbutts. André whips him into the ropes for the boot, but Hogan avoids it. He comes off the other side and nails André in the head with the loaded Hogan Hammer lariat. André goes down, and Hogan slips outside to return the foreign object to Blassie.

Hogan raises his arms outside as André sits in the ring, bloody. Vince comes to ringside with a mic to "have a word with André."

Hogan and Blassie leave, and André lurches out of the ring. "Hogan! Come here!" he shouts, blood dripping down to his chest.

The feud continued through to the end of 1980, drawing huge houses everywhere André and Hogan wrestled. But by the next year, Hogan had left World Wide Wrestling Federation after a disagreement with McMahon Sr. over his featured role as "Thunderlips" in the film *Rocky III*. He wound up in Verne Gagne's AWA, where he morphed into the promotion's leading babyface.

No matter how you slice it, there is little doubt that Hogan's rivalry with André represented a landmark moment in his career. Taking on the Giant night after night marks a crucial rung on Hogan's climb to the very pinnacle of professional wrestling.

HOWARD FINKEL: "Who knew what was going to happen seven years later, but back then, André and Hogan was a very interesting match because the roles were reversed, with André being the babyface and Hulk being the heel, managed by Freddie Blassie. We just didn't have a clue what we would be seeing seven years later."

4

André was at the top of his game as 1981 began. In February, he

won rare championship gold, teaming with Dusty Rhodes to defeat

the "Cowboy Connection," Bobby Jaggers & R. T. Tyler, and win

NWA Florida Tag Team titles. But after one defense—against

Nikolai Volkoff & Super Destroyer—the titles were vacated, and

left inactive until 1986. ■ Back in World Wrestling Federation,

André faced off against Killer Khan, the Mongolian Giant, and their first match together ignited one of wrestling's most legendary feuds.

Though he was billed as hailing from Mongolia, Killer Khan (born Masashi Ozawa) was in fact Japanese. Khan first encountered André while training at New Japan's famed dojo. The Giant's future nemesis was given the honor of running errands for André, including carrying the star's bags backstage.

The six-foot-five Khan received the Mongol Giant gimmick from the legendary Karl Gotch, known in Japan as "the god of Pro Wrestling" in honor of his defining role in developing the "strong style." Khan came to America in 1979 and worked his way around the territories, wrestling André in a few Georgia Championship Wrestling Tag matches in 1980. Later that same year, Khan was brought up to New York and World Wrestling Federation. He feuded with World Heavyweight Champion Bob Backlund and Intercontinental Champion Pedro Morales before being matched against André on May 2, 1981, in Rochester, New York.

The match immediately entered the history books. According to Khan, his intent was to kneedrop onto André's chest from the top turnbuckle. But when the Giant began to rise, the Japanese wrestler ended up landing on André's left ankle. The Giant might have been huge, but his ankle was no match for three hundred pounds of Killer Khan. The bone fractured . . . or did it?

"This wasn't an angle," Khan told writer Keith David Greenberg, but in truth, André had injured his ankle the previous evening at home, putting his weight wrong as he got out of bed.

TIM WHITE: "He made it to the ring just to put Khan over. They had to put the heat on somebody, so they put the heat on him. André would always say, 'Khan broke my ankle. I might have broken it the night before, but he broke it again.'"

VINCE McMAHON: "Killer Khan accidentally fell on André and broke his ankle. Khan was a good guy and very respectful to André. He was all upset when it happened, but André didn't hold it against him. He didn't kill him, didn't beat him up. He knew it was a freak accident because when you're in the ring, shit happens. It's the old expression: it's not ballet."

Whatever the truth, the bimalleolar fracture was repaired by Dr. Harris S. Yett, orthopedic surgeon at Boston's Beth Israel Hospital. Dr. Yett explained the difficulties involved in the operation to *Sports Illustrated,* noting how two enormous surgical screws were needed to mend the broken malleolus. What's more, two tourniquets had to be used to take in André's massive thigh. Dr. Yett described the Giant's cast as the biggest they ever had to make.

HOWARD FINKEL: "I don't know what we did to get the stink off of it, but we preserved it all these years, and it's a great conversation piece."

A nine-foot bed was required for André's stay at Beth Israel, and special crutches had to be made for his recuperation, as the biggest available were still not big enough to support the Giant's colossal frame.

Little more than a month after his "injury" in the Khan match, André returned to World Wrestling Federation television. Coming out on crutches for his first on-camera interview since the injury, he discussed his surgery with Vince McMahon.

June 8, 1981: Madison Square Garden, New York, NY

"Ladies and gentlemen, this is a very special segment of our program this week," says Vince McMahon, standing outside the ring. "It gives me great pleasure to introduce to you without a doubt the most phenomenal athlete of all time, here with us, the one and the only André the Giant."

André emerges on crutches, his hair huge and wooly, his sports jacket checked black and white. "How you doing?"

"Terrific," replies McMahon. "The question is, how are *you* doing?"

"I'm feeling very good. In fact, I've got good news for you."

"We can stand some good news. What is it?"

"Tomorrow I'm going back in the hospital to take off my cast," André says, smiling widely.

"That is really good news. So tomorrow the cast comes off. You obviously, André, have been exercising and things of that nature, have you not, to keep the ligaments loose or whatever?"

"Yeah. In probably four or five more weeks I'll be back in the ring, maybe before that. The doctor says if everything's okay, maybe in two weeks."

"So as soon as the cast comes off then you're gonna be thinking about stepping back in the squared circle. Let me ask you, André, do you feel, do your doctors or what have you feel, that it's wise to go back into the ring so soon?"

"We're going to find out tomorrow after they take off the cast," the Giant explains. "They going to take some more X-ray and then I'm going to be ready, I think maybe two or three weeks and Freddie Blassie, he better get Killer Khan in shape because I be ready to chase him everywhere."

"André, I'm sure it's frustrating for you to be in the hospital and to listen to Fred Blassie—"

Speak of the devil, Blassie emerges from the back. "You're not invited," scolds McMahon.

"I don't care if I'm invited! Why do you got this palooka on here for? What are you asking him for? You see the leg's broke (pointing with his cane). He's all through! He's washed up!"

"What are you talking about, I'm washed up?" André asks, leaning in toward Blassie. "You say I'm not gonna wrestle anymore, well, I give you news, I'm going back in that ring."

"You're going back on what?" Blassie rages, as the fans begin hurling debris at him. "You're all through! This ain't nothing but a palooka! He's all through! The man is through!"

The Giant at last has heard enough and swings his crutch at Blassie's head, sending him back against the ring apron. André loses his balance and falls forward, catching himself on the apron. Vince tries to help him up as Killer Khan runs out, picks up the steel crutch, and smashes it across André's neck, just barely missing McMahon's head. André goes down, and Blassie takes a shot at his cast with his cane. Vince stands over the fallen Giant, chasing Blassie off and giving André cover.

The heels run off. André gets to his feet and tears off his sports coat in a rage. Unfortunately, his broken ankle keeps him from following and he leans back against the apron, massaging his neck.

The televised assault on his injured ankle gave André the time he needed to fully heal from his surgery. Finally, after two and a half months, the Giant was ready for action. André returned to face his nemesis with payback on his mind.

July 20, 1981: Madison Square Garden, New York, NY

"There may be many wrestlers and many giants," says the ring announcer as André comes to the ring, "but there is only one giant . . . ooooh, I'm getting out of here. . . . André the Giant!"

André—in blue tights and red boots—and Khan lock up immediately. André powers him into the corner and is chopping away as the bell rings. A headbutt sends Khan down and rolling out to the floor. Khan holds his head and reels around the concrete, while André calls for him to get back into the ring. Khan gets up on the apron, and André challenges him to meet him right in the center. "Come on." He gestures, smiling broadly. The ref tries to approach André, but the Giant tells him to get into the corner and stay out of his way. Wisely, the official complies.

Finally, Khan reenters and attempts a kick to André's chest. His foot gets caught, and André pushes him back against the buckles, laughing as he refuses to relinquish his grip on the Killer's boot. He twists it and flips Khan over the ropes, holding on to the ankle as Killer dangles upside down. Khan tries to escape André's grasp by grabbing on to the ropes, but André ties the ankle in between the top two ropes and squeezes. The ref tries to intercede, but André commands him to the other side of the ring.

Khan shakes his head in agony. André kicks the Killer's trapped boot and releases the ropes, letting Khan tumble off the apron to the cold concrete, where he sells his injured ankle. As Khan tends to his foot, the crowd begins stamping, urging the match to proceed.

Khan limps up onto the apron, rolls under the ropes, and sits back against the buckles, waving his hands in a fruitless bid for mercy. André approaches, and Khan kicks out at his ankle with his uninjured left leg in an attempt to fell the Giant. No such luck—André

steps down on Khan's right boot, and stomps repeatedly on his damaged ankle with his other foot. Again, the ref comes close to break it up, but André sends him into the opposite corner. Still trapping Khan's foot, he continues to work Killer's injured ankle. Khan tries to flee through the ropes, but André maintains his hold and keeps stamping away.

André reaches over and puts a facelock on Khan, then chops at his chest. Khan slips back under and leans against the turnbuckle, pleading for André to relent.

Killer Khan goes to
work on André's ankle.

André responds by grabbing the top ropes and putting a boot
under Khan's chin, forcing him backward. From the corner of his eye,
André sees the ref approaching, and without releasing the pressure
on Khan's neck, he admonishes the ref back to his corner.

Khan is now on all fours, his upper body through the ropes on
the apron. André resumes his stomping attack on Killer's injured
ankle, but Khan rolls free to the floor.

"Come on," André says, waiting patiently for his opponent to
return to the ring.

Khan tries to climb back in. Unable to get leverage with his wounded leg, he lifts his left leg onto the apron and slowly pulls himself up with the ropes. André gives him the time to stand up against the turnbuckle, then attacks, chopping and grabbling hold of Khan's braid and pulling him out into the ring. He slams Khan with a gutwrench suplex, then grabs hold of his left ankle and drags him to the center of the ring. Khan squirms out. André spits into his hands, reaches down, and hammers at Khan's forehead. Khan no-sells a boot between his shoulder, prompting André to reach down and lift him up and over with a vertical suplex.

The Giant takes Khan's left ankle and pulls it out wide and drops an elbow. Khan pleads for leniency, but André takes hold again and rises into an anklelock. He twists Killer's boot hard as Khan writhes in agony. He flips Khan onto his belly, ties up his legs, and drops his weight onto his back.

With Khan's ankles locked, André leans down onto them and claps Killer's ears. He holds the ankles together with a knee and, taking Khan's wrists, surfboards

André puts down Khan.

him backward. Khan wants to submit, but the ref scurries away after André shakes his head.

André flips Khan over, still crossing his ankles, and leans in with a headbutt. Khan escapes to the corner and chops at André. A clap causes the Giant to fall back on the ropes. Limping, Khan claps André's ears a second. Reeling, André hits the canvas. Killer drops a fist to André's recently healed ankle, and then works his other leg against the rope. André takes his free leg and crashes it down on Khan's head to the crowd's delight, but can't rise in time to prevent Khan from continuing to work the ankle. Khan locks hold, and André gets his other boot onto Killer's chest and pushes him across the ring. Khan quickly comes back and locks onto André's ankle once more, flipping him over and pushing down hard.

At last, André kicks Khan away and gets to his feet. Khan comes toward him and takes a big boot to the face, a chop, and a headbutt. Limping, André whips Khan from corner to corner, then headbutts him face-first onto the top rope. He pulls the second rope up and over Khan's neck and chokes, pulling the ropes—and Khan's head—back and forth. The ref approaches and André swats him away and out of the ring. He continues bouncing the ropes, as SD Jones, Rick Martel, and Tony Garea come into the ring to convince him to stop the carnage. The bell sounds at 12:24, with both wrestlers disqualified.

André shoves the babyfaces away and squeezes away at the now unconscious Khan. Finally, Martel, Garea, and an official pull André off, freeing Khan from the ropes. André rushes back toward him and gets one last boot in before Khan rolls out to the concrete. André rages in the ring awhile, then raises his fist in triumph.

André and Khan wrestled up and down the eastern seaboard, drawing packed houses everywhere through the summer and fall. Killer Khan discussed André with writer Keith David Greenberg in Freddie Blassie's memoir, *Listen, You Pencil Neck Geeks,* explaining the Giant's preference for working tight—that is, applying holds and blows with legitimate force to create realism and intensity in the ring.

"We hit each other with very hard chops," Khan recalled. "If I went loose on André, he'd get mad and give me a good hard one, and say, 'Come on! What are you doing? Let's go!'"

The Mongolian Giant also detailed one of André's deadliest moves, one that saw him taking full advantage of his disproportionate physiology.

"I was lying on the mat," Khan said, "flat out, straight up, looking at the ceiling. And here comes André with this humongous ass, and he just sat on my face. At that moment, I actually thought I was going to die."

The program continued though the end of the year, though its true culmination came in November's now-classic Mongolian Stretcher match at Philadelphia's Spectrum. The rules were simple: the object of the match was to incapacitate the other wrestler to such a degree that he could be placed on the stretcher and taken out of the ring.

November 14, 1981: Philadelphia Spectrum, Philadelphia, PA

ANDRÉ VS. KILLER KHAN

André powers Khan into the corner to start, and hits a headbutt that leads Khan to run out to the apron. André grabs his head and pulls him back over the ropes. A smiling chop is followed by a kneelift, and Khan rolls across the ring to the outside. André reaches through the ropes and grabs Killer's hairlock. Taking Khan by the wrist, he pulls him up and in, and then whips him into a big boot. Killer goes down, so André stands over him before dropping onto him with his leg and his butt, perhaps not sure which one to go with so early in the match. André gets up and tells the ref to bring in the stretcher. The ref and a ring official try to roll Khan onto the stretcher, but he's having none of it.

On his knees, Khan lunges for André's ankle, but the Giant catches him. Khan gets to his feet, his head between André's legs. André takes the back of Khan's tights, lifts him up, and drops for a sit-down piledriver. He tries to finish it with a falling headbutt, but Khan rolls away and André hits the canvas. Both wrestlers stay down and sell, with Khan the first to rise. Shrieking like a Mongolian maniac, he puts the boots to André's head, then takes the formerly injured ankle and ties it between the bottom ropes. André howls in pain as Khan kicks at the recently healed joint. He makes wild barking noises with each kick, until the ref intercedes and tries to free André.

"C'mon, get away from there," the official says, but Khan pushes him away and continues to work on the ankle. "C'mon, get off that foot!"

Khan keeps at it, kicking away. "C'mon, Khan, step back from there."

Reaching over the top rope, Khan takes the ankle and pulls it upward. André reaches for Khan's tights and yanks him to the canvas. As Khan adjusts his trunks, the ref begins to loose André's leg. Screeching, Khan drops a knee to André's head. Unfortunately, the ref cannot untie André, so Khan goes to the second rope. He slips and lands on his feet, then tries to cover by dropping another knee. He calls for the stretcher, which looks tiny next to André's supine figure. Khan, the ref, and the ring official try to roll André onto the stretcher, but cannot budge the Giant. The official attempts to untie André but says, "I can't get his foot out!" With the ref's help, André is at last freed.

Khan pushes André toward the stretcher, but he rolls over it and gets up, taking the stretcher with him. He swings it at Khan, barely hitting the Killer's head and shoulders. Khan, however, sinks into the corner as if he'd been concussed. André cuffs the side of his head, and then grabs hold of an ear. A big headbutt puts Khan down, but when the official places the stretcher onto the apron, André kicks it away.

The ref tries to explain the rules to André, who prefers to suplex Khan. André favors his left leg as the ref fetches the stretcher. With the official, they manage to get Khan onto the stretcher, but he pushes them away before they can pick him up.

Khan kicks out at André's ankle, but only catches air. Grinning ear to ear, André stalks his Mongolian prey, who tries and fails once again to kick the Giant's ankle. André reaches down, takes Khan's ankle, twists, and drops onto it as the Killer screams. Khan tries to beg off, but André repeats the maneuver, twisting the ankle a bit further before falling onto it. André takes both of Khan's ankles, crosses them, and then drops his chest onto them. Khan sits up and tends to his ankles, so André kicks him in the face. He takes Khan's ankles under his arms, then falls back, with Khan's neck under the ropes.

André gets revenge on Killer Khan.

The ref breaks the hold and, as André gets up, fetches the stretcher. André tosses it over the ropes, preferring to continue his assault. The ref argues, the official puts the stretcher back in, but André kicks it out. Four sit-down splashes lead to the stretcher's return. The officials try to get Khan onto it, but he holds on to the bottom rope. André pushes the official out of the way and hits a series of rapid-fire buttdrops, crushing Khan. The stretcher returns, only this time, Khan grabs the apron. Still, they get him on it and try to pull him out under the ropes. But Khan holds on, and the officials yank the stretcher out from under him.

André puts Khan in the corner for a huge chop, and then takes him down with a headlock suplex. A big buttdrop and splash finish Khan off. The stretcher is brought in, and Khan is rolled onto it. Prone, he is removed from the ring at 9:57. A squad of red-jacketed Spectrum employees carry the Mongolian Giant away as the ref raises André's arm in victory.

Apart from the rivalry with Khan, André spent much of his time that year wrestling in Japan. His increased weight and overall lack of conditioning manifested in a notable decrease in André's in-ring mobility. Fortunately, he maintained his stamina and psychology.

In Japan, André largely worked as a monster heel. Among his greatest feuds were with Junior Heavyweight Champion Tatsumi Fujinami. The two worked a classic Little/Big match, with the smaller Fujinami—less than 200 pounds—getting in a series of offensive moves before being caught and squashed by André. On December 10, 1981, André & Rene Goulet defeated Antonio Inoki & Tatsumi Fujinami to win New Japan's Second Annual MSG Tag League Tournament. André pinned Fujinami at 8:05. The previous year, André & the Hangman came in third behind Hulk Hogan & Stan Hansen and winners Inoki & Bob Backlund.

André worked regularly with Hansen, both as opponent as well as tag team partner. Their hard-edged, fast-paced matches together were among André's most brutal and dramatic. The Giant's respect and comfort level in working with the notoriously tough Texan saw him allowing a rare body-slam in a classic New Japan Pro Wrestling showdown.

STAN HANSEN: "I guess André was only slammed a couple times, and that was one of them. That just goes to show what André thought of our matches. I owe a lot of my success in Japan to the fact that André and I had our matches. He got me over in Japan and I owe him that for sure.

"André was a smart enough businessman to know that even though he was 'the Seventh Wonder of the World,' or whatever they called him, in order for him to continue to do great business and enhance his status, he needed somebody to *wrestle* him. With me, he found an opponent that he could go out and have a lot of different style matches that the Japanese couldn't have with him, for whatever the reasons. I think he realized that here was an opponent that maybe could make these matches something that's gonna stand out.

"We both took each other out of our norm. I think he found in me somebody that would fight him. He found in me an opponent that people wanted to see in real matches, not just the typical André-the-strong-man type of match.

"I've heard a lot of people say they dreaded working with him because there wasn't a lot they could do. André would just dominate. But for some reason, he took a liking to me and enjoyed my style. Without his wanting to go and have a great match, it would've never happened. So for whatever the reasons, André and I, we had some good matches."

At home in America, André v. Killer Khan proved a milestone, in terms of its box office success as well as its popularity with fans. Nineteen eighty-one ended with the bouts named "Feud of the Year" by *Wrestling Observer;* the Mongolian Stretcher match at the Spectrum was declared "Match of the Year" by *Pro Wrestling Illustrated.*

André the Giant was, without doubt, the top wrestling Superstar of his generation, beloved and feared by millions around the world. The wrestling business would undergo a seismic shift in the months to come, and André's star power would greatly contribute to the extraordinary changes.

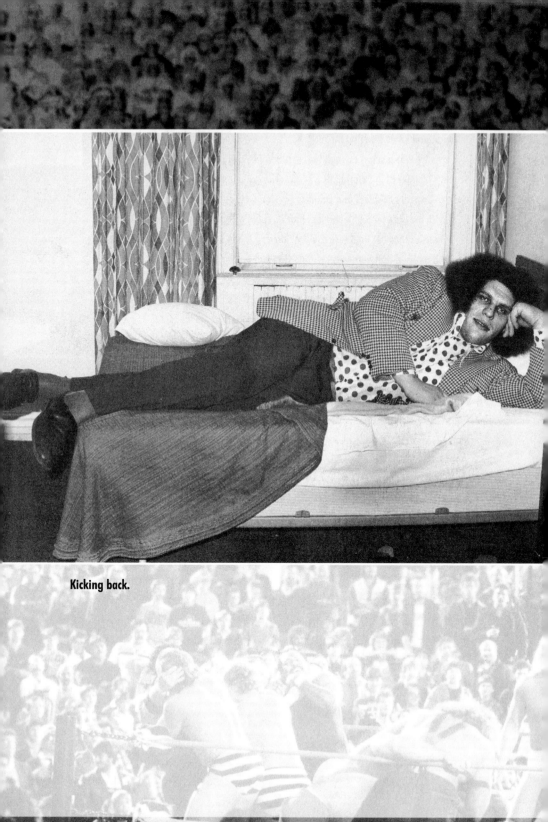

Kicking back.

5

In 1982, Tim White began working for World Wrestling Federation, manning the merchandising booth that traveled with the show. The Providence, Rhode Island, native was planning a career in law enforcement, and took the job as a way of passing time before entering the FBI academy in Quantico, Virginia. Little did White know that he would enjoy a long career in the wrestling business, both behind the scenes and in the ring as a referee.

Most significantly, he would become one of André's nearest and dearest friends, though their first meeting was not an auspicious one.

TIM WHITE: "Back then it was old-school, the wrestling. The wrestlers' locker room was the wrestlers' locker room. I mean, nobody except wrestlers went in there. I didn't know all these rules when I went in.

"Chief Jay Strongbow was the lead agent running the show. He had asked me earlier in the hallway to bring him something from the merchandise booth. So I went up and put it in a little bag, then I went back down and said, 'Where's the Chief?'

"They said, 'He's in the locker room.' So I walked right into the locker room. I walked through that door like I belonged, and André was sitting there playing cards. I got about three steps, he looked over at me and goes, 'OUT.' I went, 'But I'm here to give—'

" 'Go home.' He went to stand up, and I just turned around and ran for my life. When I got outside, my heart was pounding. Finally the Chief came out and goes, 'You can never walk into a locker room like that. You knock on the door, ask for me, I'll come outside.' And I learned. But the first time André and I ever looked at each other, he gave me the wrestler's rush out of that locker room. I was scared to death.

"That was my first encounter with André. After that I stayed far away from him and any of the guys, 'cause I felt like, I don't belong near the wrestlers, my job is to do the merchandise. Well, Arnie—God bless him, I loved him like a second dad— every night he'd come up to me and Mike Breen, who was a great friend, we worked together doing this stuff, and say, 'Where are you guys staying tonight?'

"See, Arnie wanted to make sure, right down to the little guys out front selling the programs, you're on the road, you are part of our team. And we'd say, 'We don't know,' and he'd give us a place.

"The boys had built a book—when we're in Scranton, here's where we stayed, they give us a rate, like that. So we started staying at the hotels that they did. And of course there'd always be a lounge in the hotel or else believe me, none of us would be staying there. Because at the end of your day, you wanna sit down and relax.

"Arnie would see Mike and I come in and he'd put us over with André. He'd go, 'Hey, there's those kids.' And André goes, 'Who are they?' and he'd say, 'Oh, they're good kids, they're good kids.' After a few times of seeing us around, finally André said, 'Come on over here, boys, have a drink with us,' and that started it. That started it. We started talking, and then our natural chemistry came out.

"As we got to know each other, I just saw what a real nice human being he was. Because of his being a giant and a big, huge star—at that time, André and Muhammad Ali were the most recognizable athlete celebrities in the world—the people never got to know him. You can't hug the whole world.

"But he really was the greatest guy. The people in his closest circle he loved to death. He made himself the brunt of his own jokes, he just wanted you to be happy. Imagine that? He wanted *you* to be happy."

White bonded with André and Skaaland and, before long, was invited to travel with them. Later, when Skaaland began spending less and less time on the road, White took over his role as André's regular traveling companion.

TIM WHITE: "Arnie used to be the driver. He was the one that used to drive, and they'd run together and travel together. I became the third wheel, and when Arnie started to get off the road, it was kind of a handoff. He picked me, just like André picked Hogan to carry on. Arnie felt, being André's best friend, that I would be a guy that would care about him and take care of him."

HOWARD FINKEL: "André, Arnie, and Timmy were like the three amigos. They were inseparable when they were all on the road. They just had a blast wherever they went. They could drink, they could eat, they could be merry."

TED DIBIASE: "I had a tremendous time with the guy. Traveling with André, you couldn't buy anything. Nothing. We'd go somewhere to eat, he'd pick up the tab. We traveled a lot with Tim White. We had one of those great big conversion vans and Tim would drive, with me and André sitting in the back watching movies and drinking beer."

SHANE McMAHON: "The André van was a cool thing. André didn't fit anywhere. We tried to find big cars, but it was hard for him to be comfortable. Finally my dad got him the André van, which was a custom coach with a pop top for extra headroom, a big captain's swivel chair to make it easy for him to sit comfortably. He'd get in, and the van would tip."

TIM WHITE: "We found a place in Long Island that did custom vans. We pulled all the seats out, put a TV and a phone and a big captain's chair in the back. It had everything. It was state-of-the-art back then. That's what we used locally. The two of us were just amazed every time we picked up the phone and were able to call France while we were driving down the highway.

"Now, when we had to go to the Midwest or California, part of my job was to call camper rental places to find something that André could fit in and ride comfortably. Several times we had an RV. When I got an RV, André would give me a list of the guys he wanted to ride with us, like Gorilla and Pedro. Oh my God, it was hilarious what went on.

"These guys, they were the legends of the business. I'm driving down the highway with Pedro and Gorilla and Arnie and André, everyone laughing, telling stories, playing cards. I loved it. The travel, the guys, the wrestling. I don't know how I got so lucky."

Mile after mile of excessive drinking and long-distance driving has its charms, but it also has its dangers. As it traveled along America's highways and byways, André's traveling saloon would occasionally run afoul of local authorities.

TIM WHITE: "We got pulled over for speeding a couple of times, quite a few times, because we were always in a hurry to get to the next place before they closed.

"Once in St. Louis I had to do the field sobriety thing outside the car. I only had maybe one or two beers in the locker room, so I was good with it. Now this police officer wasn't really on the ball. When he didn't see anyone in the passenger seat, he assumed I'm the only one in the van.

"He says, 'Okay, license, registration.' I said, 'You're pulling me over for the speed, I suppose?' He goes, 'Yeah. You been drinking?' I said, 'Yeah, I had a beer or two,' and he asked me to step out of the van.

"So he's got me touching my nose and standing on one foot and doing all this shit. He goes, 'You're okay but I'm gonna run your license now.' I get back in the van, and all of a sudden, André's hand comes out of the back with a beer. The officer jumps back, like, 'What the—' He looks in the van and goes, 'Oh, my God, that's André the Giant!'

"André says, 'Congratulations on passing the test, Timber,' and hands me a beer. 'Go ahead, drink it,' the cop says. 'I don't care, that's André the Giant in there!' We laughed our asses off all the way back down the highway."

Of course, one couldn't live entirely on the road. André made his home in a sprawling 200-acre ranch in Ellerbee, North Carolina. A lifelong aficionado of Western films, the Giant populated his homestead—dubbed "the AJF Ranch" after himself, his friend, former traveling companion, and estate manager Frenchy Bernard, and Frenchy's wife, Jackie—with a variety of livestock, including horses and longhorn cattle.

TIM WHITE: "Somebody told André that he'd get all sorts of tax breaks if he raised livestock. 'This place would be perfect for you,' they told him. 'It's huge and it's out of the way so you can have your own retreat.' He went down there, made the deal.

"The ranch was beautiful. It had a tree growing right through the middle of it, skylights, big decks, a huge gazebo in the yard.

"He had some of the most hellacious parties. Typical André, they lasted a day or two. Never ended. I remember André telling me that they found Albano passed out in the woodshed one time."

Squashing Big John Studd, *WrestleMania*.

6

When Vince McMahon took charge of World Wrestling Federation in 1983, he changed the very nature of the business. Though wrestlers traditionally traveled from one outfit to the next, each one covering a particular region, McMahon's newly nationalized promotion required Superstars to work only for him. André had been a hugely valuable commodity for the various territories, and

McMahon knew that in order to build his brand, he'd have to maintain control over the Giant's career. In 1984, he signed André to a contract that excluded him from working anywhere other than with the company, though he did allow him to continue wrestling with New Japan.

VINCE McMAHON: "We were in competition with all those other promoters, so I couldn't have André, who was one of our greatest assets, go work with them. I don't think André appreciated that too much. It's ironic—André never bitched about a payoff. After those old promotion days were over and he was strictly working in our organization, he made more money than he'd ever made. But that wasn't it with André. He wasn't about the money. The fact that he was earning three times more than he ever did before didn't really mean that much to him.

"When he was in the territorial system, he wanted to be paid top dollar, whatever top dollar was. And in some of those small markets, it wasn't a lot of money. Then, when I wouldn't let him go and he was only working here, he made three times as much or maybe even more. But that didn't mean that much to André. He wanted to be there with the top earners, but the money didn't mean anything to him.

"He was missing those days, he was missing those promoters that he had good times with. The other promoters were all pissed off at me, naturally. These were my dad's friends, these were André's friends, and I'd made them enemies. And now I wouldn't let André go and perform for them."

"André was the first internationally recognized athlete in our business, so therefore he was a tremendous asset to me. Of course Hogan came on the heels of that and we were expanding, getting more and more exposure. But André was definitely instrumental in our initial success."

JERRY LAWLER: "Vince Jr. bought out his dad and the following year he started showing World Wrestling Federation shows on the USA TV network. That cable exposure meant that many local promotions had to compete with a national power, and they didn't have the money or talent to do it. . . . Vince started signing all the top stars and buying out other promotions. . . . Soon he didn't have to buy the territories, he could just roll over them.

"A lot of people had said that Vince's dad would never have done what Junior did. He was more of a traditionalist and a mild, easygoing kind of guy. He probably wouldn't have let him buy all the territories, mostly because of the alliance that he'd been part of. That was the business as he knew it, and he wouldn't have wanted to be the guy to change that.

MICHAEL KRUGMAN

"[Vince's] expansion plans caused the other territories to fall by the wayside. What Vince did was sign up nearly all the good wrestlers. It was easy to do because all the guys wanted to get on cable. They knew they'd be seen all over the country rather than just on regional TV. . . . So from the AWA in Minneapolis, for example, he hired Bobby Heenan, he hired Hulk Hogan, he hired Jesse Ventura, he hired Gene Okerlund, all the top guys. Then he went right back into Minneapolis with those guys and all of his wrestlers too and promoted shows. Fans would see all the guys they were used to seeing, plus all these other stars. . . . This happened all over the country."

TED DIBIASE: "I spent the better part of the first twelve years of my career in Mid-South. It was a long, tough territory, the trips were ridiculous, but Bill Watts was a tremendous promoter and very savvy. By the time Bill realized what Vince was doing it was too late for him to make a move."

André was without doubt the preeminent big man in professional wrestling, but he was not the only one. Promoters everywhere had matched André with other behemoths, including Don Leo Jonathan and Ernie Ladd.

McMahon followed suit in this respect, knowing that pitting André in a titanic program with another big man would generate enormous attention and, of course, huge box office returns. Other than André, the biggest big man under contract was one John William Minton—known far and wide as Big John Studd.

Billed as six-foot-ten, 364 pounds, Studd was trained by another legendary big man—and André rival—Killer Kowalski. The renowned heel gave his pupil his first big break by teaming as the Executioners. Their faces hidden under black masks, the duo won WWWF World Tag Team gold in May 1976. Known simply as Executioner #1 and Executioner #2, Kowalski and Minton dominated the WWWF tag team division for much of the year, though their reign ended in ignominious defeat when Executioner #3—the infamous Nikolai Volkoff—interfered in a title match against Chief Jay Strongbow & Billy White Wolf. The Executioners were stripped of their championship, and the two wrestlers moved on to continue their respective singles careers.

From there, Minton hit the road hard, working under an assortment of monikers like Chuck O'Connor, Captain USA, and The Masked Superstar II. In 1977, he adopted the handle that he would soon make famous. Wrestling as John Studd, he defeated Bruiser Brody to win the NWA American

Heavyweight Championship, a title he held for only two months. Studd found a steady base of operations with Jim Crockett's Mid-Atlantic Championship Wrestling, where he won tag team gold with both Ric Flair and later, his future partner Ken Patera.

Of course, in those territory days wrestlers weren't bound by promotion, and Studd often ventured north to work for Atlantic Grand Prix Wrestling, as well as for Verne Gagne's AWA. His AWA career included a number of successful programs, against Dino Bravo and Mad Dog Vachon, as well as several unsuccessful title shots against promoter/champion Verne Gagne. In 1981, Studd won NWA gold once more, defeating Angelo Mosca for the Canadian Heavyweight title. Feuds with Ric Flair and Blackjack Mulligan followed, as well as a NWA Georgia Tag Team Championship with Super Destroyer in 1982.

Later that same year, Studd was brought to Eddie Graham's Championship Wrestling from Florida by J. J. Dillon, where he was put into programs with Barry Windham, Cowboy Ron Bass, and of course, the promotion's biggest star, Dusty Rhodes. Before the year was out, Studd teamed with Jim Garvin to win the first-ever Global Tag Team Championship tournament. The title reign was short-lived, dropping the championships to Windham and Bass just two weeks later.

Studd landed on his feet soon thereafter, signing with the dominant World Wrestling Federation. With "Classy" Freddie Blassie as his manager, Studd was quickly put into the title chase against World Wrestling Federation Heavyweight Champion Bob Backlund. Though he failed to capture the gold, Studd earned a reputation as a big man to be reckoned with. Blassie pushed the point by holding weekly bodyslam challenges, with thousands going to the wrestler who could lift and drop Studd to the mat.

On February 15, 1983 at Allentown, Pennsylvania's Agricultural Hall—the site of the company's monthly *Championship Wrestling* tapings—André answered the challenge.

Blassie and Studd's Bodyslam Challenge is now at $10,000. Debris is being flung immediately upon their arrival. The challenger is announced initially as Chief Jay Strongbow, but the Chief comes out from the back and signals a change in plans. The curtains part and a smiling André emerges, to Studd's shock and dismay.

Studd tries to weasel out, but the crowd demands the Challenge take place. André stands grinning in the middle of the ring, waiting for Studd to take his shot. "Come on," he gestures, pointing at the canvas in front of him. "Right here."

Blassie walks up behind Studd. As André scoops up Studd, Blassie wraps his arms around his wrestler's waist. André tries to lift Studd twice before getting wise and shoving Studd into the ropes. Blassie turns to scurry away, but André shoves his shoulders, causing the Classy One to tumble to the canvas, bills flying out of his hand. Backed into the corner, he begs off and shoves some cash at André, who tosses it away. Studd attacks with a double ax-handle to André's neck, then hammers with forearms to his shoulders. A series of boots double the Giant over in the corner, but André fights back with wild chops. Studd drops and rolls out under the ropes.

VINCE McMAHON: "Studd was six-ten and about 350, a good-sized man. But not even close to André. Studd was a nice guy, but he was scared to death of André. He always thought of himself as this big giant—which he was—but André was a legitimate giant. In any event, André sensed that John didn't have any balls, and that was that. If you've got no nuts, you really shouldn't be in the business, especially if you're a big guy."

TIM WHITE: "He didn't respect Big John too much. He had problems with John, he had problems with Dino Bravo, he had problems with a few other guys. But when I got into that with him, 'Don't worry, boss,' would be his answer to me.

"I liked Big John. I always saw him trying to be André's friend, and it was kinda pathetic because you could see he wasn't buying into it."

SHANE McMAHON: "André didn't like anybody else that was remotely big. He wanted to be the only giant, because that was his thing."

Beginning in March, André and Studd battled on a regular basis, including a number of six-, eight-, and ten-man Best-Three-Out-of-Five Falls matches, alongside such top stars as Bob Backlund, Rocky Johnson, Jimmy Snuka, Tony Garea, and Chief Jay Strongbow vs. major heels like Don Muraco, the Wild Samoans, Mr. Fuji, and Sgt. Slaughter. Steel Cage matches and further Bodyslam Challenges became a staple of their feud, with bloody bouts in Boston Garden, New Jersey's Meadowlands, the Los Angeles Sports Arena, and the Philadelphia Spectrum.

"He's wrestled against Mulligan, other big men, and he's worked his way up to me," Studd told *World Wrestling Federation's Victory* in November 1983. "As far as I'm concerned, I'm the best big man in professional wrestling. He has a lot of people buffaloed that he is the main man of wrestling. That might have been true a few years back, but I'm ready for him now."

"Before John Studd it was Don Leo Jonathan," responded André. "He was the first time I wrestled against another big guy. His last match—I'm sorry to say—I put him in the hospital."

April 20, 1983: Fieldhouse, Hamburg, PA

ROGERS CORNER W/BIG JOHN STUDD

"There's only one man in this business that might stop Big John Studd," says the legendary "Nature Boy" Buddy Rogers, hosting his *Rogers Corner* interview segment. "and I for one believe that André the Giant just might do it."

"I'll tell you something, Rogers," declares his guest, Big John Studd. "I'm gonna tell all you people out there, I've given André the Giant—and this is the last time I'll call him 'Giant' on your spot—every opportunity in the world to wrestle me, and I have a contract in front of every promoter in the entire United States, it says John Studd's name on it and André the Giant. All he has to do is sign it. As far as I'm concerned, you talk about size, take a look at this fist right here, it's as big as your head. [Studd gets up, opening his robe.] Take a look at this body right here, take a look at it! Three hundred sixty-eight pounds of solid muscle. The man stole $10,000 from me, and I'm tired of going to all these arenas and seeing all you people having these signs that say 'André the Giant Is #1' when he hasn't proven himself. To be number one he has to beat John Studd, the giant of professional wrestling! And then, when we meet in the center of the ring, no matter where it is in these United States, and I show you, Rogers, and I show all you people out there that John Studd is the only giant, you will all be bringing the right poster and that is 'Big John Studd the Giant Is #1.'"

"Well, that remains to be seen," concludes Rogers, "and I still think André might cut the job."

April 25, 1983: Madison Square Garden, New York, NY

ANDRÉ THE GIANT VS. BIG JOHN STUDD

Studd comes to the ring and announces, "Tonight's the night that Studd slams André the Girl! C'mon, André the Girl, I don't have all night!"

André comes in, climbs over the top, stares down Studd, and shoves him. Studd shoves right back. André shoves again, as does Studd. The bell rings, and Finkel runs out of the way as André shoves, now with two hands, sending Studd into the corner.

"Tonight's final bout is the Battle of the Titans, one fall or to curfew," says ring announcer Howard Finkel. "Introducing first, to my right, from Los Angeles, California, weighing 364 pounds, Big John Studd! His opponent, from Grenoble in the French Alps, weight 492 pounds, the Eighth Wonder of the World, André the Giant!"

A shoving match ensues before Studd even gets his robe off. André chops his chest, sending him back and over the rope to the apron.

"Everywhere André the Giant goes, people recognize him," says color commentator Pat Patterson. "All over the world, this man cannot hide from no one. I told him one time, why don't you put a hat on, maybe they won't recognize you."

André smiles as Studd stretches and challenges him. They lock up and André pushes Studd into the corner. Studd complains that André grabbed his hair. They lock up again and Studd lands a blow to André's shoulder. They stare down, locking up again; Studd continues to work on André's left arm and shoulder. Big chop sends him back. Lock up, André goes right for the slam, Studd hooks the top rope. Ref breaks it up, but André pushes Studd back, his hand covering Studd's face. Studd reels from another big chop but comes right back, working the shoulder and arm. Studd locks onto the arm, dropping André down.

"It's not the left arm that gives you the power for the slam," notes commentator Gorilla Monsoon, "it's the right one."

Studd holds André's arm out and drops an elbow. André gets up, lands a right, but Studd maintains his hold, putting André back down onto the mat. André sells hard, gets to the ropes, but Studd won't let go, working the shoulder. He lands another right breaking the hold. Studd comes in for a double ax-handle, but André ducks into a bearhug. Studd starts squeezing André's head, going at his eyes. André kidney-punches out, and then two big chops and a big right send Studd back into the ropes. He comes off with a knee that Gorilla says "looks very, very low to me."

A big boot and a chop put Studd down. He gets right back up, they lock up, and André gives him a headbutt. Studd goes to one knee, then rolls out between the middle ropes. Referee John Stanley gets to seven before Studd comes back in. André gets him into the corner, hand on Studd's face, chop, two big butt shots, another right, chop, but Studd goes back to the shoulder. André goes shoulder-first into Studd's midsection, sending him hard into the turnbuckle. He sets up a headbutt, but Studd reverses and tries for the slam. He tries to lift three times, but André turns it into a headlock. He swings three big chops and Studd is whipped into the ropes for a Giant-sized boot to the sternum; Studd rolls out to the apron. André grabs his hair, stands him up, big right and chop chop chop, reaches over the ropes and gets Studd set for the slam, but Studd hooks the top rope between his ankles. André drops him to his back, then sit-down slam on his chest. Studd rolls out to the floor and heads up the aisle. The referee counts him out at 8:22 as the crowd goes wild.

However, the countout victory does not satisfy André, who grabs the mic from Finkel: "I want Studd back in the ring, I'm not going to leave the ring before he come back in this ring!

BIG JOHN STUDD: "I'll meet him anywhere, anytime, in any kind of match. If he can beat me, then I'll say he's a better man. . . . I've never seen a wrestler come out of a steel cage without being hurt, and André doesn't want to get hurt. My goal is to become Number One. That means if I have to hurt him, then I'll have to hurt him. That means he'll have to retire from wrestling or he'll have to get on national television and tell everyone that, hey, he's Number Two, and that John Studd is Number One. That's my object, that's what I'm after. That's my prize, my championship."

ANDRÉ THE GIANT: "I don't like to be in a cage. I go into the cage against John Studd not for myself, but for the people. I just want to show the people I can beat him. If he wants to get me in the cage, I'll go."

June 11, 1983: Boston Garden, Boston, MA

ANDRÉ THE GIANT VS. BIG JOHN STUDD
IN A STEEL CAGE MATCH

André starts by tearing Studd's face against the wire mesh, drawing blood. He follows with a big chop, and then whips Studd into the ropes for the big boot. Studd ducks and nails André with a clothesline. The Giant doubles over; Studd lands a double ax-handle into André's back, sending him flat onto the mat. A weary Studd hits the canvas himself and begins crawling for the door. André rises in time to grab Studd's left boot, dragging him away from the door, then drops a big leg onto the back of Studd's neck.

"That could terminate your career, a move like that," notes Gorilla Monsoon.

André stands up and, rather than leave the cage, steps on Studd's head. Studd manages to grab André's enormous right ankle and pulls him down, but the Giant lands a hip directly onto Studd's head. André gets to one knee and lands a big fist to Studd's forehead. André stands up, raising a fist to the screaming crowd, as Studd inches backward toward the center of the ring. André reaches down, grabs a handful of Studd's mane, and effortlessly lifts his six-foot-ten opponent and slams him down hard. He climbs to the top turnbuckles and leaps off, landing a sit-down splash onto Studd's chest.

"This match is over!" exclaims Monsoon. The crowd goes wild as André calls for the cage door to be opened and steps out, fist raised in victory.

$30,000 18-MAN BATTLE ROYAL FEATURING ANDRÉ, BIG JOHN STUDD, HULK HOGAN, THE MASKED SUPERSTAR, MOONDOG REX, SAMULA, MIL MASCARAS, DAVID SCHULTZ, BOB BOYER, MR. FUJI, TIGER CHUNG LEE, IVAN PUTSKI, TONY ATLAS, PAUL ORNDORFF, ROCKY JOHNSON, JIMMY SNUKA, AND THE TAG TEAM CHAMPIONS ADRIAN ADONIS & DICK MURDOCH.

Studd spends the early part of the match hanging outside on the apron. Shultz and Snuka are eliminated in the first moments, followed soon thereafter by Hogan's tossing out Moondog Rex. André tries to dump Fuji, who catches onto the ropes. André bounces the ropes in an attempt to loose him, but to no avail.

"It's pandemonium everywhere," notes Vince McMahon on commentary.

André kicks back in the far corner, and then gets into an exchange with Tony Atlas. Bob Boyer runs at André, who gets a boot up and puts him down. André lies down on Boyer, followed by the remaining contestants piling on, bar Hogan who prefers to observe the mayhem. Afterward, Orndorff kicks away as the official extracts the deflated Boyer from the ring.

In the corner, Studd traps André with a facelock from outside on the apron, opening him up for blows from Orndorff. He escapes and hits his opponents with a noggin knocker.

Studd paces around the floor as Lee gets eliminated amid the chaos. André chokes out Atlas, who pitches the Masked Superstar over. Superstar pulls Atlas out, and they go at it outside. Orndorff is thrown over by Johnson, who goes through the ropes and gets pitched headfirst into the post by Mr. Wonderful. Despite the referee's protests, Orndorff lifts Rocky and smashes his head again, splitting him open. Orndorff beats Johnson a bit longer, and then sends him flying under the ropes into the ring. Samu and Murdoch double-team Johnson, who ducks a flying crossbody, sending Samu over the top. André grabs Murdoch's throat for Johnson. They go toe-to-toe and together, tumble out to the floor where their exchange continues.

André chops at Fuji, and then throws him out. Meanwhile, Hogan dumps Adonis, leaving the two face-to-face as Studd battles Mascaras and Putski in the opposite corner. Studd rids himself of his competition just as Hulk and André begin trading blows. They lock up and fall against the ropes, allowing Studd to come up behind them. He grabs André's trunks and leverages him over, then does the same to Hogan, winning the Battle Royal at 13:28.

The crowd boos as Studd raises his arms in victory. André climbs back in, but Studd quickly makes his escape to the outside. Hogan gets into the ring and demands Studd come back to face him one-on-one. André stalks Studd outside until finally Studd has no choice but to go into the ring. André follows, so Studd bolts back out. Hogan goes after him, as does André. Studd tries to flee into the ring, but André and Hogan grab his boots. They pull him out and take turns holding Studd's arms back for shots to the head. Studd goes down to his knees, and Hulk comes from behind and claws his face. André and Hogan raise their arms together as Studd is presented his $30,000 check in the ring.

Nineteen eighty-four proved an eventful year for André. He appeared in two major Hollywood films, Blake Edwards's *Mickey & Maude* (alongside Big John Studd, Chief Jay Strongbow, and Gene LeBell) and Richard Fleischer's *Conan the Destroyer*. He plays—uncredited—the god Dagoth, a rubber-suited horned monster conjured up by Arnold Schwarzenegger and his merry band of barbarians.

As his program with Studd continued, André was invited to appear on an early edition of what would become one of the World Wrestling Federation's most enduring segments, *Piper's Pit,* hosted by the one and only "Rowdy" Roddy Piper.

"Here we have, of course, this week on *Piper's Pit,* André the Giant," introduces Piper. "Supposedly the biggest man in the world ever. It's a pleasure to have you here. Where are you from, André?"

André, his hair wild and woolly, just stares at his insolent host.

"I'm sorry," says Piper. "Do you speak English? André, where. Do. You. Come. From?"

"None of your business," snarls the Giant.

"If the questions are too hard for you, I will try to bring them down a little so you can understand. I understand, big body, little, tiny, weeny brain. I can understand that, that's very simple. Let's get right down to facts. Is it not true that John Studd himself took the largest man like yourself, supposedly, in the world, and picked him up and slammed him? Is it not true that John Studd slammed you?"

"Never," answers André with a grin.

"Are you telling me that John Studd never slammed you? You trying to tell me, at 540 pounds, whatever you are, that you cannot be slammed?"

"Are you understand English or not? I told you that one time already."

"At 520 pounds, if I'm given five minutes, *I* could slam you myself! I don't care, you're saying John Studd, at 520—"

André stands up and grabs the Hot Rod by the collar of his T-shirt. He yanks him up onto the table, and then shoves him to the floor. Piper gets into defensive mode, but André takes another fistful of T-shirt. As Roddy tries to remove the red tee, André uses it to toss Piper toward the camera. The Giant stalks off as Piper returns, shirtless and raging.

"You think you're tough! Come on! You ain't nothing! I'll tell you one thing right now! You wanna fight, André? You're gonna find out one thing! *You do not throw rocks at a man who's got a machine gun!*"

> **RODDY PIPER:** "There was this behind-the-stage joke that he had been doing with me. I'd ask him a question, like 'Is that your water there, Andre?'
>
> " 'None of your business.'
>
> "It was just one of those stupid things that had been going around the dressing room. So when I got out there on *Piper's Pit* and asked him the first question, it was 'None of your business.'"

As part of his continuing efforts to bring wrestling's greatest talents to World Wrestling Federation, McMahon hired manager Bobby "The Brain"

Heenan away from Verne Gagne's AWA. Heenan was one of the sport's wittiest and most provocative heels, a verbally gifted performer whose management of such tag teams as the Blackjacks and Nick Bockwinkel & Ray Stevens led to the acquisition of a long run of championship gold.

Initially hired by McMahon to manage Jesse "The Body" Ventura, Heenan soon took the reins of Big John Studd's career. Also falling under Heenan's aegis was former Olympic weightlifter-turned-wrestler Ken Patera, who with Studd, formed the first World Wrestling Federation incarnation of the Heenan Family, an ever-shifting stable of heels that began in the AWA with Bockwinkel, Stevens, Bobby Duncum, and Blackjack Lanza.

With Heenan serving as mouthpiece, Studd's feud with André increased in its intensity. The program reached a fever pitch when André teamed with babyface "Special Delivery" Jones in a classic Tag match against Studd & Patera.

November 13, 1984: Mid-Hudson Civic Center, Poughkeepsie, NY

ANDRÉ THE GIANT & "SPECIAL DELIVERY" JONES
VS. BIG JOHN STUDD & KEN PATERA

On commentary, Vince McMahon notes that André & Jones were "pitting their skills against two of the strongest men in the world today, not just professional wrestling."

Patera and Jones lock up to start. Jones into the ropes, Patera drops, Jones hooks Patera's left arm as he bounces back, brings him to the corner, and tags André. André headbutts Patera, goes to work on the arm, delivers another headbutt, and tags Jones in. SD continues to work the arm, but gets caught in a backbreaker over Patera's knee. Studd tags in and begins beating on SD's back. Studd sends Jones into the ropes, right back into a big elbow. SD goes down and gets stomped by Studd. Patera is tagged in as Jones tries to get back to his corner, stopped by Studd. André reaches for Studd as SD gets beaten down by Patera. Jones is whipped into the ropes, comes off with a kick to Patera's chest. Headbutt sends Patera reeling back into André's corner.

SD tags André and goes for one more shot at Patera, who catches him and flips him over the top to the concrete floor, his head hitting the steel railing. André leads Patera to the opposite corner, where he chops at his chest and then squashes him against the turnbuckle. He backs up once, twice, and Patera gets a knee up, right into André's kidney. As André doubles over, Patera climbs onto the middle ropes, places a boot on André's back, and then drops an elbow into the back of his head. He hammers away, big rights to the back of André's head, and then hooks on—barely—a full nelson.

Studd jumps in, and the two begin double-teaming André, together suplexing him over into "an unbelievable slam." Studd drops an elbow, Patera drops an elbow, Patera grabs André and holds him down as Studd puts the boot to him. Studd holds André down by his knees as Patera gets onto the middle rope and drops a knee to his head. More elbows as the ref finally calls for the bell. The double-teaming continues, with André taking a nonstop rain of elbows and boots.

"André is taking a brutal beating from Studd and Ken Patera," says Vince. "Never have I ever seen André the Giant downed like this before, never."

The heels get André to his knees, Patera holding his arms behind his back. Heenan gets on the apron and pulls a pair of orange-handled scissors from his pocket. Studd takes the scissors and begins cutting off big clumps of André's bushy mane.

"Oh, no," moans McMahon. "Oh. This is humiliation. This is 'shear' humiliation."

"They're cutting his hair?" asks his shocked broadcast partner, the legendary Bruno Sammartino.

"This should not happen to any athlete," protests Vince as debris begins flying into the ring. "André is unconscious. He's being held up, literally, by Patera and Studd, continues to rape, Studd and Patera *rape the dignity* of André the Giant, who has been recognized as one of the greatest athletes of all time. Heenan keeping SD away as Studd and Patera continue to rape André the Giant's dignity, look what they're doing to this man."

Studd cuts away at André's hair as Patera stomps on his back, Heenan kicking at SD as he attempts to climb into the ring.

"I can't believe it," says Bruno, "that nothing is happening to stop

MICHAEL KRUGMAN

this, this is ridiculous. They won't stop, look at this [shot of big clumps of hair and a green peanut M&M on the canvas], both of them. Oh, my . . ."

"A nightmare," Vince agrees, "a complete nightmare. This is one of the most despicable displays of conduct in the history of World Wrestling Federation."

Heenan, Studd, and Patera circle the ring, displaying handfuls of hair as cups and assorted debris pelt them.

HOWARD FINKEL: "For John Studd and Ken Patera to go ahead and do what they did to André's hair, that was sacrilege. Studd would bring the hair around and show everybody. If eBay was around back then, it would've been worth a gold mine."

December 1984: Mid-Hudson Civic Center, Poughkeepsie, NY

PIPER'S PIT W/STUDD, PATERA, AND HEENAN

"The greatest array of wrestlers in the world today," says Roddy Piper, introducing his guests. "[They] made history by taking André the so-called Giant and making a complete blithering idiot of him. I'd like to ask one question, you first Mr. Heenan, was it premeditated?"

"Oh, yes," says the Brain. "It was planned from the very beginning. You probably wonder, why? Well, it's simple. We wanted to demoralize this Giant, so-called Giant. We wanted to take his dignity from him and we wanted to embarrass André the Giant. And I think we did a heckuva job.

"Did he look silly! I ain't never seen nobody look sillier in their entire life."

"That's because he's already a big goof anyway, everybody realizes that," interjects Patera. "It was premeditated, and the thing was, we didn't realize how easy it was gonna be to knock the man unconscious and do what we did to him, and that was clip his hair and humiliate him."

"It also proved that there really is only one giant in professional wrestling," declares Piper, "and that's John Studd. Get up, show 'em the real giant!"

Studd rises from his seat, holding up the bag of André's hair. "This is something all you people will remember forever and ever and ever—André the Giant is in this bag! And you know what, Mr. Piper?"

"What?"

Studd opens up the bag. "Pick a lock."

"Pick a lock?"

"By having us on your program, you may pick a lock of hair," Heenan explains.

Piper is positively gleeful at receiving such a prize. "Ha! This is André's hair? It's got fleas in it, man. It's dirty and nasty, but I want one. [Pulling out a clump.] Oh! Ha ha! It's mine! André, it's been a pleasure!"

January 21, 1985: Madison Square Garden, New York, NY

ANDRÉ VS. KEN PATERA (W/BOBBY HEENAN)

"Privately, André vowed to me that it was just a matter of time and he would pay these gentlemen back," says commentator "Mean" Gene Okerlund.

"Well, he has to, Gene," notes his broadcast partner, Gorilla Monsoon, "because he was humiliated on that particular day."

"Stripped of a great deal of dignity, it's going to be very difficult to come back."

"Well, if anyone can, this individual can. . . ."

"I concur," Okerlund concurs.

". . . because this is not your run-of-the-mill nine-to-fiver, this guy's gonna make these two individuals pay."

"Is he ever."

Patera gets into the ring. André gives him a knee to the midsection, a big right, and then chops him into the corner; a headbutt sends Patera to the mat. He rolls out and into Heenan's arms.

"André's telling the referee to get in the corner and get out of the way and let me do my thing here," Gene explains.

Patera gets back in; André stands before him, seemingly unstoppable. Patera readies a punch; André gestures. "Come on, then."

Patera climbs back out to the apron. He gets back in, goes to another corner. André turns to him, rubbing his hands together, ready and waiting. Patera makes his move and lunges toward the Giant, but André open-hands him below the belt. Patera doubles over; André swings a big boot to the butt, sending Patera running to the ropes and out to the floor. Heenan consoles Patera, one arm around his wrestler, the other hand on the apron. André places his big blue boot on the Brain's hand. Patera tries to pull the huge foot off and gets his own hand stepped on with André's other foot. He reaches over and bashes their heads together, the heels each reeling backward as the 22,000 fans in a sold-out MSG crowd roar.

Patera gets back in and raises a fist; André just grins his huge toothsome smile. Patera makes his move, but André grabs him and wraps his two huge hands around Patera's throat.

"Like a rag doll," Monsoon says, "he's shaking him, choking him."

"Like a child!" adds Mean Gene.

André goes back onto the ropes and smashes his fist into Patera's sternum. He stumbles forward and goes face-first onto the canvas. André grabs him up and chokes him with his singlet strap, shaking him violently back and forth. Reeling, Patera manages to roll out of the ring. André just misses grabbing him by the hair. Patera gets back in, holding a hand up as if to say, Don't come any closer. André shakes his head, rubbing his shortened hair and making scissor gestures with his fingers to remind Patera of why he's about to be destroyed. Patera just looks sad. André approaches; Patera gets his fists up in defensive position and lands two rights to the Giant's jaw to little or no effect. André chops him down. André gets a bearhug on, squeezing Patera between himself and the turnbuckle. Headbutt, reverse knife-edge chop, Patera goes down. He rolls back up, but André grabs him and sends him into the ropes. André goes for a backdrop, but Patera comes back, boot extended. He begins punching André, landing four strong shots, stunning André.

Sensing his opportunity, Patera goes to lift André for a bodyslam, but André breaks it up with a knee to the midsection. A big boot sends Patera down once more. André lifts Patera up and hits an atomic drop; Patera bounces up and over the top rope. A handful of hair brings Patera back up onto the apron and over the top into the ring. André sends Patera into the ropes and right back into a boot. Patera rolls to the apron, but another handful of hair lifts him up, back against the ropes. A shot to Patera's sternum drops him; he falls into the ring ass first between the bottom ropes. André takes a seat on his neck and shoulders. Patera ends up on his back. André stands directly on top of him, the crowd going mental. Patera rolls out as André steps off.

The ref tells André to be careful, but André rubs his shorn head, explaining why he's breaking the rules. André finally follows Patera to the floor—punch, chop, and throws him into the steel railing. Pleased with his work, André, ever mindful of the regulations, rolls back into the ring.

Patera is down on the floor; André is debating with the ref. Heenan slips on his brass knuckles and climbs to the top turnbuckle. He leaps up, rather ungracefully, and lands the knucks into the back of André's head, sending him down and taking the ref with him. Heenan kicks and punches André's enormous back as the Giant tries to regain his footing. André gets up, and Heenan starts punching him, the knucks doing their job, shaking up André and sending him down to the mat. Heenan gestures to Patera, who climbs up to the top. He goes for the splash, but André gets a boot up in time, right to Patera's chin. Heenan tries to help Patera, but André grabs their heads and pushes them into the corner, his back pressing down against them both. After a couple of big butt shots, he whips Patera across the ring into the opposite corner.

André slaps Heenan repeatedly, then whips him toward Patera, who gets down in time to avoid being hit by the Brain. Heenan, however, winds up in the corner, draped over the top turnbuckle. André takes Patera and tosses him toward the corner, knocking Heenan backward to the floor. A headbutt puts Patera down, and he bails out. The ref holds up André's hand as Heenan and Patera stumble and crawl up the aisle. The cops escort Patera to the back as the crowd goes crazy.

PIPER'S PIT W/ANDRÉ

Roddy Piper welcomes André to his show. His associate, "Cowboy" Bob Orton, stands behind him, arms folded.

"Hello." Piper rises to greet his guest. André takes the waiting chair and throws it off the set. He stands close to Roddy, intimidating him with a slight smile.

"Mr. Giant, sir. Mr. Giant, I would just like to explain to you that I have been a fan of yours for a long time, and I think that you're a terrific person."

He moves his own chair behind him, and introduces Orton. "This is my bodyguard, Ace, and he's been a fan of yours, and I think that is a terrible, terrible thing what John Studd and Ken Patera did to you, by taking you and cutting your hair in the ring. I'm a hundred percent on your side, sir!"

"First of all," says André, "next time you get me on the *Piper's Pit,* get a chair in my size. I don't like those small chairs. Another thing, about John Studd and Ken Patera, I will say one thing. I'm gonna get even, my way."

Orton claps and nods his head, but André glares at him, sensing the phoniness of the applause.

"I agree that you're gonna get even your way, sir," Piper says. "And I'm a hundred percent behind you like I said, and what those guys did to you was terrible—"

André points a finger in Piper's face, interrupting. "I don't want you to say 'sir.' I want you to say 'Mr. Giant.'"

"Mr. Giant," Roddy continues, extending his hand, "it's been a pleasure having you here, sir . . . Mr. Giant. It's been a pleasure."

André just scowls and walks off, saluting the crowd but ignoring Piper's hand.

Piper and Orton pause, then take a look to be sure the Giant is gone. "What an idiot," Roddy laughs. "Are you kidding me? What a jerk!"

"I thought he looked bad with *long* hair," drawls Ace.

"He looks ridiculous! Let me tell you something, I've seen John

Studd right beside me, and John Studd is bigger than André the Giant!"

The crowd roars its disagreement, but Piper continues. "Are you kidding me? Let me tell you something, it's obvious, *quite* obvious, the bigger they are, the tinier the brain!"

Roddy puts a foot on the table and an arm around Orton's shoulder. "That ain't the problem in our case. This is Ace, my bodyguard. I loves my bodyguard. Ha, ha. André, you're such a goof."

JOHN STUDD (W/BOBBY HEENAN) VS. JIM YOUNG

Heenan takes the mic after Finkel introduces Studd, who is waving a plastic baggie filled with André's shorn locks. "Holding in his hand, $15,000 and the bag of hair of the head of the dummy, André the so-called Giant."

Howard Finkel informs challenger Jim Young that if he can slam Studd, the $15,000 prize is his. Young immediately tries to scoop up Studd, but to no avail. A dropkick shakes Studd up, but Young is still unable to lift the big man on his second attempt. A forearm across the back and a clothesline puts the kibosh on Young's offense. Studd covers—taking a handful of hair—and gets a one-count. Studd lifts Young and drops him across the ropes, then goes for another cover, this time getting two. Studd lifts Young up and slams him just as André arrives, removing his sports coat during his walk up the aisle.

Studd hammers him into the corner the moment he gets into the ring. André chops and headbutts and punches, while Studd continues to throw forearms. A chop to the throat puts Studd down, and he immediately rolls out to the floor.

André wants more, but Heenan keeps Studd from reentering the ring. "They were going at it like animals," says Vince McMahon on commentary. "Two giant-sized animals!"

Finkel announces Studd as the winner by disqualification at 1:15. The crowd chants "André! André! André!"

BIG JOHN STUDD: "Giant? I'm the real giant and a giant killer besides. I don't need Ken Patera nor anyone else to help me put André down on his face again. And if that ox of a Frenchman thinks I hurt his pride before, wait until I get a second chance to do it again."

In 1985, with World Wrestling Federation now dominating the industry, McMahon unveiled plans for a major event, dubbed *WrestleMania*. Slated for March 31 at New York City's Madison Square Garden, the show would officially confirm the company's status as a national promotion by being broadcast across the country on closed-circuit TV. *WrestleMania* would be headlined by World Wrestling Federation Champion—and burgeoning pop culture icon—Hulk Hogan, teaming up with *The A-Team*'s Mr. T in a match versus top heel Roddy Piper (and his bodyguard, Cowboy Bob Orton) and Paul "Mr. Wonderful" Orndorff.

To add broad appeal to the show, McMahon brought in a star-studded roster of celebrities, such as flamboyant piano player Liberace, New York Yankees manager Billy Martin, Radio City Music Hall's Rockettes, and "the Greatest" himself, Muhammad Ali. Most significantly, McMahon cross-promoted with the newly created MTV by involving pop star Cyndi Lauper in the Women's Championship program, a relationship that became known as "The Rock 'n' Wrestling Connection."

Of course, no World Wrestling Federation supercard would be complete without an André the Giant match. He was pitted against his archrival Studd in the biggest Bodyslam Challenge of all, with $15,000 on the line for the winner.

FINKEL: "Hulk Hogan was the goose that laid the golden egg, make no mistake about it. But André was an attraction unto himself. That's why he got the name 'the Eighth Wonder of the World.' André was unique, and nobody ever challenged that. The perfect man for André at *WrestleMania* was John Studd. There was no doubt about it. You had two big behemoths, and back then, big was better and better meant box office."

On March 15, André promoted his upcoming match at *WrestleMania* with a visit to *Tuesday Night Titans*, the World Wrestling Federation's hilarious takeoff of the classic late-night talk-show format. The program was hosted by Vince McMahon, who sat behind a desk not unlike that of Johnny Carson or David Letterman. And like Carson, Vince was joined by an amiably sycophantic sidekick in Lord Alfred Hayes.

"Welcome back to TNT," says McMahon, shaking André's huge hand. "My goodness, I think you're larger now than when you were previously on TNT. Are you gaining weight, André?"

"A little bit."

"A little bit?"

"Almost five hundred now." The Giant grins.

"Almost five hundred pounds?"

Lord Alfred Hayes is appropriately stunned. "Phew! Gosh!"

"A long way from since you first met me first time," André says, turning to his old friend.

"When you were seventeen," Hayes remembers. "Oh gosh, a long way."

"You fellas go a long way back," explains McMahon, "to when André was seventeen."

"When I first start, yes."

"And Alfred was old even then," jokes Vince.

"Ha ha, thanks a lot." Lord Alfred laughs.

"At that time," André notes, "I was only two hundred and seventy pounds."

"Two hundred and seventy pounds, André."

"Yeah."

"You had a devastating dropkick too," recalls Hayes.

"Is that right?" asks McMahon. "Do you find now, with your weight, the mobility is still there? Do you find that it's an asset when you're meeting, let's face it, you're meeting, well as a matter of fact, you're meeting a giant in his own right, on March 31, a man who's very close to the four-hundred-pound mark now, he's huge, Big John Studd?"

"Right, then you get another guy, you get Ken Patera, who can push five hundred pounds over his head," says André, noting, "but he never did it with me."

"No, I'm sure a barbell, balanced as it is, is totally different than the way your weight is distributed."

"I'll tell you one thing," rebuts the Giant. "I pick up four hundred pounds before."

"I have no doubt about that," agrees McMahon. "What we'd like to do is

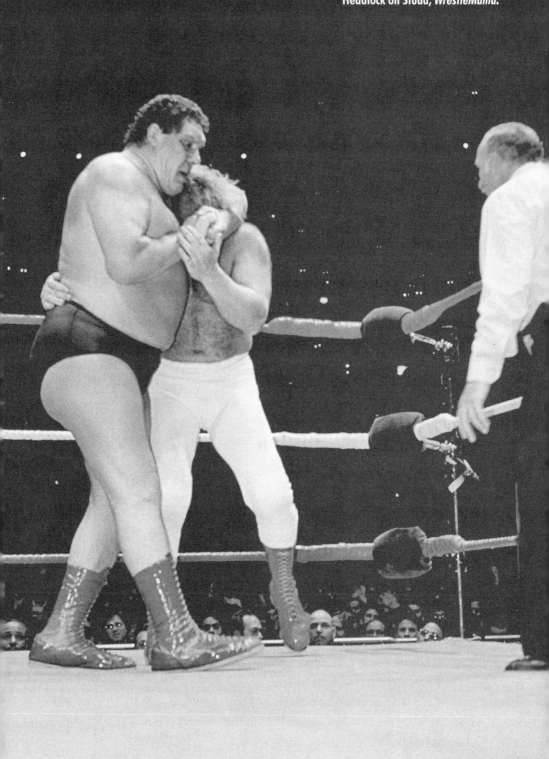

Headlock on Studd, *WrestleMania.*

take you back, take you to a match, this matchup, very, very important because it pits André the Giant against Ken Patera. Bobby 'The Brain' Heenan, and this is in Madison Square Garden, and this is a match that André the Giant positively had to win."

The match—billed as "The Battle of the Behemoths"—is screened. "That was the very first match you'd had since Heenan, Patera, and Studd attempted to rape your dignity," says McMahon upon its conclusion. "You were determined more than ever to right the wrong, but you didn't quite do it all the way. On March 31, there's an awful lot at stake at Madison Square Garden, as fans watch literally all over the world via satellite or on closed-circuit television all over this country. A tremendous amount at stake, because this is the final chapter that you can write, be it André finally for the first time, bowing in defeat to Big John Studd, who's bulked up to almost four hundred pounds, looks better than he's ever looked in his life. Fifteen thousand dollars on the line as well, as they have placed fifteen thousand dollars in jeopardy should you slam Big John Studd.

"I wonder, there have been a number of things brought, a number of questions asked by Bobby Heenan and others, is André the Giant willing to put up anything? They're willing to put up fifteen thousand dollars—"

"I will to tell you," André interrupts. "I put my hair up already. They cut my hair."

"No, I understand that—"

"They got my hair," the Giant says. "But I'm going to tell you one thing, I don't come into the ring to be a loser. I'll come into Madison Square Garden—not just Madison Square Garden, but there will be all over the world for this match—but believe me, I don't come in there to get beat. I come there to win."

"Okay, they're putting up fifteen thousand," argues McMahon. "And Heenan makes, I think, a good point, to a certain extent. What's André the Giant putting up? I mean, shouldn't André the Giant put up something if they're putting up fifteen thousand dollars? Regardless of who wins this match, and it could be, as you well know, for the first time, bowing in defeat. Then again, it could be you finally writing all the wrongs. But they're putting up fifteen thousand dollars. Bobby Heenan thinks that you should put up something, as a matter of fact."

"Why I have to put something up? They want to lose that money, I will take that money."

McMahon refuses to drop the point. "All right, but Heenan thinks that maybe you should put up something like, if you don't slam Big John Studd, then you have to retire from wrestling. How do you think about that?"

André takes a long pause to think over the challenge. "Bobby Heenan say that?"

"Bobby Heenan, Ken Patera, they all state that you should put up something, and they think that's the only fair thing for you to put up. That if you can't slam Big John Studd, then you retire from wrestling. If you do slam Studd, of course you don't retire—"

"And I win that ten thousand dollars."

"Fifteen. Fifteen thousand dollars," corrects McMahon. "But don't you think you should put up something, André?"

"I don't think so."

"Okay, but there are gonna be people that state that there's a bit of a yellow streak running down your back if you don't put it up, if you don't put something up, there's gonna be people that state there's a big yellow—"

André is infuriated by Vince's insult to his courage and integrity. He rises up and grabs Vince by his tie, yanking him up out of his chair. "I will tell you one thing, nobody call me yellow. And I will take that slam, and I will take that fifteen thousand dollars, and I will walk out that ring."

With that, André drops McMahon back behind his desk and storms off the set. Lord Alfred calls out to his longtime mate.

"André . . . ," he says, and then turns to McMahon. "Gosh, I guess you upset him."

JIM "J.R." ROSS: "[Studd] was probably the first guy that really became a rival of André the Giant to that level that people had concern. And certainly the culmination of that, their Bodyslam Challenge at the first *WrestleMania* was certainly a very memorable night for big men in our business."

WRESTLEMANIA: BODYSLAM CHALLENGE—ANDRÉ THE GIANT VS. BIG JOHN STUDD (W/BOBBY "THE BRAIN" HEENAN)

Before the match, "Mean" Gene Okerlund interviews Studd and Heenan. "André the Giant," he begins, "putting his entire career on the line—"

"Oh, man, this bag is heavy, man," butts in Studd. "This is what it was all about. The fifteen thousand dollars that we used for bait. [Heenan opens the bag of cash, displaying crumpled singles and fives.] John Studd, the only giant in wrestling, seven-foot-plus, nearly four hundred pounds of solid muscle. And this was what we wanted, to prove to the whole world that I am the giant, and in a few short moments, along with this fifteen thousand dollars, you're gonna see me in the ring and you're gonna see the last match of 'Andréa,' because he retires when he can't do it. . . ."

Mean Gene reaches into the bag, but Heenan pushes him off. "Bobby Heenan, I'm just trying to count the money here—"

"Keep your hands to yourself, pal," says Heenan. "For fifteen thousand dollars and a haircut we're eliminating André the Giant from professional wrestling. Oh, yeah, a lot of gladhanders around here today"—Studd reopens the bag, Mean Gene reaches in and pulls out a handful, Studd slaps his hand, scattering bills on the floor— "keep your hands outta there, pal. Only two people are gonna see this money, that's Studd and myself, oh three, the people at the bank when we deposit this money—"

"That's right, we're banking it," says Studd.

"—but not the Giant," says the Brain. "He's retired. He's done! He's done!"

"Stand by," says Okerlund, again attempting to get a hand into the duffel full of money. "It's upcoming—"

"Don't you touch our money," says Heenan.

Moments later, Howard Finkel is in the ring announcing the match: "Introducing first to my left, the manager, Bobby 'The Brain' Heenan. This is the fifteen-thousand-dollar Slam match"—Studd holds up the open duffel full of money—"one fall will win this contest, and the rules, if the gentleman to my left is slammed, he loses fifteen thousand dollars in cash." [Studd displays a fistful of bills.] "If his opponent does not slam this man in the ring, he will retire from professional wrestling. And now, to my left, from Los Angeles, California, weighing 367 pounds, Big John Studd! And his opponent, from Grenoble, in the French Alps, weighing 476 pounds, the Eighth Wonder of the World, André the Giant!"

"Look at the big grin on his kisser, Jesse," says Gorilla Monsoon. "He looks very confident."

"I'll tell you what," responds his broadcast partner, Jesse "The Body" Ventura. "He better be confident, Gino Monsoon, because he's stated that if he does not slam the Giant Studd, he will retire. So the wrestling fans of the world may be, just maybe, getting their last look at André the Giant as a professional wrestler."

Studd shows André a fistful of cash as he enters the ring, then gestures how André will have to slam him to get it. Studd tries to hand the duffel to Heenan to hold, but André demands that it be given to an unbiased official. The bell rings, and Studd attacks with punches and forearms. André is forced into the corner, where Studd drives rights into his gut and chin. But four knife-edge chops to the throat push Studd off, with a headbutt stunning him to his knees. A kick rolls Studd out to the floor, where he confers with Heenan. André, for his part, waits patiently.

Studd climbs back in, and André wastes no time, wrapping his hands around his opponent's traps and backs him into the corner. He chokes Studd violently against the ropes as Heenan yells to the ref, "Break it!" A roundhouse right doubles Studd over for a knee. A right to Studd's kisser sets up a squash in the corner and another shot to the face. Studd responds with a knee below the belt and an attempt at a slam. André doesn't budge and throws Studd off with a knee to the belly.

Chops and a bearhug wear down Studd as the fans begin chanting, "Slam! Slam! Slam!" André lifts Studd up, and Studd rakes his eyes with a forearm. André, however, refuses to release the bearhug. Studd pushes at André's face, but the Giant only squeezes harder. Finally, André releases, and hits a forearm against Studd's kidneys. Studd turns, and André nails another blow to the lower back. Studd

André shows Studd who is the true giant, *WrestleMania.*

backs into the corner and throws a forearm at André, who catches him and turns him around in a facelock.

Punches and a headbutt wear down Studd. He whips Studd into the ropes for a backdrop, but Studd raises a boot, which the Giant catches before impact. Studd begs for mercy as André laughs. Hold-

MICHAEL KRUGMAN

ing Studd's foot, he hits a big right and a sidekick to Studd's thigh. Studd drops and takes another kick to his leg.

André chops Studd in the corner. Studd turns to Heenan, so André kicks at his leg again and again. As Studd reels from the kicks, André scoops him up and slams him flat at 6:06. Studd holds his lower back as the duffel is passed to André. He reaches in and tosses a handful of bills to the crowd. Heenan runs in and grabs the bag from behind and scurries up the aisle. Studd follows but isn't as quick as the Brain, giving André time to yank a fistful of hair before he too gets away.

In the back, Mean Gene awaits. "André the Giant, I'll tell you what, 23,000 and millions around the world, you finally did it. Big John Studd slammed. Where's that money?"

"I don't know," grins André. "It disappeared somewhere, but I don't care about that money. I just showed to John Studd and the Weasel and I showed to all the wrestling fans, I can give him that slam. And I did it."

"You did indeed. Many saying that perhaps this would be the occasion for the retirement of André the Giant—"

"No, no! No way. No way. I'm not ready to retire."

Mean Gene throws it back to the announce table, where Jesse Ventura rightly refers to the match as "the slam heard 'round the world."

BOBBY HEENAN: "André slams Studd, then goes over and grabs the bag away from the referee. I was supposed to grab the bag away from him before me and Studd leave, but André says, 'Let me have a little time with the bag.'

" 'Do anything you want,' I said, 'you're the boss, big man.' So he reaches into the bag, grabs two or three big handfuls, and starts throwing it to people in the audience. People were going nuts, so I ran in the ring after two or three throws and grabbed the bag. André let me have it—if he wanted to empty the bag, he would have. I went back with the bag and saw Vince. I thought, 'Oh man, am I in trouble! I didn't get the bag back quick enough.' But he never said anything to me, never said anything to the Giant."

HOWARD FINKEL: "There were some doubting Thomases out in the crowd that thought there was nothing in the bag but sawdust or pillow feathers. When the match was over and André dove into that bag and started throwing the money around, I'm telling you, it was just an amazing moment. It made André even more of an attraction than he was before."

7

In the months after *WrestleMania*, André disappeared from the

World Wrestling Federation spotlight. He spent most of his time

away wrestling in Japan, including a few cross-promotional

matches with New Japan's Antonio Inoki. Upon his return, the

Giant picked up where he had left off and resumed his feud with

Bobby Heenan and the Heenan Family. André battled regularly

against Family members Big John Studd and King Kong Bundy, in both singles matches as well as Tag Team matches in which he paired up with Hillbilly Jim, Tito Santana, Capt. Lou Albano, and Hulk Hogan.

THE BODY SHOP W/JESSE VENTURA

"This week in *The Body Shop*," Jesse says, resplendent in tuxedo shirt and canary yellow boa, "I guess it's old home week. Because I got a guest coming in here that to my understanding, as the way I see it, come on in here, big fella . . ."

The camera pulls back to reveal André, smiling broadly, his hands on his hips. He's wearing a silk beach shirt and very short shorts.

"If you wanna talk to me," he says, "come closer."

"I'm getting there," Ventura says, accepting André's authority, even over his own segment. "As I understand it, André, the way I hear it, you are retired. How is retirement?"

"What do you mean, retired?"

"The word that I heard. I heard from Bobby Heenan, Big John Studd, that they had put you out to retirement. I gotta say, you looking good! It must agree with you. You gotta nice suntan, looks like you just got in from the beach, you milking cows and stuff now?"

"No, I'm still wrestling," André says, looking somewhat perplexed. "I just come in from Hawaii, but I still wrestling. I never retire in my life, no way. I been wrestling in Australia and Japan, New Zealand, Australia, and I just come back."

"You haven't retired?"

"Not at all. And I will tell you one thing, maybe it will surprise you, and it will surprise John Studd, but I even put some weight on now." André grins, rubbing his belly.

"You put some weight *on*," Ventura responds, incredulous.

"Yes, sir."

"*On*. Can I ask you, how much you weigh?"

"Can you pay me, for a dollar a weight," André asks, then corrects himself. "A dollar a pound."

"Will I pay you a dollar a pound?"

"Ya."

"An English pound?"

André laughs, perhaps amused at the surreal turn the interview seems to have taken. "Well, I tell you how much I weigh. I weigh five hundred and twenty pounds now, okay?"

"Five hundred and twenty pounds!" Ventura exclaims. André reaches out and fingers the feather boa. "Hey! Hey! Get your hands off my threads, man! Whatchu think you're doing! I bring you out here, I bring you out on my program, and you start insulting my clothes. Get away from me, you big coot! Get the guy off my program!"

André yanks the boa from Jesse's neck, mocking his host. He begins softly whipping it into Ventura's face as Jesse continues to rage.

"I won't stand for this anymore! I ain't standing for it from you! No giant, no nothing!"

The camera fades to black as André pokes further fun at Ventura's fashion sense.

WrestleMania was such a phenomenal success that World Wrestling Federation presented its sequel a year later. And as with any good sequel, it was obliged to be bigger and better than its predecessor.

After the original spectacle, it was decided that one ring would not possibly be large enough to contain WrestleMania 2. In fact, the supercard would require three rings, at a trio of arenas across the country—the Los Angeles Memorial Sports Arena, Chicago's Rosemont Horizon, and Nassau Veterans Memorial Coliseum in Uniondale, New York.

Each venue would have its own main event, with André headlining a Twenty-Man Battle Royal in Chicago. In the ring with him would be a diverse lineup of Superstars, including Big John Studd, Tony Atlas, Bret Hart (in his WrestleMania debut), Jim "The Anvil" Neidhart, Ted Arcidi, Danny Spivey, Hillbilly Jim, King Tonga, Iron Sheik, B. Brian Blair, "Jumping" Jim Brunzell, and in their only WrestleMania appearances, wrestling legends Pedro Morales and Bruno Sammartino.

To make the match even more extraordinary, World Wrestling Federation invited a number of the NFL's top stars to participate, including Chicago

Bears' All-Pro offensive tackle Jimbo Covert, Dallas Cowboys' defensive end Harvey Martin, Pittsburgh Steelers' lineman Ernie Holmes, Atlanta Falcons' Bill Fralic, and San Francisco 49ers' Russ Francis (the son of famed wrestler/promoter Ed Francis).

Of the football players, there were none bigger—both in terms of fame and sheer size—than Chicago Bears defensive lineman William "The Refrigerator" Perry. The six-foot-two, 300-pound Fridge had become a cultural icon during Da Bears' Super Bowl–winning season, celebrated for his enormous bulk and charismatic presence. In short, Perry was the perfect fit for a role at *WrestleMania 2*.

August/September 1986

"HOW BIG IS BIG? A LOOK AT HOW SOME ATHLETES MEASURE UP"

William "The Refrigerator" Perry, 6-foot-2-inch, 308-pound sensation of football's Chicago Bears . . . is a mere pygmy next to André the Giant. While the gridiron star boasts of a ring the diameter of a half-dollar, the circumference of André's finger is the size of a silver dollar. As a 12-year-old in Grenoble, France, he intimidated other sixth-graders with his 6-foot-3-inch, 200-pound frame. Two years later, he was up to 340 pounds. While the average human wrist is 7 inches, André's is 12—the same as a western lowland gorilla!

"The guys in other sports make me laugh," [King Kong] Bundy says. 'It's a joke how 270 pounds means a giant in the NFL. That's a paperweight to me." About William "The Refrigerator" Perry: "I'd eat soup off his head."

[Jimmy Hart] says that football players lack intelligence: "William Perry might be big, rough and tough," he rhymes, "but he's not hard to bluff. Because he's just a football player."

A secret dress rehearsal was held a few days before *WrestleMania 2* for the benefit of the untrained football players. Afterward, Ernie Holmes ran off at the mouth, bragging how he was the toughest guy in the bunch, much to the annoyance of all around him. Finally, André said what everyone was thinking: "You talk too much, you know what I mean?"

Duly chastised, and well aware of André's power, Holmes shut up.

WRESTLEMANIA 2: BATTLE ROYAL

Keeping with *WrestleMania* tradition, the event featured a number of celebrities—guest timekeeper was Clara "Where's the Beef?" Peller, while football legends Dick Butkus and Ed "Too Tall" Jones served as guest referees. Best of all, former NFL superstar and longtime André rival Ernie Ladd joined Gorilla Monsoon at the announce table.

The participants, in order of introduction: Jimbo Covert, Pedro Morales, Tony Atlas, Ted Arcidi, Harvey Martin, Danny Spivey, Hillbilly Jim, King Tonga, the Iron Sheik, Ernie Holmes, B. Brian Blair, Jim Brunzell, Big John Studd, Bill Fralic, Bret Hart, Jim Neidhart, Russ Francis, Bruno Sammartino, William "The Refrigerator" Perry, André the Giant.

André, in babyface yellow trunks and boots, goes at it with Studd immediately. They take a corner, and André chops and chokes Studd. Eventually Studd joins the fray and is replaced by the Hart Foundation. André stacks them up and shoulderblocks the team in the corner. He soon goes into the melee and returns to action with Studd. They part, and André challenges Francis, who begs off. André doesn't care and tosses him over the top. Francis, however, catches a rope and pulls himself back in before his feet hit the floor. He comes right back at André, who headbutts him to the mat.

Bored, André goes back to Studd and chokes him in the corner. Chops are followed by hair-pulling by both men. Perry goes for Studd, so André diverts his attention to Fralic. He tries to get him over the top, but Fralic holds on to the ropes. Martin intercedes, and is soon joined by Morales. André puts all three into a corner and shoulderblocks. Fralic and Martin keep punching at André's belly, but he simply wraps his arms around their shoulders. Finally, André swats

Battle Royal, *WrestleMania 2.*

Martin away, while Morales holds Fralic for some chops. Fralic slips out and André takes a moment to rest up in the corner.

After a time, he walks over to where Studd and Perry are brawling and takes Studd's arms from behind, holding him for the Refrigerator's attack. André soon grabs hold of both big men for a noggin knocker. Perry falls and immediately heads to the next corner, where the Hart Foundation is waiting. André and Studd continue, with André squashing and butt-blocking his nemesis against the buckles. He tries to put Studd over the top, but Big John wraps his legs around the ropes. From behind, Hart and Francis attack André, though Bruno quickly yanks the Hitman away. Iron Sheik comes over and works on André's back. Bruno comes back and removes the Sheik as Studd comes off the ropes, back into the ring.

André stalks Francis and throttles him in the corner. To his credit, Francis keeps attacking, with shoulderblocks to André's midsection actually doubling the Giant over against the turnbuckles. A big headbutt sends Francis flying, but he comes back for more. He wraps his arms around André as Studd runs over and hits André with a double ax-handle. Studd kicks Francis in the gut and goes to work on André. The Giant falls, taking a seat in the corner. Studd is distracted as Perry tackles the Hart Foundation, though both avoid elimination. Studd and Perry face off. Perry tackles Studd, and then tries it again. Studd gets his elbow up and tosses the Refrigerator over.

Meanwhile, Francis and Hart battle, while André rests on one knee. Perry reaches up to shake Studd's hand but pulls him over when he agrees. Francis rests in one corner while the Hart Foundation works on André. They move over to Francis, but André tosses them off and headbutts Francis himself. The Harts hit a double dropkick on André and he gets tied up in the ropes. With André trapped, they go to work on Francis, pitching him up and over.

André is loose, and the Hart Foundation pounds at him in the corner. Hart shoots the Anvil into a tackle on André, doubling him over. They each grab a leg, but he kicks them both off. Neidhart whips Hart into André, but the Giant gets a boot up and Bret goes down. André, now enraged, takes Anvil by the beard, lifts up the Hitman, and hits a noggin knocker. He lifts Neidhart by the goatee and

MICHAEL KRUGMAN

The Hart Foundation tries a double dropkick, *WrestleMania 2.*

shoots him into the ropes for a big boot, which bounces the Anvil over. Hitman goes up top, but André catches him and presses him over onto his partner to win the Battle Royal at 9:13.

"André the Giant, the winner of more Battle Royals than any man in the history of professional wrestling," notes Gorilla Monsoon upon the match's conclusion.

Later that same month, André returned to Japan for a series of tours that would keep him in action for the next three months. Among the highlights of his itinerary was a match with New Japan Pro Wrestling's Akira Maeda in Tsu, Japan. Maeda had been one of the top names in Japan's renegade UWF promotion, known for their stiff, full-contact style and their condemnation of other styles of professional wrestling. When UWF went under, he returned to his first home, New Japan, and pioneered a blend of submission and pro spots that made him a Superstar.

Maeda never lost to anyone but Yoshiaki Fujiwara, whom he considered a real competitor. As a result of that, and his vocal disdain for pro wrestling, Maeda received minimal cooperation from visiting Western wrestlers such as André.

When the two iron-willed wrestlers met in the ring, it was clear from the bell that there was going to be trouble. The Giant refused to sell for Maeda, shrugging off his shooter gimmick by no-selling submission holds and even going for his opponent's eyes. It wasn't long before the match spiraled out of control, with neither man willing to lose.

Maeda attempted to take out André's increasingly weak knee, shoot-kicking, then immediately backing away. After fifteen minutes, he finally toppled the Giant with a single-leg takedown. Even down, André remained the power. He challenged Maeda to pin him, knowing that his opponent understood one of the cardinal rules of wrestling: no one pins André. Still, Maeda made a point of asking another wrestler at ringside if he could cover the Giant, but was told no.

In the midst of this chaos, NJPW promoter Antonio Inoki ran down the ring and called for the bell, not even bothering to explain why. The abrupt ending infuriated André, who complained that he wanted to go back to the ring and continue the match. However, Inoki was not about to let that happen—even an angry André was less dangerous than allowing such a strange and revealing match continue.

Back in the United States, André became embroiled in an altogether different controversy, one that ultimately led to his storyline suspension from World Wrestling Federation. The Giant was to resume his long-running program with Bobby Heenan and the Heenan Family with a Tag Team match pitting him and the partner of his choice against Big John Studd & King Kong Bundy on an April installment of *Prime Time Wrestling.* However, when André missed the match, an infuriated Heenan began calling for the Giant's suspension. It took weeks of on-air campaigning, but the Brain eventually got his wish.

Greg Valentine & Brutus Beefcake are squashing George Wells & Mike Saxon when Bobby Heenan interrupts Vince McMahon at the announce table.

"I've got some big news for you and everybody in professional wrestling and everybody out there," declared the Brain. "As of this week, that mess with André the Giant, where he walked . . . he didn't even show up for the match with Studd, in that Tag match. He didn't even represent himself. Well, I had a meeting with the president of World Wrestling Federation, Jack Tunney. I told ya I was gonna get something done and something has been done. As of this week, André the Giant has been, listen to this, suspended from professional wrestling."

"I have some difficulty believing that one," says Vince.

"Well, I'm gonna make a formal announcement later on, but right as of now, André the Giant is formally suspended from professional wrestling. He didn't even have the courtesy, the class, or the dignity to show up at the hearing, or to be represented. I told you what happens when you mess with me. I told ya I was gonna rid wrestling of André the Giant, and *I did it!*"

"We thank you, Mr. Heenan, for that bit of, uh . . ."

"Anytime I can deliver news like this, it's my pleasure."

There was, of course, a legitimate reason for André's "suspension" and diminished presence on World Wrestling Federation television. First and foremost was his deteriorating health. His acromegaly was affecting his back and spine at a rapid pace, causing him to walk slowly and with a significant stoop. The pain was so debilitating that André began wearing a back brace under his singlet, just to keep himself standing upright. Though his brute physical strength and indefatigable charisma were still unmatched, the mighty Giant was breaking down. However, this consummate professional was careful to keep his weakened condition from the fans. André became more and more detached from the real world, spending much of his time with the trusted fellow wrestlers with whom he didn't need to fake better health.

TIM WHITE: "His health was getting worse. It was getting harder and harder for him to move. And he would never say how bad things were."

Some two months after André's suspension, World Wrestling Federation began heralding the impending arrival of Japan's hottest tag team. The masked Machines—Giant Machine & Super Machine—were coming to America to establish themselves as the number-one team in wrestling.

One look at the seven-foot-four, 500-pound Giant Machine was enough for any fan to know who was hiding behind the black mask. The Machines gimmick had been originated the previous summer in New Japan Pro Wrestling. Under the aegis of manager Ichimasa Wakamatsu, André had teamed with "Super Machine" Bill Eadie (the name was a play on his "Masked Superstar" character) and "Super Strong Machine" Junji Hirata as the Machine Gun Army.

In May, André went to perform in his final tour with New Japan Pro Wrestling. The tour's historical highlight was a June 17 battle in Nagoya that saw André tapping out to an armlock by Antonio Inoki, said to be the Giant's only career loss by submission. While in Japan, André—that is, Giant Machine—also found time to sit down in a Tokyo teahouse to introduce himself and Super Machine to the fans.

June 24, 1985: Mid-Hudson Civic Center, Poughkeepsie, NY

"Mean" Gene Okerlund interviews the Machines in Japan.

Okerlund—wearing his tuxedo, natch—enters a Tokyo teahouse. "I have finally found them," he says, dropping to his knees at the table. "I cannot believe it, the Giant Machine and the Big Machine."

"No, no, *Super* Machine."

"The Super Machine, I beg your pardon, from Sapporo, Japan, weighing 130 kilo. And you of course, are the Giant Machine, at 220 centimeters tall and 230 kilo, is that correct?"

"Hai."

"Yes, that is, that's very high."

"Hai."

"Gentlemen, I cannot believe it, educated in English schools,

The Machines.

you're very articulate apparently in the English language, I can't believe it."

"Yes," says Super Machine, "educated right here, the University of Tokyo. Master's degree in education. Also, master's degree in business administration."

"I see."

"He is also educated in the University of Tokyo."

"Tell me, the anticipation of the fans in the United States for the Machines, the Giant Machine and the Super Machine, your thoughts?"

"We are. Very, very happy," says Super Machine, selling the language gap. "About going to. Your country. It is an honor. A great honor for us. Because we have been told by our mentor, our stable-master, Wakamatsu-san . . ."

"Ah," nods Mean Gene.

". . . in order to be, not only good in your country, in order to be good in the world, you must go to United States."

"Number one," agrees Okerlund, holding up a finger.

"Number one," translates Super Machine. "*Ichiban.*"

"*Ichiban.* Right now, the two of you are number one in Japan, hopefully to be number one in the United States and the world."

"And the world, that is correct. We are also told, in order to be number one in the world, we must fight in World Wrestling Federation."

"In World Wrestling Federation. That too, gentlemen, *ichiban.* Very curious, any talk of a manager in the World Wrestling Federation?"

"We have an adviser now, Wakamatsu-san, here in Japan. He has been in contact with one Lou Albano. . . ."

Mean Gene pays rapt attention, a finger to his lips as he listens. "Oh, Captain Lou Albano! Yes! He's very popular, very famous manager in World Wrestling Federation."

"Wakamatsu-san says Mr. Albano-san will take care of us, guide us, give advice. . . ."

"Oh, he'll take care of you," agrees Mean Gene. "Listen, I'm very curious, competition, in the United States, in World Wrestling Federation, have you heard about any of the competition there? It's second to none."

"We challenge everybody," says the Giant Machine.

"Everybody."

"Including Hulk Hogan?"

"Hogan-san," nods the Giant.

"Hulk Hogan-san, number one in world now," says Super Machine.

"Yes he is, *ichiban*. How about the Magnificent Muraco? I've got a couple for you, Big John Studd and King Kong Bundy, you've heard of them?"

"Yes," says Giant Machine. "Anytime. Anytime."

"Anytime . . . say, you know something? Your voice sounds familiar, and I get the distinct impression that I've met you someplace before."

"Never. Never. First time I see you."

"Perhaps you are mistaken," says Super Machine. "We are very popular here in Japan, I'm sure you have seen us. . . ."

"Maybe in wrestling magazine," suggests the Giant . . . erm, Machine. ". . . In magazine or on television.

"Maybe I've seen you on TV or in a magazine here in Japan. . . ."

"Hai."

"It makes sense. That's a good point, gentlemen, I thank you. We're looking forward to seeing you in the United States as part of World Wrestling Federation, the Giant Machine and the Super Machine."

The Machines bow respectfully.

"From Sapporo, Japan, and the island of Fu Yu Tu."

"Hai," says the Giant.

HOWARD FINKEL: "Obviously you're not going to hide who it was under a mask. But it was a novelty. It was hilarious. Everybody knew who it was. It was all designed to keep André in the mix. When you have a guy who is as tall as he was, you have to be innovative. You have to be creative. You have to try and keep this guy in the mix, because André was ours exclusively. We were national now, we weren't regional anymore, so we had to come up with ways to keep him fresh."

"GIANT MACHINE/SUPER MACHINE: NEW ENTRIES FROM JAPAN"

Giant Machine is a mammoth piece of work. He stands about 7 feet 5 inches and weighs over 500 pounds. In his size, he resembles the . . . grappler from France, André the Giant, who has left the ring since he was suspended by the company for failing to show up for a match [with King Kong Bundy and Big John Studd]. This resemblance has not gone unnoticed. In fact, Bobby "The Brain" Heenan, manager of Stud and Bundy, has charged that if the Giant Machine were unmasked, he would be revealed as André.

The Giant Machine denies the charge. He claims to be a graduate of Tokyo University and gives his home as the small northern island of Fu Yu Tu, once part of Japan but occupied by the Soviet Union since the end of World War II.

NEW FROM JAPAN: THE GIANT MACHINE
by Ed Ricciuti

Like many other imports that threaten domestic competition, the Giant Machine has sparked a heated controversy. Typical of Japanese products, the Giant Machine seems patterned after an existing model that has long been a success in the ring. The immense frame of the huge masked wrestler bears an astonishing similarity to that of the veteran mat warrior from France, André the Giant, who has been suspended by President Jack Tunney for failing to show up for a match with Big John Studd and King Kong Bundy. Like André, the Giant Machine weighs upwards of 500 pounds. He has the same hamlike hands, massive, sloping shoulders, and legs like columns in front of a courthouse. Star commentator "Mean" Gene Okerlund noticed the similarity when he interviewed the two Machines in Tokyo shortly before they came to this country in

August. The Giant Machine got rather testy at Okerlund's suggestion that he was in any way similar to the Frenchman, and the commentator let it go at that.

Heenan . . . is convinced that under the black-and-silver mask that hides the face of the Giant Machine are features not of a Japanese, but of a Frenchman. Heenan gets livid every time he talks about it. "He's no more Japanese than I am," screams Heenan. "The Giant Machine is André. He's so scared of Studd and Bundy he's got to hide his ugly puss. We got that Frenchman out of wrestling, and now he's trying to sneak back in disguise."

The Machines and their newly acquired manager, Captain Louis Albano (who, ironically, was André's manager), have challenged Heenan's team. "We know of Big John Studd and Bundy," says Super Machine, who does most of the talking for the two Japanese. "They are huge and very good wrestlers, but we can beat them."

Super Machine, attempting to put Heenan's charge about Giant Machine's identity to rest, readily provides verbal biographies of the Japanese tag team. Super Machine gives his native city as Sapporo, on the northernmost large Japanese island of Hokkaido.

Heenan, however, remains adamant. "Japanese?" he yowls. "No way. Jack Tunney should unmask those frauds. And if he won't, Studd and Bundy will, in the ring. And then we'll send the Machines to the scrap heap."

July 15, 1986: Mid-Hudson Civic Center, Poughkeepsie, NY

Ken Resnick interviews President Jack Tunney & Bobby Heenan re: André.

"Mr. Tunney, I understand that you have a clarification on the suspension of André the Giant."

"Yes, let me just explain something, Kenny," says Tunney. "Suspending André the Giant was one of the worst things I had to do as president. However, I had no choice. He failed to appear for a couple of matches that he had contracted for. Also, he failed to appear for the hearing, which I really can't understand, because

The Machines, clockwise from left: Big Machine, Giant Machine, Super Machine, Capt. Lou Albano.

André is not that type of man. Very dependable man, and great athlete."

"Obviously something unusual on the part of the Giant."

"Well, this is what I can't . . . it doesn't make any sense, really, because he's just not like that."

Heenan barges in. "Mr. President, may I congratulate you on your decision. You have made my day. You have made my *life*. You talk about André the Giant, how he's an honorable man. I told you about him, you shoulda listened to me! People shoulda listened to me. He chickened out, he backed out, he didn't even have the gumption to show up for a hearing. And now he's back, or he's trying to come back, with somebody else as a partner, calling himself the Giant Machine. The Super Machine's his partner. You know it, I know it, we all know it. That is André the Giant!"

"They're Japanese wrestlers," replies Tunney, to Heenan's disbelief. "They have Japanese passports, it's . . . could be Giant Baba."

"Mr. President, please. Don't make yourself look bad in front of the people. That's *André the Giant*. I know it. The man *speaks* like André the Giant. There's no Japanese wrestlers seven-foot-five. You know that and I know it. *Thirty of 'em* aren't seven-feet-five!"

"Mr. Heenan, if you can prove that that's André the Giant, I'll suspend him for life."

"You mean if those masks come off, you will suspend him for life?"

"Absolutely."

"Well, those masks'll come off, I guarantee it. He shows one foot on this soil, he shows one face around this ring or anyplace, those masks are coming off. And I can guarantee that, 'cause I'm the Brain."

"Just a moment," Tunney cautions, "control yourself. You could be suspended also."

"But . . . ," Heenan sputters, backing off. "Hey, pal, you don't have to worry about me. I'm clean!"

Don Muraco and Mr. Fuji guest-host Jesse Ventura's *The Body Shop*.

"A hot August night in World Wrestling Federation," begins the Rock. "Myself and Mr. Fuji have the pleasure of speaking with Bobby 'The Brain' Heenan, who is never, never short for dropping bomb-shells on the world of professional wrestling."

Bows are exchanged between the two managers.

"Well, I suggest you hit the air-raid shelters," says Heenan, "because I'm gonna drop something on you right now like you've never seen before. I have now, I am managing two of the greatest wrestlers from Korea in the history of professional wrestling."

"Ooooh!" says an excited Muraco.

"Gentlemen," says Heenan, inviting over two large wrestlers wearing brown paper sacks on their heads. "First of all, from Seoul, Korea, this is Kim Duk."

Big John Studd . . . er, Kim Duk poses with his thumbs in his waistband.

"This gentleman over here is also from Korea," the Brain continues. "This is Pak San."

King Kong Bundy . . . that is, Pak San stands with his hands on his hips. He seems more comfortable with the bag on his head than his teammate.

"Now these two men are the biggest wrestlers in the history of wrestling from Korea. Now—"

"No doubt," interrupts Muraco, "no doubt in my mind why they call you 'the Brain,' Mr. Heenan!"

"That's right," Heenan agrees, then resumes. "Now, you and I know one thing. Isn't this absolutely ridiculous?"

Studd and Bundy de-bag themselves.

"What a wonderful way of fighting fire with fire," growls Muraco.

"Y'know, we didn't fool anybody out there," bellows Big John Studd. "Everybody knew it was the Giant Studd, and King Kong Bundy, just like Andréa [sic] is not fooling us, and I understand, if we prove to the whole world that that's Andréa underneath that mask, it's all over for him! His entire career will be shattered!"

"You've already hospitalized him one time," says Muraco to Bundy.

"You know, Magnificent One, I'm gonna do it all again! You know, you saw the way the masks came off us. We're gonna do the same thing to André and his little partner."

"I'm gonna guarantee one thing," promises Heenan. "Those masks, if they get in our way, they're coming off. I had the man suspended, he's *done*! There's only one giant, and his name is Studd. And Bundy. That's it. Simple. Cut and dried."

"Magnificent moments," rasps Muraco in conclusion. "What a way to heat up the hot summer, fighting fire with fire!"

One week after the Machines' in-ring debut, André's old rival Blackjack Mulligan put on the mask to portray a third member of the team: Big Machine. André was in such physical torture from his rapidly degenerating back that he could barely wrestle. Big Machine was there to pick up the slack in the ring, while also allowing André to maintain his crucial presence in World Wrestling Federation. Over the following few months the Machines, accompanied by manager Capt. Lou Albano, battled back and forth with the Heenan Family, often in Six Man Tag matches that also included managers Albano and Heenan.

Unfortunately, André's condition worsened, and even a nonwrestling role in the Machines proved too difficult. To maintain the tag team's star quality, Big & Super Machine would be joined by a number of other easily identified masked Superstars, including Animal Machine, Piper Machine, Crusher Machine (a.k.a. the legendary Reggie "The Crusher" Lisowski), and of course, the Hulk Machine. But by October, the gimmick had run its course. Big & Super did the honors for Studd & Bundy in what would be Capt. Lou Albano's final World Wrestling Federation match.

Despite his infirmity, André did spend some of his time "off" working on what would ultimately be one of his greatest triumphs—*The Princess Bride*.

An inimitable blend of comedy and adventure, fantasy and satire, the film's fairy-tale milieu was a perfect fit for the true-life Giant. When director Rob Reiner and screenwriter William Goldman considered who should play the role of Fezzik, an immense Turkish giant in league with a band of out-laws, André was the clear first choice.

While his previous acting roles had merely capitalized on his immense size, portraying Fezzik revealed a well of innate charisma and larger-than-life presence. Joining a cast that also included Mandy Patinkin, Wallace Shawn, Cary Elwes, and Robin Wright, the inexperienced André stole every scene in which he appeared, delivering a warm and irresistible characteri-zation that has become a cinema classic. Though his back pain was such that some stunts proved unfeasible, André rose above it, following the wrestler's credo of always working through pain and illness.

> **TIM WHITE:** "He was in excruciating pain during that whole movie, and look how great he did. Look how great he did."

Immediately after *The Princess Bride* wrapped production, André finally took measures to deal with his agonizing back pain and booked a major spinal surgery at London's Cromwell Hospital.

> **TIM WHITE:** "They had to cut his back open and widen the spine, which was a very, very tricky operation. I was told it took three or four months to assemble the operat-ing room, because they needed bigger scalpels, they needed bigger everything. They had to have a special crane in there, in case they had to move him. But the guy sweating the most was the anesthesiologist. He wasn't sure how much it would take to knock him out."

The surgery proved a success, though André required significant recuperation time. Fortunately, the Cromwell Hospital offered a number of additional accommodations that were certain to ease the Giant's postoper-ative pain.

> **TIM WHITE:** "They set up a videotape machine and they served us beer in the room. The office sent us hundreds of tapes—movies and wrestling clips and all that—and a VCR. I sat there all day with him and we kept pushing the buzzer, order-ing four more Heinekens, six more Heinekens."

In November, André was quietly reinstated in an active role in World Wrestling Federation. The news was announced while André was still in London, prompting a rare international interview.

INTERVIEW FROM LONDON WITH GARY DAVIE

"Big news just in from headquarters," says Davie. "World Wrestling Federation president Jack Tunney has just announced that the controversial suspension of André the Giant has been suspended. That's right, André the Giant, now free to return to World Wrestling Federation action."

He brings out André, who says, "It's great to be back, believe me."

"So you're about to return to the World Wrestling Federation action. That must've been a tough time for you, being away."

"It's tough time, but I'm gonna surprise all the wrestling fans, and believe me, I'm gonna have a big surprise for you. I'll be back, all the way, just like I used to compete before."

"You've had a good time in Europe, but obviously you've missed all your pals."

"I had a very good time, and what I did, I don't gonna disappoint all the wrestling fans." André grins, teasing his work on *The Princess Bride.* "I think wrestling fans will be happy what I did during that time I was suspended. But now I'm more than happy to be back in the ring. And anybody, anywhere, believe me, I'll be there."

8

André's appetite for living was the stuff of legend, befitting a real-life giant. He could and would consume quantities of alcohol that would knock most men unconscious. André's prodigious consumption—which earned him the title "The Greatest Drunk on Earth" from the humor magazine *Modern Drunkard*—has been recounted by anyone who ever had the pleasure of knowing him.

Tales abound of thirty-six-hour booze-fueled card games, of stolen horses, and of quickly drunk cases of fine wine.

There are those who attribute André's Falstaffian lust for life to his being told it was doubtful he'd survive past the age of forty. Perhaps it was the knowledge that he was destined for a shortened life, or maybe it was the chronic physical pain that he endured almost every waking moment. Possibly it was the loneliness that comes from being a French-speaking giant in a regular-sized world. Of course, it could simply be that André was just very, very thirsty.

JERRY LAWLER: "Every night after his match, he would drink two cases of beer. Not two six-packs, two cases! Forty-eight beers, every night! Those beer bottles looked so tiny in his huge hands."

JACK BRISCO: "We used to drink a lot of Budweiser. André could put his hand around a can of Budweiser and you couldn't see any parts of the can, it would totally disappear in his hand. That's how massive his hands were."

TIM WHITE: "He drank wine like most people drink ice water. That wasn't drinking to him."

TED DIBIASE: "If you're with André, you've got to drink. I mean, you just have to. He'd say, 'Drink, boss.' 'Okay, André, I'll drink.'"

SHANE McMAHON: "At one point I remember him drinking this Mexican whiskey that had fermented snakes in it. Not worms, snakes. I remember looking at it and being so freaked out. He offered to give me a drink of that Mexican whiskey, but I was like, 'No way!' He knew I was scared to death when he offered it to me.

"But there were a few times where we had a couple of beers together. I didn't drink very much, so after a few beers, I was like, 'Whoa.' He got a big laugh out of that—'Ho, ho, ho, ho!'—because he knew I was wasted. He got a kick out of that. It was kind of a rite of passage. André got to drink with my grandfather, then my father, and then me, the kid. It was a very cool thing for both of us, I think."

STAN HANSEN: "He was without a doubt the biggest drinker I've ever seen, but I never saw him drunk. No matter how much he drank, he was always very easy to get along with."

TED DIBIASE: "As many times as I was out with André, I think there might have been one time where he got a little silly but I never saw him sloshing drunk. He would drink all night and then just get up and walk out of the bar like it was nothing."

VINCE McMAHON: "André and Bobby Heenan are walking out of the Savoy Grill in New York. It must be six in the morning now, because they stayed open for André. They've been drinking all night. André's standing on the corner with Bobby, who can hardly stand up. He says, 'Bobby, I think I'm going to be sick.' By the time Bobby looked up at him, André gave this one big '*Wwwuuuuuhhhh*' and like a gallon of vomit just regurgitated right out of his mouth. As it did, this taxi was going by and it splat right on the front windshield. The taxi driver obviously couldn't see and had to slam on his brakes so he didn't hit anything.

"André, as soon as it was over, just says, 'Feeling better' and walked away."

TIM WHITE: "When there were people around in the bar that he didn't like, he'd pass gas. He could control it and it was god-awful. I mean, it was loud and it was strong. There would be a couple of smart-asses, we'd tell 'em right off the bat, No autographs, please, we're just having lunch, leave us alone. They'd say something like, 'Oh look, big fucking wrestler won't sign an autograph for my kid.' I'd see him get into the launch position, he'd give me the look and do the tilt. He'd let one go and people would just scatter. He was a funny guy. What a sense of humor."

SHANE McMAHON: "André, uncharacteristically, got smashed one Saturday night at the bar. Arnie was also just completely smashed. Finally André said, 'I'm going to sleep,' and put his head down on the table. The other boys there didn't know what to do. You can't move 550 pounds, especially if he doesn't want to be moved. They decided to put a couple of tablecloths over him, let him sleep it off.

"So Sunday morning comes and the restaurant shifted over to its brunch service. Eventually André starts waking up and he has no idea where he is, he's got table-cloths on him."

TIM WHITE: "We were doing it day after day. And then eventually I needed to crash. I would say, 'I love you to death, André, but I gotta lie down. This is too much.' I'd tell him, 'I'm not even having one beer today.' 'Okay, boss.' Then we'd go out, and he'd look at me, 'Not even one?' 'No, not one,' I said. About three hours later, he'd say, 'Not even one?' 'All right, fine, let's order.' I couldn't take it anymore, so I gave in."

"Of course, André needed time off too. He's a human being, like anyone else. We'd see a spot in the schedule where there would be two or three days off and he would shut down. He'd say, 'Timber, if you wanna do anything for the next couple of days, go and do it.' Then he'd order water and fruit to his room and not come out for about a day and a half. He'd finally get some rest and detox himself. He was very smart. He knew that even he couldn't burn it that long and not drop. So when we had those two days, I'd do the same thing he would do. I'd go get gallons of water, some fruit and stuff, and I wouldn't come out of that room for two days."

"The road itself is tough enough, but when you just keep rolling like that . . . The thing with André, it wasn't all about drinking. He just loved to be out there and having fun."

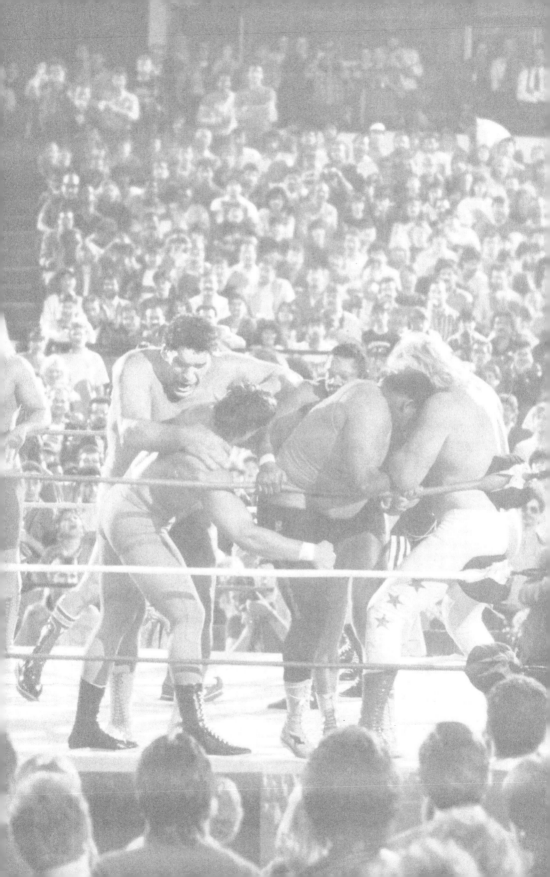

André vs. Hogan,
WrestleMania III.

9

On January 23, 1984, Hulk Hogan escaped the Iron Sheik's dreaded Camel Clutch to win his historic first World Wrestling Federation Championship. Gorilla Monsoon branded the birth of an era at the match's conclusion: *"Hulkamania is here!"* ■ A victory party was held in the locker room for the new champ, with all the top babyfaces in attendance. Among the wrestlers offering congratulations to Hogan were Rocky Johnson, Ivan Putski, and of course, the promotion's biggest Superstar, André.

HOWARD FINKEL: "I think there was great respect. There was definitely great respect from Hogan toward André. And I think André gave it back. Again, if André liked you he'd be your friend for life. If he didn't like you, he'd pull no punches. He would, in his own way, let you know that he wasn't fond of you."

From that point on, Hogan's star ascended higher and higher. He became one of the most recognized faces on the face of the earth as McMahon turned World Wrestling Federation into a true pop culture phenomenon. The Hulkster main-evented to unprecedented houses, appeared all over TV, was featured on the covers of countless magazines.

Needless to say, Hogan was to headline his third consecutive *Wrestle-Mania*, an event McMahon was determined to make even bigger than before.

He decided that *WrestleMania III* would be held in Michigan's Pontiac Silverdome, the domed stadium home of the NFL's Detroit Lions. Such an enormous venue required a suitably massive main event, but McMahon had something special in mind.

VINCE McMAHON: "André had pretty much cashed in his chips by then. He was in England, filming *The Princess Bride*, so I went over to talk to him and he was not feeling well. His back was really, really bothering him. He was all hunched over. He was pretty much ready to give up the business. He wasn't sure if he was going to retire in France or just what he was going to do.

"So I went over and talked to him and I said, 'Boss, I've got an idea. I think this will be the biggest thing you've ever done and in all likelihood probably the biggest thing anyone will ever do.'

" 'What is it?'

" 'Well, this is what I want to do. The Pontiac Silverdome is the biggest arena in the world, it's 93,000 seats, and I want you to headline it with Hogan.'

"And he couldn't do it. He wanted to. He was intrigued, but he knew his body wasn't up to it.

"After the operation, he came back and needed to rehab. I said, 'Boss, you've got to train.' He had never trained before as such, and didn't have to. So I told Timmy White, 'You've got to get him to train,' and he ultimately relented."

MICHAEL KRUGMAN

TIM WHITE: "I picked up André in the morning, probably four hours after he went to bed, and we drove over to Vince's beautiful home in Greenwich. He has a gym in his house the size of most Gold's Gyms—you know how Vince works out. He had talked André into doing some training, so we set up this little program and he stuck with it.

"We had it all mapped out and André was religious, he'd do everything. Then we'd go out into the kitchen off the gym and he'd start drinking.

"Vince would come up from his workout and stop dead. He'd go, 'Ugh. It's nine thirty in the morning and you're having a couple of beers. What am I gonna do with you guys?' I said, 'Hey, there's the chart. He's doing everything every day.'"

VINCE McMAHON: "André came over to the house to train, twice a day. I had started taking a protein powder drink—Metabolol—after working out. I know the amount I was doing, so it stands to reason that André's got to do twice mine. So every time he was there I gave him a big shake, twice what I was taking.

"André kept up with his training, and every time I'd bring him a shake after his training. The Boss would say, 'You don't mind if I don't drink shake?'

" 'Not if you don't like the taste of it,' I said.

" 'No, I like the taste,' André said. 'Make me fart.'

" 'Okay, then you don't have to drink the shakes anymore.'

"He was training for the first time in his life, for this one match that he knew would set all-time records."

SHANE McMAHON: "I was just starting to work out then, so I saw André almost every day. It was so funny to see him on those machines, because everything was so tiny. I had to teach him form, tell him things like 'Keep your back straight.' He had never lifted a weight in his career. My dad and I always said, 'Can you imagine if André actually trained? He'd have a thirty-inch arm!'"

VINCE McMAHON: "André was so proud of himself. He was feeling good leading up to *WrestleMania*, at least he was feeling better than he was. A lot better."

As the biggest babyface in the business, Hogan needed an opponent who was a heel of equal stature. Having been a heroic and popular figure for most of his career, André agreed to turn. In the months leading up to *WrestleMania III*, World Wrestling Federation television was dominated by

the tale of André's anger at being mistreated by his world champion pro-
tégé, a rage that saw him turn to Hogan's archnemesis, Bobby "The Brain"
Heenan, for managerial guidance.

Though Hogan and André had of course battled before—with André as
the babyface—*WrestleMania III* was sold as the first in-ring meeting between
two legends, one of whom had been undefeated for more than a decade.
André vs. Hogan became the most anticipated professional wrestling
matchup in history and a true highlight of what would become known as
the '*Mania* Era.

HULK HOGAN: *"I was at the pinnacle of my popularity, the biggest attraction in
wrestling at the time. And the guy I would be going up against had been the biggest
attraction in wrestling up until that time. There was no telling what we could draw
with a combination like that."*

January 5, 1987: Meadowlands, East Rutherford, NJ

PIPER'S PIT W/ANDRÉ, JACK TUNNEY, AND HULK HOGAN

Piper, enters, chewing gum. The trophy sits in the foreground: "Nineteen hundred and eighty-seven and I'm still alive! In the true fashion
of *Piper's Pit,* I have something, as you can tell, very prestigious and
possibly the most important bit I have ever done in my life. Obviously,
we have here a presentation, and to do the presentation I would like
President Jack Tunney to please come on out here and issue this
presentation." Tunney comes in through the archway and stands
directly behind the trophy, which obscures his face.

"Thank you."

"Pleasure to have you here."

"Ladies and gentlemen," says Piper, "we're delighted to help
honor a very special man on a very special occasion. Let me read
what it says on this trophy [putting on his glasses and opening a
folder]. 'Three years ago this week you captured the heavyweight
championship belt in a memorable battle. You're one of the greatest
professional athletes in the history of sports. You are a champion who

has raised wrestling to heights never before scaled. You are one of America's most patriotic citizens. You are loved and idolized by men, women, and children of all ages. You are the single most recognizable star in the entire world. We salute you on the third anniversary of your reign. Let's all honor the one and only Hulk Hogan.'"

Hogan comes to the set, wearing the World Wrestling Federation Championship belt. Smiling, he lifts up the trophy and shows it to the fans as Piper chews his gum. "It's yours," says the Hot Rod, sticking the mic in Hogan's face.

"Unbelievable! You know, January 23, 1984, when I won the world title, I knew there was something special, man [cut to the locker room celebration, with André smiling and pouring champagne on Hogan and Mean Gene, then shaking Hogan's hand]. I knew there was some kind of electricity. But I never believed, three long years down the road, thousands of people just like you would all turn into *Hulkamaniacs*. To receive an award for something that I believe in— the training, the saying the prayers, the eating the vitamins—to be rewarded for living the thing, this is unbelievable! This has got to be just as great as when I won the world title, this has got to be just as great as the first time I saw you *Hulkamaniacs,* and from here, it's higher and higher we go. This is unbelievable. Unbelievable!"

Enter André. With a huge smile lighting up his face, he puts a big hand on Piper's and Hogan's shoulders, startling the Hulkster.

"Ladies and gentlemen," Roddy announces, "Hulk Hogan's best friend, André the Giant! I'm sure you have come here for congratulations, and I'm sure you'll have something to say."

"Three years to be a champion, it's a long time," André booms, lacing his fingers together thoughtfully. He turns to face Hogan, grinning and extending his huge hand.

"It's a long time, yeah," agrees Piper.

André and Hogan shake, with Hulk grasping his friend's enormous hand in both of his own. As André turns and leaves through the archway, Hogan massages his palm, expressing some surprise at the strength of the Giant's grip.

PIPER'S PIT W/ANDRÉ, JACK TUNNEY, AND HULK HOGAN

Piper comes out and sells his Hair match at *WrestleMania III*. He then
points out the trophy and says, "We have a real special *Pit* again this
week, as you can see, starting this year off right. We had an exceptional
one last week and without further ado, I'd like to again bring out President Jack Tunney, come out and please present this special award."

"Thank you very much, Roddy," says Tunney. "We're very pleased
to honor another extraordinary hero. I'll read what's on the trophy
[putting on his glasses]: 'This man is the all-time greatest athlete in
the history of wrestling. This man is the only undefeated wrestler in
wrestling history. Please join me in saluting the one and only André
the Giant.'"

Tunney moves to stage right as André comes out, a toothsome
smile lighting up his face. "In living color," says the Hot Rod, shaking
André's hand. "André the Giant!"

André waves to the cheering fans.

"This is a very special and prestigious award," says Piper, "and
very deservedly so. You are a tremendous athlete, and I am proud to
be part of giving you this award. I'm sure that you must have some
things to say to your many, many fans."

He holds the mic up for André, but the Giant just smiles and
waves. After a moment, he decides to speak. "Well, yeah. I got only
one thing to say—"

Just as he begins his acceptance speech, André is interrupted by
the arrival of Hulk Hogan, in full ring gear and wearing the championship belt. He rushes out and, with no preamble, picks up the trophy
and hands it to the Giant.

"I'm more excited about this than you are, André," he says as
André raises the trophy aloft. "Y'know, this is about time, man, that
they recognize the greatest athlete of all time! Not only is he undefeated, man, André the Giant is the greatest role model. When I had
to pattern myself, I wanted to be like André. His sense of fair play, the
sportsmanship, the way all over the world he's been kind to all the
little kids, André the Giant is number one. I'd like to thank you for

recognizing, in my book, the real champion of superstars all over the world, that's André—"

But André is displeased about being upstaged by Hogan at his own award presentation. Rather than listen to the champ extol his virtues, he puts the trophy down and simply walks off. Hogan watches the Giant go, looking perplexed as he tries to get a round of applause out of the crowd.

"I'm sure that . . . ," says Piper, turning to discover that his guest of honor has left the set.

"That's the biggest package of modesty you'll ever see," says Hogan, clapping his hands together. "How about, for André?"

Cut to: Gorilla and a red-rhinestone-tuxedoed Bobby Heenan behind the news desk. "Boy, what tremendous accolades from the World Heavyweight Champion," says Monsoon.

"Please!" disagrees the Brain. "You talk about the things I do, how despicable they are. You talk about how I'm a fountain of misinformation. . . ."

Over the next few weeks, Roddy Piper and Jesse Ventura met to broker some kind of truce between the two friends. After much negotiation, it was agreed that André and Hogan would both appear on an upcoming *Piper's Pit* to resolve their differences.

January 6, 1987: Hershey Park Arena, Hershey, PA

Gorilla Monsoon does a stand-up interview with André, his eyes heavy-lidded and his face unshaven.

"André the Giant, a whole lotta speculation going here in World Wrestling Federation," Monsoon begins. "I'd like to clear the air at this point in time. Will, in fact, you be here next week to meet, one-on-one, in a discussion with World Heavyweight Champion Hulk Hogan?"

"I'll be there," the Giant replies, pointing a finger to the camera and the audience at home.

PIPER'S PIT

Piper and Jesse Ventura are in the *Pit.* "I promised it to ya this week," Piper says. "I ain't gonna fool around—"

"Hey, I've got one thing to say, Piper," says Jesse, grabbing the stick. "My man is here. The man who I promised is here. What about you?"

"My man, you're talking about?"

"My man's here. My man's here."

"Ladies and gentlemen," introduces Piper, "would you please welcome [punching the table] the Heavyweight Champion of the World, Hulk Hogan!"

Hogan enters. "My man is here!"

"I'm impressed, and I don't impress easy," says the Body. "Now, for this discussion, may I present, fifteen years undefeated, the Eighth Wonder of the World, seven-foot-four, five hundred pounds, André—whoa!—the Giant!"

To the shock and surprise of all three men, Bobby "The Brain" Heenan leads André through the arch. A stunned Hogan takes the mic, "Wait, what's going on here? Hold on, man. What are you doing with him? You guys aren't together, come on, man. André, what are you doing here with Heenan? André, listen, man, you can't be here with him. Don't you know what Heenan's done to me, to these people out here, since you've been gone?"

Piper puts the mic to André, but the Giant just stares coldly.

"It can't be so," Hogan beseeches. "André, listen to me, day one, when I set my eyes on you, brother, you're the reason I got in professional wrestling. You're like a god to me, a role model. You can't be here with him, man. You're the one that took me all the way from nothing to the world's title. André, you can't be with him, man."

Heenan tries to interrupt. "Let me tell you something—"

"No no, wait one minute," pleads the Hulkster. "You're the one that taught me, man, about respect for the fans, about helping the kids. You're the one that taught me about good sportsmanship.

With Bobby "The Brain" Heenan.

You set the mold for me to follow, man. What are you doing here
with him?"

André just stares at Hogan, a steely glint in his eyes.

"I'll tell you what he's doing here with me," explains the Brain.
"He's sick and tired of you and what you stand for. Let me tell you
something, Hogan. You're the one that for three years as world champion used this man. You're also the vermin that made this man, I can't
tell you what I think about it, you used him, they gave him a trophy.

But no, that wasn't good enough. It was a littler trophy than yours and you had to walk out and steal that moment. You're so jealous of this man, you can't stand it. This is the man that for fifteen years is undefeated, but did you ever once—"

Hogan pulls back the stick. "No, man, you're wrong! You're wrong, you're wrong! When I won the world title, he poured champagne over my head, it was like a bond of friendship. You're wrong, Heenan!"

"Did you ever once, once in your life, offer him a championship match? You laughed behind his back."

"No, André, listen," begs Hogan. "It's not happening. Tell me it's not so, man. Even though you came out here with him, you don't have to leave with him [pleading, gripping André's shoulders]. It's not happening!"

"Take your hands off my shoulders," André says flatly. Hogan complies, bowing his head in disbelief.

"He's got one more thing to say to you," adds Heenan as André puts a finger under Hogan's chin to lift his face up.

"Look at me when I'm talking to you," says the Giant. "I'm here for one reason—to challenge you for a world championship match in *WrestleMania.*"

Ventura is flabbergasted by the challenge, mouthing "Whoa!" Hogan is even more dismayed.

"André, please, no, it's not happening, man," he moans, his head bowed in supplication. "We're friends! We're friends, André, please!"

"You can't believe it? Maybe you'll believe this," says Heenan as André grabs Hogan's collar and tears off his shirt. He throws it to the floor and leaves with Heenan as Hulk drops to his knees and picks up the gold cross that André yanked off along with the yellow T-shirt.

"André? What are you doing, man? You can't leave like this, man! What are you doing, André? You can't . . . my cross . . . the shirt . . . what's wrong with him, man? You can't leave like this!"

Piper joins Hogan on his knees. "You're bleeding," he says softly, noting the blood on Hulk's chest.

"It's not happening! André, come back, man! You don't have to leave like this! What is he doing?"

"You're bleeding," Piper says again, helping a rattled Hogan to his feet. "Take it easy. Come. Come on."

Piper puts his arm around the heartbroken Hogan's waist and escorts him away.

HOWARD FINKEL: "For André to rip the cross off of Hulk Hogan was one of the single most dramatic moments in our industry. Here you had Hulk Hogan, who was the train that just kept on running. The ripping of the cross by André was the very first seed that we planted for *WrestleMania III*, and as the precursor to what we wound up with, was executed perfectly. People were stunned, legitimately stunned, by what had happened. It just absolutely floored the audience to watch that."

RODDY PIPER: "It's funny how things go. One sentence helped to bring in 93,000 people. Andre reaches and grabs the cross off of Hogan, Hogan went down, and all of a sudden I went, 'You're bleeding.' Cut! That probably was the strongest statement ever said on *Piper's Pit*. I don't know how to explain it. It was a very powerful statement, and such a simple one."

January 26, 1987: SunDome, Tampa, FL

PIPER'S PIT

The Hot Rod emerges and grabs the stick off the tabletop. "Are you people half as confused as I am?" he asks, massaging his brow. "You're doggone right. Three weeks ago, we came on, the beginning of 1987 and presented an award for Hulk Hogan, who has managed to be the World Heavyweight Champion for three years in a row. The next week we come out, we give another nice award to André the Giant, for fifteen years of pro wrestling without a defeat [pounding the tabletop]. The next week, yes, the next week, Gravel Gertie, the Aunt Jemima of professional wrestling, Jesse 'The Body' Ventura, comes out, and he starts stirring up all kinds of stuff. I don't know what's going on, so the next week comes on, you folks saw it, we got André, we got Hulk Hogan, the world's champion. Next thing I know, André the Giant is tearing the clothes off the World Heavyweight

Champion, and if that don't beat all, if that don't beat all [pounding the table for emphasis], he says—"

Cut to André: *"I'm here for one reason—to challenge you for a world championship match in* WrestleMania.*"*

"Ain't that the damnedest thing?" Piper continues. "So, I follow Hogan out, I followed Hogan to his dressing room, I go to the dressing room, I'm serious, I go to the dressing room, he's sitting down like this, I've never seen him like this before, man. He's sitting down, he's got his head down, and I said, 'Hey, Hogan, what's wrong with André?' And Hogan just kinda looked up at me and I looked at him and his eyes were all kinda steamy, and his eyes, and he put his head back down, between his legs, I said, 'Hogan, what's wrong?' And he just kinda goes like this to me [flicking a hand away]. Then I said, 'All kinds of people have been asking me questions.' I said, 'There's only one man in the world that can tell us if he's gonna accept this challenge or not.' [Putting up a hand] But wait, wait . . ."

Hogan appears in the archway.

". . . I saw Hogan in the hallway, I said, 'Hogan, are you coming on the *Pit*? There'll be nobody else there. . . .' "

Piper finally sees Hogan, rubbing his eyes, holding his torn shirt and cross, looking hangdog. "Ladies and gentlemen, the World Heavyweight Champion, Hulk Hogan!"

The champ is forlorn and barely responsive.

"Yo. Yo, look at me," demands Piper. "Look at me in the eye. Hulk, I don't understand something, man. Look at me in the eye, please [Hogan finally looks up]. What's going on with André?"

Hogan pauses and looks away.

"Please, look me in the eye. I've always known you to be a man at least, look me in the eye and tell me what's going on with André. We want to know!"

"You don't understand, man," Hogan says. "I worshipped the guy. He was like a friend, man. Everything he was, I wanted to be like him. I watched him on nationwide TV, that's the reason I'm here!"

"Wait a second; I thought he's your best friend."

"I thought so. I thought so, man. Like I said, that's why I'm here. I patterned my whole life after him, man. The courtesy, the way he treated people, in and out of the ring, man. The way he was a good sport, brother. That's what I wanted—"

Piper tries to interrupt.

"No, no, no," says Hogan. "I knew I couldn't be as big as him, man. I wanted to be just like him. I watched him move, man. I watched him treat people."

"Treating people?" Piper interjects. "Ripping clothes off is not my idea of treating people right."

"When I saw him with Heenan, you're right, man. I knew he'd changed. When he was with Heenan, I knew he was a different man. I knew Heenan had got to him. I knew something was different. We used to fight for the same things; we used to fight because we believed in the straight and narrow. When I saw him with Heenan, I don't know if it was jealousy, greed, the money, something had gotten to him. But when he pulled this shirt, man, when he ripped the cross off my chest, he didn't just tear it off, he dug in and tore my heart out, man. Why didn't you just take a stake and drive it in my heart, André? You know something? Now that he's with Heenan, it's all changed, man. He's different!"

"Tell me, yes or no! Are you or are you not gonna fight him in *WrestleMania III* for the world heavyweight championship? Yes or no?"

"Yesssss!" Hogan avows, the sound of his affirmation morphing into a lion's roar.

February 16, 1987: New Haven Coliseum, New Haven, CT

PIPER'S PIT

Piper comes out and runs a brush through his hair. "Three weeks, I'm letting it grow, man! Three weeks we got till the biggest extravaganza in the history of professional wrestling, *WrestleMania III,* and I'm damn proud to be the man that runs Adonis out of town, baldheaded, brother! I've got something else. I talked to Bobby Heenan and Bobby Heenan—ha, somebody said he's a weasel, ha ha—and I said to myself, why should I talk to Bobby Heenan? I would prefer to hear the words from André the Giant himself, why he is doing this [André enters, followed by Heenan]. So I would like to bring out, as my guest, André the Giant."

"You want to talk to somebody, you talk to me," says the Brain. "You want to talk to André the Giant, you talk to me. Anybody out there wants to do any negotiations, anything concerning this gentleman, you talk to me. Another thing, I'm sick of you and everybody else out here calling me names, calling me 'weasel,' saying I—"

"Who called you weasel?"

"Everybody did! Saying I poisoned this man's mind. I haven't done a thing but awoke him to the fact that people like you, Hulk Hogan, they used him. They laughed at him. They stabbed him in the back. Well, now it's time for *us* to do a little stabbing in the back!"

"Wait, wait, wait, wait," Piper cuts him short. "I want you to listen to this now. This weasel here is saying—excuse me, Mr. Heenan is saying that Hulk Hogan has been stabbing in the back and Hulk Hogan has been doing all this, this is *WrestleMania,* this is a big thing, for the World Heavyweight Championship, I don't want to hear you talk no more, I want to hear right from André the Giant—"

From behind, Capt. Lou emerges and puts his hand on Piper's shoulder. He takes the stick.

"André. André, what have you done? To all these people out here, to me, your former manager, listening to the halfwit devious brain of the weasel, Bobby Heenan. André, what have you done? You've let the people down, you've disgraced yourself and your family and all the fans out there. I was your manager! You know something, I hope that the Hulk whips your butt, what do you think of that?"

André, who had been looking away, a grim cast on his face, turns to Albano. He approaches menacingly, his chest at Capt. Lou's eye level, sending his former manager cowering from the *Pit.*

"Wait, wait, whoa, whoa, whoa," Piper says, trying to regain control.

"Whoa, whoa, nothing!" Heenan says, grabbing the mic. "Who does anybody think they are to come out here [pounding the table] and belittle me, belittle this man! Everybody in wrestling is gonna answer to him! They're gonna pay!"

André continues to stare out at the crowd as Piper pulls the stick back. "Nobody's belittling nobody, but you're gonna have hell to pay to get the World Heavyweight Championship!"

He slams the mic onto the table and pushes Heenan out of his way, leaving his own set. Unfazed, André looks steely-eyed out at the crowd.

THE SNAKE PIT

"There's something about intimidation," Jake "The Snake" Roberts says, "because, you see, that's the way I've always run my life, by intimidating people. Because if you can make people fear you, then you've got 'em one step closer to where you want 'em, and that's in the palm of your hand. Now *WrestleMania III*'s coming down, it's two weeks away, there's a lot of things happening, a lot of questions to be asked."

Bobby Heenan, in blue rhinestone dinner jacket and red bow tie, emerges from the cave entrance while the Snake discusses his own *WrestleMania* match with Honky Tonk Man. André follows and Roberts turns to chat.

"I gotta ask you, why?" he says, holding the mic up to the Giant.

Heenan takes Jake's arm and brings the stick toward himself. "Don't talk to him. You talk to me, if you wanna talk to him."

"Why?"

"Why what?"

"Why," Roberts asks, gesturing toward André, "against Hogan?"

"Why?"

"After all this time."

"Because Hogan has used this man for the last time," Heenan says as the camera goes in close to André's dead-eyed stare and stone-faced expression. "Fifteen years undefeated, this man never got his fair shot at anything. People laughed at him, stabbed him in the back, and used him. Well now, in *WrestleMania*, we're gonna use Hulk Hogan to get to what we want, the Championship of the World!"

"Don't you realize, André, how much respect you've lost from all the people?"

Heenan pulls the mic back. "*You* pick *me* a winner!"

"Pick you a winner of this match?"

"Right. You pick me a winner."

"Well, I tell you," Roberts says, "I respect faith, but doubt has always taught me an education. It's a very big man. Now I wanna know why? Why don'tcha do it on your own, instead of having Heenan do it?"

Again, André says nothing, and Heenan guides Roberts's mic to his mouth.

"Maybe you don't understand. Maybe you're dumb and thick like Hogan. And I'll tell ya something, Hogan. If you're as dumb as I think you are, it's gonna be a piece of cake. 'Cause right now, the sheer picture of this man, the size of this man, you're shaking! You can't talk to anybody, you can't do an interview, you can't do a thing without the sweat pouring off of your body! *WrestleMania*, Hogan, is the end of *Hulkamania.* We've got a new heavyweight champion of the world, André the Giant!"

"When worlds collide," Jake muses, "something has to give. I agree with that. But what?"

February 27, 1987

André and Hogan sit across from each other, staring over the championship belt. At the head of the table is Jack Tunney, flanked by Mean Gene and Heenan, with assorted personnel standing around. Everybody other than the wrestlers themselves is arguing until Okerlund gets the proceedings under way.

"Gentlemen, gentlemen, please," says Mean Gene. "We are here for the most auspicious signing of any heavyweight title match in history, as you all know. Let me introduce, just for the record, some of these dignitaries who are with us at this time, for this historic event. First of all, Bobby 'The Brain' Heenan, representing the challenger, the Eighth Wonder of the World, from Grenoble, France, André the Giant.

"To my right, the Heavyweight Champion of the World, from Venice Beach, California, Hulk Hogan. And to my immediate left, the distinguished president of World Wrestling Federation, Mr. Jack Tunney. Mr. Tunney, you can get on with the proceedings."

Hogan is breathing heavily, eyes locked on André. Cameras are clicking away as Tunney begins preparing the contracts.

"Would you please sign on the dotted line, Mr. Rousimoff—"

"Whoa, whoa, whoa," interrupts Heenan. "Slow down here, Mr. Tunney. Mr. President. Few things I want to go over with you first. When we had a discussion about this championship belt—"

"Yes," says Tunney as Heenan reaches across the table for the title.

"—I want a new championship belt. This one was made and designed for *this* human being—and I use that term very, very loosely. I want one made that will fit a *man.* Fit a *giant* of a man. Somebody that can represent the world of professional wrestling. Not like *this man.*"

The Brain tosses the title belt back onto the table toward Hogan, who is continuing to snort and stare at André.

"And another thing," he continues. "I just want you to get one thing straight, Hogan. Fifteen years, this man's gone undefeated. The three years you've been world's champion, you've talked behind his back, you laughed at him, you never *once* gave this man an opportunity. Now he's got that opportunity—"

Hogan slams his hand down on the table in a rage. "Sign it if you're gonna sign it!"

André grins at his opponent's loss of composure, a crooked Mona Lisa smile across his face. He picks up the pen, affixes his name to the contract, and passes the paperwork back to Tunney, all the while keeping his eyes locked on Hogan's. Tunney slides the contract to the champ.

"You can sign under his name, Mr. Hogan."

"I'll sign a lot of things," pants the Hulkster, "signed a lot of contracts. Never thought it would come to this. What's wrong with you, man? Both of you, you're both *sick.* You're both sick. If you wanted a title shot, all you had to do was ask me. I'd-a gave you anything, man. André, you were bigger than the world title to me. Yeah, I'll sign it.

You'll get your chance at *WrestleMania*. When you tore my shirt off, man, when you tore the cross, you tore the heart and soul outta all the little Hulksters, man. Not just me. Well, you're gonna get your chance, man. You're gonna get your chance."

"Now you signed that contract," André replies calmly, "you think I tell you everything you know in professional wrestling? But I didn't. Believe me, *WrestleMania III* will be your last lesson."

The Giant continues in French as Hogan huffs and puffs. Finally, he slaps the table and points an angry finger in André's face. "Speak to me in English when you talk to me! As far as I'm concerned, it's not signed in ink. It's signed in blood!"

They both rise. "You want me to speak in English, I will speak in the ring at *WrestleMania*," André says, putting up a hand to leave. "*Au revoir.*"

March 10, 1987: Hara Arena, Dayton, OH

PIPER'S PIT

"We ain't far from *WrestleMania* now, are we, man?" asks Piper, pounding the tabletop. "*WrestleMania III* . . . And now, without further ado, I'd like to bring out President Jack Tunney, please."

"Hello, Roddy, how are you?" says Tunney, holding a black velvet bag.

"Good, good. You've got a little present for me?"

"Not that you don't deserve it, however, this is a little different."

"What've we got?"

"I've been charged with getting a new world's championship belt, at Bobby Heenan's insistence. Now this is large enough to fit André the Giant, if necessary. Let me show it to you, it's beautiful."

"Let's get that sucker off there," Piper says, helping to remove the bag. "Ho, ho. That's a big sucker there! That's a giant belt, for sure! He's a little trim, is he? Well, I don't know. I know one thing for sure. . . ."

Heenan and André come out. The Brain picks up the belt and examines it.

"Hi, Weasel," greets the *Pit*'s host. The Brain turns and glares at him. "I mean, Mr. Heenan."

"You've finally done something right," Heenan says, shaking Tunney's hand. "You finally have done something that I've asked for. And I want all you people, all over the world, to get used to a certain sight, because you're gonna be seeing a lot of this. You're gonna be seeing the new next Heavyweight Champion of the World, André the Giant!"

André spreads his arms wide as Heenan places the belt around his waist.

"Wait a second," Piper says, giving André the chance to speak. "What?"

"I say, this one fit!" André booms, throwing the title belt over his shoulder.

"Well, you're an awfully big man," says Piper, "but I wanna . . . just one, I've never done this before, just take a little poll. This guy is wearing the World Heavyweight Championship belt right now; we're just a little ways before *WrestleMania,* do you think, in any kinda way, he deserves to wear it now?"

The crowd boos, gesturing thumbs-down.

"If it doesn't fit, and you do win, I'll be sure to increase it myself."

"I have to just say one thing," André says, staring down at the Hot Rod. "In one week, finally you gonna see a real champion."

Heenan and André leave the set.

"Finally," Piper notes, "finally, old sourmouth there, he has got himself a belt, he has got himself a manager, he has got himself a fight with Hogan. The only thing he ain't got, is he ain't won yet, man."

March 10, 1987: Hara Arena, Dayton, OH

Announcer, TV Pitchman, and former Milwaukee Brewer Bob Uecker was enlisted as one of *WrestleMania III*'s celebrity guests. In advance of the event, the man known as "Mr. Baseball" is granted the dubious task of interviewing the challenger to the World Wrestling Federation title.

"Hey, Bob Uecker here with Bobby 'The Brain' Heenan and André the Giant. You guys gotta be feeling pretty good, last week, throwing Hulk Hogan out of the ring, gimme a break, willya?"

"That's why we're here," Heenan says, noting Uecker's orange sweater. "I see you've been to a garage sale too. That's why we're here. Are you ready for your announcement?"

"What announcement?"

"You know, you been practicing? Are you prepared?"

"I don't practice announcing," Uecker says proudly.

"Well, you better practice. You gotta say one important thing."

"What?"

"André the Giant, the new World's Heavyweight Champion," Heenan explains.

"Come on, say it," scowls André.

"Wait a minute, I don't—"

"Say it!"

"Come on!"

"André the Giant, the new World's Heavyweight Champion," stammers Uecker.

"No, with some enthusiasm," insists the Brain.

"Better than that," demands André.

"André the Giant! The new World's Heavyweight Champion!"

"Better than that!"

"ANDRÉ THE GIANT!" yells Uecker. "THE NEW WORLD'S HEAVY-WEIGHT CHAMPION!"

"Finally got something right," allows Heenan.

"TALE OF THE TAPE: HOW HULK AND ANDRÉ MEASURE UP"

Hogan's great stature and physique do not come near matching André's overwhelming size and bulk. . . . André comes out on top in all but the arm department. Only in terms of biceps and forearms does Hogan outmatch the Giant. . . . André has the edge in all else, especially height and weight. The last-mentioned category, in fact, is where Hogan gives away the most—more, for that matter, than usual. His bout with André is the first title defense made by Hogan at a weight of less than 300 pounds.

Hogan—Height: 6'8", Weight: 294 lbs, Neck: 21", Chest: 58", Biceps: 24", Forearms: 18", Wrist: 9", Hands: 13½", Thighs: 30½", Calves: 20"

André—Height: 7'4", Weight: 525 lbs, Neck: 24", Chest: 71", Biceps: 21", Hands: 16", Wrist: 11", Forearms: 17", Thighs: 36", Calves: 22"

April/May 1987

"THE PROS RATE ANDRÉ AND HULK"
by Keith Elliot Greenberg

Rowdy Roddy Piper: "They're gonna punch and punch and kick and smash and whack. It's not gonna be pretty. But it's gonna be good! André has one thing on his side—he's ugly. One look at his puss and you wanna run back to the dressing room. . . . André's gonna come at him, and Hulk's not gonna budge. He's gonna stand there in the middle of the ring and take everything that André gives him. Then, he's gonna pick up that big backstabbing Giant, and he's gonna slam him into the mat. And then the referee's gonna get on the canvas and lift his hand and say three words: One-Two-Three."

Big John Studd: "Hogan is quicker than André. He knows how to bounce off the canvas and take a man off his feet. If a wrestler's not careful, Hogan'll roll him up for the pin. And—I'll even admit it—his short-arm clothesline is painful. But André's clothesline is more painful. And his kicks can take a man's head off. Also, André's angry. He finally discovered that Hogan's friendship was just Hulk's way of ducking him. Have you ever been near André when he's mad? I've been. He's vicious."

" 'HULKAMANIA IS DEAD': HEENAN VOWS TO END HOGAN'S REIGN AT WRESTLEMANIA III"

[André] is a man many have called the world's greatest athlete, an overpowering presence who seems to hark back to the days when, legends say, giants walked the earth. André has never been beaten, not by any single opponent, and not in the thunderous donnybrooks of Battle Royals. In *WrestleMania 2,* for instance, he emerged the victor from a Battle Royal that included not only wrestling greats but some of the biggest, toughest brawlers from the NFL. André waded through some of the most formidable men in the world, tossing them about like children. In the end, only the Giant stood in the ring.

"I told André that I was the only one who could get him what he wanted," says Heenan. "I'm the world's best wrestling manager. I could get him Hogan's belt and the glory that goes with it. . . . André has always been the real champion, the man who should wear the belt. But the company never gave him the chance because they know he could beat Hogan as easily as I'd swat a fly. But now, I've given them no choice. Hogan must face André or quit. André knows that I've made this possible. So we're together. No more *Hulkamania.* It's time for reality. And reality is that no one in the world can beat the Giant."

As *WrestleMania III* approached, McMahon was faced with a decision as to how the match should play out. Should André the Giant remain the unstoppable monster, or should the hotter-than-hot new Superstar prevail?

With *Hulkamania* running wild and business booming, it was obvious that Hogan should come out on top. McMahon confirmed the finish with André, but Hogan was kept in the dark until mere hours before the big show.

VINCE McMAHON: "Hogan was scared to death. 'What's he going to do?' Of course, Hogan *should* have been scared to death. 'Are you sure André's going to do this for us? I mean, are you really sure?'

MICHAEL KRUGMAN

"Hogan would not say anything to André, like, 'Hey, are you going to do this job for me?' He had too much respect for André to come out straight and ask him. Instead he would beat around the bush—'Hey, boss, what are we going to do?'

" 'I'll tell you later,' André would answer.

"Well, later never came, and Hogan kept coming to me, 'Oh my God, am I going to win this thing?'

" 'Yeah, yeah, yeah,' I kept saying. 'It's all set, it's all set.'

"Finally I got Hogan in my room the night before the event, and that's when André let him know what was going to go down.

"After André told Hogan what he was going to do, there was a big hug and all that kind of stuff. And then, here we go."

TIM WHITE: "This is how cool André was. We stopped on our way to the Silverdome and went to Lindell's AC and had a couple of beers. Ninety-three thousand people lining up, and it was just business as normal for him.

"People were coming to me that day, 'Is he gonna do it? Is he gonna do it?' He was sitting there naked, playing cards with Arnie, with ninety-three thousand people out there, and honestly they didn't know if he was gonna do the finish or not till about eight minutes before they went to the ring.

"This is just what I witnessed, but Hogan was sweating the whole day. I think André was just holding court, like, 'Know this. Before I make *you* the guy, remember that *I'm* the guy, and always have been.'"

VINCE MCMAHON: "I was the only person that knew what was going to go on. Because of his personality, André would not have shared that with anyone. That's how closed he was in terms of the business back in the day. It wasn't anybody else's business. He also enjoyed a little bit of playing around. I mean, he knew that everybody wanted to know.

"All I knew was the finish. That's all I knew. That's all I cared to know. I knew André was going to take care of Hogan, he wasn't going to hurt him. I knew André was going to do the job for me, my dad, for the business, and for himself. But other than that, I didn't know what was going to happen."

TIM WHITE: "About ten minutes before the match, André started tying up his boots, and Vince said, 'Who do you want for a referee?' He said, 'Joey [Marella].' Then he got into the cart with Bobby Heenan and it was time to go."

Stare-down before the Main Event, *WrestleMania III*.

March 29, 1987: Pontiac Silverdome, Pontiac, MI

WRESTLEMANIA III

Vince McMahon visits the locker room for a prematch interview with Hogan.

"Heavyweight Champion of the World," says McMahon, "in the locker room, just one hour away from his moment of destiny."

Hogan takes a deep breath. "Well, you know, they said it was my last ride, man. Yesterday when I finished hangin' and bangin', when I jumped on the Harley, man, as I went through the intersection, as I headed for the mountains, some of the nonbelievers in the gym said, 'See ya later, Hulksterman. This is your last ride.' It ate me alive, brothers. When I felt the fury as I ripped, as I tore the shirt [ripping and tearing off his shirt, Vince grimacing while holding the mic], as I headed for the sunset, man, I looked down, brothers, and as the sun beamed off the gold in my eyes [holding his cross], I realized that sooner or later you gotta live and die and you gotta face the truth.

"And for you, André the Giant, it's time to face the truth, brother. Because when I think about what you and I have to do, man, what I have to do is nothin'. All I have to do is merely beat a seven-foot-four, 550-pound giant. But André, you gotta face the truth, brother. In its purest form, man! The purest truth there is, man! The training, the saying the prayers, the eating the vitamins.

"And to beat me, man, you've gotta beat every *Hulkamaniac*, every little Hulkster in the world, everyone that plays it straight, all the ones that don't take any shortcuts, brother. And they usually say, if the dirty air don't get ya, the politicians will. But in this case, it's gonna be *Hulkamania*. And the reason it's going to get you, man, it's the purest form of the truth there is. And I can't wait to see you go down at the feet of *Hulkamania* in front of 90,000-plus in the Silverdome. Whatcha gonna do, André the Giant, when the real truth, the 24-inch pythons, and *Hulkamania* runs wild on you?"

Later, Mean Gene interviews André and Heenan.

"With me at this time, manager Bobby 'The Brain' Heenan," introduces Okerlund. "And I'm privileged to be standing next to the most extraordinary athlete of all time. He is not elected, until this date, to challenge Hulk Hogan for the heavyweight championship. And this afternoon at *WrestleMania III*, Bobby Heenan, your man, André the Giant, will be doing just that."

"You bet he's going to be doing just that," Heenan says. "He's going to become the Heavyweight Champion of the World, and I'll tell you why. First of all, the man is undefeated in over fifteen years as a professional athlete. Hulk Hogan has never been in the ring or met a man bigger than him, stronger than him, taller than him, that weighs more than him, and with a burning will inside more than André the Giant.

"You see, Hogan, a few short hours from now that clock is ticking. And it's ticking in our direction, not yours. *Hulkamania* is over. *Hulkamania* is dead. The door's going to be shut on the history books of Hulk Hogan once and for all. There is a new Heavyweight Champion of the World. The odds-on favorite in Las Vegas and all over the whole wrestling world, they're picking André the Giant. Nobody can defeat this man. Nobody even can come close to defeating this man. And Hogan, I know it's happening to you now because it's happening to me. The butterflies are in my stomach. The adrenaline's flowing through my veins and I'm getting ready. 'Cause I'm gonna manage the Heavyweight Champion of the World. And Hogan, hey, you've had three good years. You've got nothing to look back on. But it's all over. André the Giant, the new Heavyweight Champion of the World."

"The biggest heavyweight title bout of all time," Mean Gene declares. "André the Giant to meet Hulk Hogan."

As the main event approaches, Mean Gene interviews André and Heenan once more.

"And André the Giant, just moments away from now you're stepping through the ropes and into the ring to meet Hulk Hogan, in the *biggest* title match of all time. I want to get your thoughts."

"Gene, you see me now," rumbles André. "And I'm going to the ring, and believe me, it's not going to take me too long to come back right in front of the camera with the World Championship belt around my waist."

"Bobby?"

"Oh, I can feel it. Oh, the adrenaline's going! This man right here is gonna make me famous. He's gonna become the Heavyweight Champion of the World. And I'm gonna go down in the history books as the manager of the World Heavyweight Champion. I'm ready! Hogan, you better be ready!"

Right before the match, Mean Gene goes for a final thought from Hogan.

"Moments away from the biggest heavyweight title defense of this man ever," says Okerlund. "Hulk Hogan, you've gotta be ready."

"Well, you know, I hope Pontiac, Michigan, recovers, man," says the Hulkster. "I'm glad I snuck in early last night, brother. I didn't realize the interstates, the Pontiac Silverdome, was in danger. Not the 90,000-plus on the inside. It's the 90,000-plus on the *outside* of the Silverdome. Those are the ones I'm worried about. Because when I get my hands on that big nasty giant. When he faces the truth. When he feels the wrath of *Hulkamania*. The day the whole earth is gonna shake. What are those 90,000-plus *Hulkamaniacs* on the outside gonna think? I'm not worried about the people at the closed circuit. I'm not worried about the people all around the world. They'll see it! But the intensity of *Hulkamania*. The way it's turned this whole state upside down. The way the whole world's turned upside down. What are they gonna think, when the giant hits the ground, he feels the wrath of *Hulkamania,* and the whole world shakes at my feet?"

"We could conceivably blow the roof off this great facility, the Silverdome," Okerlund says as Hogan shows off the pythons.

After weeks of promotion, the match, at last, is ready to begin. Ring announcer Howard Finkel introduces the special guest ring announcer, Bob Uecker. "Mr. Baseball" comes out in his cart and is escorted to the ring by two lovely women. Uecker brings out special guest timekeeper, Mary Hart.

At last, Uecker introduces André and Heenan (wearing white tie and tails adorned with gold rhinestones). They come out in the cart amid a rain of debris. As the cart travels to the ring, they are literally pelted with trash from the angry fans.

The crowd is out of control, cheering for Hogan, who walks out on his own.

"This is the biggest match in the history of professional wrestling," says Ventura.

Mary Hart rings the bell, and the stare-down begins. André wears the cold face as Hogan, already Hulking up, says something known only to the two wrestlers. André responds with a shove, which Hogan returns. A right is blocked by Hogan, who nails André with three rights of his own. He reaches between André's legs and attempts a slam, but André falls on top of the champ for a two-count from ref Joey Marella.

Hogan crawls away, favoring his back, as André insists he had the champ pinned for three. André gets up and plants a kick to Hogan's kidneys. He goes to work on Hogan's back with his forearms, demanding Hogan get up each time he sends him to the canvas. A kneelift and a bodyslam continue the damage to the champ's lower back. Garbage rains into the ring as André scoops Hogan up for another slam. The Giant walks across Hogan, pausing a moment to put his full weight on the lower back.

"Get up," insists André.

The Giant lifts Hogan by the back of his trunks and whips him into the turnbuckles. He takes a wrist and whips him across the ring to the opposite corner. Hogan drops to his knees, holding on to the second ropes.

"What do you think of your champion now?" mocks André before lifting Hogan upright for a choke and shoulderblock.

"Again! Again!" shouts Heenan, and the Giant happily obliges.

André turns and squashes Hogan, driving his butt back with full force. Heenan calls for a headbutt, and André delivers. André throttles Hogan by his traps and attempts a headbutt, but Hogan slips away. He throws two rights, shoots off the ropes for a third roundhouse right. He goes off the ropes again, this time hitting an elbow. André teeters into the corner, where Hogan delivers a number of chops. He reaches up and with two hands, takes André's head and plants it into the top turnbuckle ten times.

Hogan nods to the crowd as André stands, dazed. He comes off the ropes for another elbow, but André raises his size-22 boot and catches Hogan smack under the chin.

"Are you all right?" asks Heenan.

André nods and rights Hogan with a handful of hair. A chop staggers Hulk further, and André locks his arms around Hogan for the bearhug, Hogan pulls at André's hair, at his shoulderstrap, to no avail. André squeezes, preventing Hogan from breathing and doing more damage to his lower back.

Hogan wilts and drops his arm. Marella raises it twice, and on the third, it stays aloft.

A dozen hard rights to André's head finally break the hold, but André maintains a grip in Hogan's tights. Hogan goes off the ropes, but his tackle barely budges the Giant. A second one pushes André a couple of steps, but he stays standing. On his third try, Hogan is planted by a chop. He whips him into the ropes and sends him flying out through the ropes with a big boot. André follows and chops him against the ringpost. He goes for a headbutt, but Hogan ducks and the Giant hits his own head—showing an awful lot of light.

Hogan lifts up the mats as André reels. He pulls André to the exposed concrete—wood, actually—and tries for a piledriver. The Giant reverses it and backdrops Hogan to the floor. André throws him back into the ring, and then rolls back in himself.

Hogan is whipped into the ropes but avoids the boot, comes off the opposite side with a clothesline that drops André to the mat. Heenan tends to André as Hogan sits straight, beginning to Hulk up. They both rise to their feet, and Hogan scoops up André for the slam. He hits the legdrop and covers—one, two, three—at 12:01.

"I never thought it could be done, Gorilla," says Jesse Ventura.

Hogan raises the belt high and thanks the guy upstairs. He lays the belt across the mat and challenges André to come back in as "Real American" plays.

André and a dejected Heenan get into the cart, debris and garbage flying at them from all sides.

BOBBY HEENAN: *"Everybody said when I put my jacket over my head at Wrestle-Mania it showed how demoralized I was that Andre didn't get the job done, that this was probably my last shining moment, that I was crushed.*

"Nope. The reason I put the jacket over my head was people were throwing cups and batteries and all kinds of stuff. I didn't want to get my eye put out, so I put my coat over my head."

With that, Hulk Hogan became the first person to beat André by pinfall or submission in the Giant's fourteen years with World Wrestling Federation. He had, of course, been beaten a number of times throughout his career at this point. In his early days working the Quebec territory for Grand Prix, he was defeated by Killer Kowalski and Don Leo Jonathan to build up returns. Jerry Lawler beat him via countout in AWA, while feuds with the Sheik—who famously never lost in his native Detroit or Toronto—were blown off with his defeating André in gimmicked finishes. What's more, André had even been bodyslammed on a number of occasions, by such wrestlers as Stan Hansen, NWA champion Harley Race, and *lucha* legend El Canek.

That said, the *WrestleMania III* slam was a momentous occurrence that received what's generally acknowledged as the biggest crowd pop ever. On a 2006 installment of WWE.com's *Byte This*, McMahon referred to it as "the most extraordinary moment in the history of the business."

Hogan scoops up the Giant, *WrestleMania III.*

HULK HOGAN: "Before the match started, I told André I didn't want to just beat him. I wanted to really give the people something they could tell their grandchildren. I wanted to bodyslam him. It was a crazy idea."

VINCE McMAHON: "Please. His idea? He didn't have any ideas in that match and he wasn't supposed to. André told him what we were going to do, André called the slam. Hogan couldn't have slammed him if he didn't want him to. He couldn't have slammed *me* if I didn't want him to slam me, much less André."

MICHAEL KRUGMAN

HOWARD FINKEL: "When Hogan picked André up and slammed him, that will go down as one of the single greatest moments in our business. It was an anointment. The guy who has never been slammed, never been taken off his feet, not even through chicanery or skullduggery."

VINCE McMAHON: "Even though Hogan was a strong guy—he thinks he's a lot stronger than he is—the question remained: Could he get André up for the slam? But when the time came, André just went up, I won't say like a feather, but he just went right on up for the big slam and the one, two, three."

HULK HOGAN: "When we got to that point in the match, my first move was to get my arm between his legs. . . . Then I had to get him to come toward me so I pushed him into the ropes, and as he came forward again I pulled him in and used his momentum to pick him up. . . . If you look at the tape of that match, you can see André's knuckles were dragging on the ground when I picked him up. He was so damned big, his leg was almost as big as my whole body.

"But somehow, I slammed him."

One million fans watched at over 160 closed-circuit venues across North America, while millions more ordered the show on home cable Pay-Per-View. The Pontiac Silverdome sold out two weeks in advance, ultimately drawing 93,173 fans, the largest recorded paid wrestling crowd ever and a world indoor attendance record that still stands today for any sports or entertainment event. The event was the first million-dollar live gate in history, as well as the biggest closed-circuit gate to date. In addition, *WrestleMania III* set a Pay-Per-View buy rate record that has yet to be equaled by a wrestling event.

Hogan's victory was a true passing of the torch—from André, wrestling's biggest star of the 1970s, to Hogan, wrestling's biggest star of the 1980s. Faced with his failing physical condition, André was well aware that his best years were now behind him. Above all else, he understood the wrestling business. If the time had come for André the Giant to pass the torch, then that match was damn well going to be something spectacular.

WrestleMania III was spectacular and more—a milestone match, in front of the biggest house in wrestling history, which, rather than closing the book on his career, only served to magnify the Giant's legend.

10

The Princess Bride opened in theaters on September 25, 1987. The film received unanimous critical acclaim, with André's performance singled out as one of the film's undeniable highlights.

TIM WHITE: "Never in my life did I ever see him nervous or on edge. Everything was, 'Okay, boss. Don't worry about it, boss.' 'Cause he ruled the world we were in. The only time I ever saw him nervous was at the premiere of *The Princess Bride.* I'll never forget, it was at the Festival of Festivals in Toronto. It was just me and André, walking down the red carpet. I looked over at him, he was shaking. He was a nervous wreck about how people were gonna view him in this movie. I mean, he never worried a lick about wrestling—he's the Boss. But now he stepped out of that world, and he's gonna be judged by other actors and film people.

"When the movie finished, everybody stood and cheered, especially when they announced André. He was as proud as he was at *WrestleMania III.*"

KENNETH JOHNSON: "André's performance is so sweet and delicious in that picture. It always tickled me when I saw it to remember that, hey man, I was there when he started out."

André had always delighted in the crowd's response during his matches. Not long after *The Princess Bride* had opened, he and Tim White slipped into a late screening of the film in order to get a first-person sense of how audiences were reacting to his performance.

TIM WHITE: "We were on the road in Regina, Canada, staying at a hotel that's connected to a mall, and in the mall is a cinema. *The Princess Bride* is playing. He goes, 'Boss, find out what time the last one is on.' It was showing at like ten thirty or something. André put his match on before the intermission so we could beat the fans out of the building.

"I went to the theater manager and said, 'As soon as the lights dim down, could we go in the back and just sit down?' So we went in and were sitting in the back, just to the side of the projector, 'cause his head would've blocked it. No one knows André's in the theater. He's finally getting to watch the movie and enjoy it just for himself.

"So the lights come up at the end, and people turn around and there he is. They all just started clapping. They couldn't believe it. Can you imagine going to a theater In Regina, Canada, to see a movie and then when the lights come up you turn around and André is sitting right there? He got the biggest kick out of that!"

STEPHANIE McMAHON: "To me, the character André played in *The Princess Bride* is very much who he was. That's how I knew him, as this sweet, loveable, kick-

Stephanie and her Giant.

your-ass giant. A big teddy bear. I doubt any of the boys would say this, but I think that André was vulnerable. We all are to some degree. I think that vulnerability is what came across in *The Princess Bride*."

André's world was an aggressively macho existence, with booze and cards and wrestling being the bond that fixed his friendships. But the real-life Giant also had a fairy-tale camaraderie with the World Wrestling Federation's own princess, Vince McMahon's daughter Stephanie. Though the Giant was also close with McMahon's son, Shane, his relationship with Stephanie was something special. In many ways, the McMahons provided André with a surrogate family, with Shane and Stephanie filling in for the nieces and nephews he saw so rarely. His relationship with Vince, however, was somewhat more complicated.

TIM WHITE: "André was never locked down to anybody. However, his heart and soul was with the McMahon family. André loved Vince Sr. like he was his dad. When Vince Sr. passed away, André cried, he was so upset. So upset. They never had a contract. Imagine that. Just a handshake. Vince Sr. and André.

"He loved Vince because he saw him grow up, he saw what a maniac he was and said, 'Yeah, he's a good kid.' But sometimes he questioned, How far is he pushing, what's he doing?

"I think he was a little bit concerned what WWE was doing, things like 'Rock 'n' Wrestling.' But he went along with it, like, 'I'm trusting you because I've seen what you've done, I've seen 93,000 people in the Silverdome.' But he wasn't one hundred percent in on it. That's going to happen with an older guy that's come through the business working a certain way and then sees it turning. He had questions in his mind, but he still respected and liked Vince a lot."

MICHAEL KRUGMAN

With Vince McMahon.

VINCE McMAHON: "André really loved my dad, and the feeling was mutual. He liked me, but he didn't love me. To a certain extent, he resented the fact that I broke up all the little territories. André enjoyed going to the various wrestling territories because he was treated like a king. But when he was just part of World Wrestling Federation, I think he didn't feel as appreciated. He was, but now one person controlled the business. We never talked about it, but I don't think he liked that.

"But my God, he loved my daughter, Stephanie. We were living on Cape Cod for a while, and we had a trampoline. Steph was bouncing on the trampoline and André comes up to the house. Very unusual, but he was in town and we invited him over for dinner. I think it was the first time that they had met. André just got out of his car, goes to her trampoline, and holds out his hand. Steph just stepped into his hand and gave him a kiss. It was just tremendous."

SHANE McMAHON: "André was always so nice to me. My dad told me it's because he was shocked that I wasn't scared of him. Usually everyone was very afraid, just based on the sheer size of the man—he was very intimidating. But kids have no fear. So I got to know André, he was my buddy. I'd sit in the locker room when he was playing cards, things like that. I always told my dad that I was going to grow up and be André the Giant's tag team partner. I was going to grow up and be big like André, not small, like my dad."

STEPHANIE McMAHON: "He was my friend. André understood me, and I understood André. I think a lot of people had a hard time understanding him, he had that very deep, booming voice with his accent, but I never had trouble understanding him at all. We kind of had a bond without words.

"André treated me like an adult. I'm not saying he treated me like one of the boys by any stretch of the imagination, but he didn't talk to me like a child. We had very adult conversations, about life and people.

"When I was about fourteen, André took me out to dinner at his favorite French restaurant. So we walk into the restaurant, and all of a sudden André starts laughing this deep, booming laugh. I said, 'André, what's so funny?'

" 'Ho, ho, ho, ho. All these people, they think I'm a dirty old man.'

"I was a little shocked. I said, 'No, they don't.'

" 'Oh, yes, they do. Ho, ho, ho, ho.'

"We talked about all different kinds of things. He ordered just about everything on the menu—I was so full by the time I left there. We really had a nice time.

"At the Garden, I would always sit by where the wrestlers came out. André would always grab my hand as he walked by, either on his way out or on his way back. He wouldn't look at me, because he was working, but he'd give my hand a little squeeze as he walked by. Always. It was just between he and I. Nobody else saw it. He was my friend. That's the only way I know how to explain it."

WrestleMania IV.

11

The Princess Bride made André the Giant a household name, intro-

ducing him to new fans that were perhaps unfamiliar with his work

in the ring. He returned to wrestling "with a little bit of swagger,"

according to Tim White. ■ "He was super proud of it," White says.

"Wrestling he almost took for granted, whereas this was new."

Between the colossal success of *WrestleMania III* and the massive star power being generated by its main event protagonists, the André/Hogan rivalry was guaranteed to continue. A new Pay-Per-View event would be held in November. At *Survivor Series* teams of five would battle it out in elimination matches. The Thanksgiving Day event—held November 26, 1987, at Ohio's Richfield Coliseum—marked the first official in-ring meeting between André and Hogan since *WrestleMania III.*

Survivor Series saw André leading a heel squad that included the Heenan Family's Rick Rude and King Kong Bundy, along with Butch Reed (with his manager, Slick) and the One Man Gang. In the opposite corner, Hogan captained the team of Bam Bam Bigelow (with Sir Oliver Humperdink), Paul "Mr. Wonderful" Orndorff, Ken Patera, and Don Muraco (replacing Superstar Billy Graham, who reinjured his hip in an earlier match with Reed).

Due to his increasingly debilitated physical condition, André was forced to spend most of the match on the apron, leading his team with sheer presence. He and Hogan had a brief mid-match confrontation, resulting in the Hulkster's elimination by countout. The teams fought until the only remaining wrestlers were Bam Bam Bigelow and André, who nailed an underhook suplex for the pinfall and the title of Sole Survivor.

ONE MAN GANG: "All the guys, we tried to pull in there. He just came in a couple of times. But he was the cornerstone of the team, he was André the Giant. We all tried to go out there and really help the match and keep him in the limelight, but not keep him in the ring so much."

Squeezing Bam Bam Bigelow, *Survivor Series.*

After the bell was rung, Hogan returned to the ring and nailed the Giant with his championship belt. The shot sent André down to the canvas and out to the floor. As "Real American" boomed though the arena, Hogan taunted the angry André with the title. The Giant had to be held back by Bobby Heenan, who fulfilled his managerial duties by challenging the cocky champion: "You want him? You'll have to sign a contract!"

Survivor Series was immediately followed by a memorable installment of *Saturday Night's Main Event.* The NBC broadcast was headlined by Hulk Hogan defending his title against King Kong Bundy, with André serving as cornerman for his fellow Heenan Family behemoth. André's interference ultimately caused the match to degenerate to the point where he was expelled from ringside. Though it was Hogan and Bundy doing the work in the ring, the Giant would always be the true star of the show.

March 1988

Reported *USA Today,* "Wrestling fans helped NBC's latest *Main Event* special (November 28, 1987) . . . tie its highest overnight rating."

Two nights earlier, a Pay-Per-View standard was achieved by the historic *Survivor Series.* An explosive lineup to 490,000 households. Considering that many watched the Thanksgiving spectacular in large groups, it is estimated that between 2 and 3 million saw teams headed by . . . André the Giant gain victories."

As 1987 drew to its close, André's letter-perfect heel turn earned him one of wrestling's highest accolades: *Pro Wrestling Illustrated*'s "Most Hated Wrestler" award. The year culminated with a major turn of events in the André vs. Hogan program, one that would have far-reaching ramifications for the entire World Wrestling Federation. Having failed to convince Hulk Hogan to sell his World Heavyweight Championship, Ted DiBiase—the Million Dollar Man–used his infinite resources to purchase André's contract from Bobby Heenan.

The son of wrestler Helen Hild and the stepson of wrestler "Iron" Mike DiBiase, Ted DiBiase was destined for a career in the ring. He attended West Texas State University, alma mater of a veritable who's who of wrestling

MAIN EVENT

Choking out Hogan.

greats, including Dusty Rhodes, Stan Hansen, Tully Blanchard, and Tito Santana. It was there that he had his very first encounter with André the Giant.

TED DIBIASE: "I actually met André in Amarillo while I was still in college playing football at West Texas State. Here I am, a college kid, and being raised in the business, I would go to matches every Thursday night. That's where I really started to appreciate the business. I was fifteen when my dad died—I admired the business, but I didn't have the eye or the intellect at the time to appreciate it for what it really was.

"André would come to town, and I'd take him out, to the bars and back to his hotel, things like that. I said, 'André, where do you want to go?' He says, 'Where does everybody go?' 'Okay, I'll take you to one of the college bars.'

"So we go to this bar and the barmaid walks up and says, 'What are you having?' André says, 'You have trash can?' She looked at him kinda funny and says, 'Yeah, we got lots of them.' André says, 'Empty trashcan, clean it out, fill it with beer and ice, bring it to the table.'

"She looked at him, then she looked at me—she knew me, because I'm a regular coming in there—and I nodded and said, 'He's serious.' So, sure enough, they brought over two or three cases of beer, iced down in a great big tall trash can, just for André. It was pretty funny."

DiBiase trained in Amarillo with fellow West Texas State alumni Terry and Dory Funk Jr. before embarking on his wrestling career. He made his bones in "Cowboy" Bill Watts's Mid-South Wrestling—"a long, tough territory," according to DiBiase—and in 1979 was brought to New York to work for World Wide Wrestling Federation. Among his tag partners during that brief run was André, whom he teamed with in a series of Six Man Tag matches against the Valiant Brothers. DiBiase also was the first-ever holder of the North American Championship, a title he lost to Pat Patterson, who then unified it with the South American Championship to create the World Wrestling Federation's Intercontinental Championship.

After leaving the company, DiBiase mastered his craft working in Mid-South, Georgia Championship Wrestling, and All Japan Pro Wrestling. In 1987, just as he was on the verge of signing an NWA contract, DiBiase was invited to join the now-booming World Wrestling Federation. He was promised a major push, with a gimmick so good that if Vince McMahon himself were to become a wrestler, this would be the character he would play.

DiBiase accepted the offer and became one of wrestling's all-time great heels—the Million Dollar Man, a filthy rich, morally bankrupt villain who would prove his motto, "Everybody has a price," by inviting fans to perform degrading acts for a handful of cash. He was accompanied by his "bodyguard," Virgil—Mike Jones—who provided extra muscle and outside interference when necessary.

The Million Dollar Man was a main event player from the start, offering to purchase Hulk Hogan's World Heavyweight Championship immediately upon his arrival in World Wrestling Federation. Needless to say, the champ declined DiBiase's offer, thus forcing the Million Dollar Man to devise a new plan for possessing the title without ever having to actually wrestle for it.

March 1988

"HIS BUCKS BUY ANDRÉ: DIBIASE SAYS HE'LL OWN HULK'S TITLE"

Ted has purchased the contract of André the Giant from the master manipulator of managers, Bobby "The Brain" Heenan.

"If I have André," says DiBiase, "I have the title."

DiBiase's pronouncement came late in December, when the sale of the Giant's contract was announced. . . . DiBiase obviously knew he was not just buying the greatest contender for the title, but a scheme . . . that would practically place the championship in André's—and DiBiase's—hands.

Heenan would be infinitely wealthy and see his greatest dream come true—the defeat and humiliation of Hulk Hogan. DiBiase could prove once and for all that his philosophy of life was supreme—money can buy anything. And, for André, there was the chance to attain the goal that has so festered in his soul it has turned the gentle Giant into a monster of mayhem—he would be recognized as the supreme force in international athletics, the World Wrestling Federation Champion.

Heenan had been outraged when DiBiase had attempted to buy the title from Hogan. "Unfair," shouted Heenan. "André should have the chance to take the title in the ring."

The Million Dollar Man promised resources that would give André a massive advantage, such as a private world-class gym staffed by the best professional trainers, in which André could become more of a Giant than before. . . . One way or another, the purchase of André's contract by DiBiase has added an astounding new dimension to the earth-shaking feud between Hogan and André.

CRAIG DEGEORGE INTERVIEWS TED DIBIASE (W/VIRGIL)

"I frankly thought we had put to rest this issue of buying the heavy-weight championship," says interviewer Craig DeGeorge, "but I assume by your presence here that, well, we haven't."

"Well, well, well," DiBiase crows, hands on his shiny purple lapels. "I told you people some time ago that Hulk Hogan was a fool, that he would live to regret not accepting the most generous offer of the Million Dollar Man. And I also told you people that I was a man not accustomed to not getting what I want. Well, I'll tell you right now, I get what I want. I buy what I want! And I want the World Wrestling Federation heavyweight title. And I told you people that I would buy it! And coming down the aisle right now, accompanied by his manager Bobby 'The Brain' Heenan, is the man that will deliver it to me, the World Wrestling Federation heavyweight title, the Eighth Wonder of the World, André the Giant."

André and Heenan, resplendent in bright red satin jacket and black neck brace, come to the stage. André's hand is on the Brain's shoulder as the two men shake hands with Virgil and the Million Dollar Man.

"What is the meaning of this?" sputters DeGeorge.

"Mr. DiBiase," Heenan says, "thank you. Thank you. Never in my life did I ever think I would have the wealth and be able to buy the things I can, and the way I can live now, financially for the rest of my life. You see, Hogan, you are a fool! I'm not a fool. I don't let opportunity pass *me* by. Mr. DiBiase, thank you again. Because all you're buying is what we planned to do anyway, guaranteed the World Heavy-weight Championship, because we're gonna beat Hogan like we've done before. Thank you."

"André, will you deliver to me, the Million Dollar Man, the World Wrestling Federation heavyweight title?"

"Mr. DiBiase," rumbles the Giant, a malevolent grin spread wide across his face, "I will tell you one thing. I will deliver that belt, the World World Wrestling Federation [sic], and I will enjoy it, Hogan! Ha, ha, ha! Oh yeah!"

"We've got it, Virgil!" DiBiase says assuredly. "It's ours!"

Though his back operation relieved some of his pain, André was still quite limited as far as his physical range. Pairing him with DiBiase kept the Giant—the promotion's top heel by far—in the center of the storyline. At the same time, it allowed him to play a less active role in the ring, with the talented DiBiase handling the majority of the actual wrestling.

TED DIBIASE: "It was a way for André to stay in the main events while protecting his injured back. Most people really didn't know how much he wrestled in pain. There were times when we walked to the ring together and he would have his hand on my shoulder to keep him balanced. In the ring, I basically did all the work."

December 11, 1987: Sam Houston Coliseum, Houston, TX

HULK HOGAN VS. TED DIBIASE
(W/VIRGIL & ANDRÉ THE GIANT)

André is announced as DiBiase's second. Hogan clears the ring upon entry, swinging the belt to chase DiBiase and Virgil out. The bell rings; Hogan pulls DiBiase in and hammers away. He whips him into the ropes for a clothesline. An atomic drop bounces DiBiase over the top.

DiBiase is tended to by his team, so Hogan comes out and cracks Virgil and the Million Dollar Man's heads together. DiBiase gets up on the apron, and Hogan grabs his head and flips him into the ring.

Virgil follows and gets the same treatment. Hogan whips DiBiase into a big boot, and then repeats the maneuver on the bodyguard. The ring cleared, Hogan points in André's direction, challenging him to come in and get pressed.

The heels pace the ring, but Hogan won't take a neutral corner. Finally DiBiase gets in and they circle each other. They lock up; Hogan gets a headlock on DiBiase, trips him down, and applies a front face-lock. The ref breaks it, and DiBiase shoulderblocks Hulk against the ropes. Hogan goes outside and DiBiase follows, bashing the Hulk's head onto the apron. DiBiase avoids a countout by rolling back in, and then goes to the apron to kick a kneeling Hogan in the skull. Hogan tries to climb back up, but takes another shot to the head. As he sits on the concrete, Virgil waves a few bills under his nose.

"That's not sportsmanship," says commentator Mike McGuirk.

DiBiase pulls Hogan through the middle ropes and nails him in the head. He stomps on the dazed champ's head. Hogan rolls toward the apron, holding the second rope in his left hand. DiBiase repeatedly steps up on Hogan's grip, landing with his other foot on Hulk's head. He drops down and chokes the champ, breaking at Dave Hebner's four-count, then resuming the hold.

A red-faced Hogan gasps for breath. DiBiase whips Hulk to the ropes, but the champ reverses and hits a forearm smash that bounces DiBiase onto his head. Scoop slam is followed by a walk across DiBiase's back, over and over until André grabs Hogan's boot and trips him up. Hebner calls for the bell at 6:06 as debris begins flying.

"André is so anxious to get at Hogan," commentator Pete "The Duke of Dorchester" Doherty says, "he grabbed him. He just wants to tear him apart."

"The referee is awarding the match . . . the referee has demanded that André the Giant leave the ring area and he has been fined $2,000 and ordered to leave the ring area."

André balks, but officials gather around him and force him to leave. The bell rings, and the match resumes. DiBiase goes to work on Hogan, twisting the champ's nose and dropping him with blows. A trio of elbow drops sets Hogan reeling. DiBiase goes to the second turnbuckle and drops an elbow smash. Cover is made but only gets two. Hogan is whipped into a clothesline. DiBiase comes off the ropes and drives a fist into the champ's forehead, then drops two more. Another cover, again only getting two before Hogan kicks out.

The champ gets to his knees and shakes it off. DiBiase punches away, but Hogan begins hulking up. He gets to his feet, waves a finger in DiBiase's face, catches the next fist, and begins returning blows. He whips DiBiase into a big boot. Virgil gets on the apron, and Hulk chokes him. DiBiase sees Hogan's back turned and runs in to smash a forearm on the champ's neck. Hulk slips out of the way and DiBiase nails Virgil, knocking him off the apron. Hogan rolls up DiBiase for the pinfall at 9:30.

Hogan poses a bit, lifts Dave Hebner to a seat on the top turnbuckle, and challenges DiBiase to get back in. The Million Dollar Man considers it, and then grabs a steel chair. He tosses it in the ring, but Hogan catches it and takes a seat in the middle of the ring. DiBiase bangs on the apron in frustration as Hogan puts on his show.

"Justice prevails," McGuirk notes.

The traditional practice in wrestling was to maintain some kind of verisimilitude on the road—for example, babyfaces should never be seen with heels, and teams that work together in the ring should travel together. Old-school to his core, André invited DiBiase and Virgil to travel along with him and Tim White in the custom André van. Suffice it to say, a good time was had by all.

TIM WHITE: "What a vanload that was, rolling down the highway."

TED DIBIASE: "I had a tremendous time with the guy. Traveling with André, you couldn't buy anything. Nothing. We'd go somewhere to eat, he'd pick up the tab. We traveled a lot with Tim White. We had one of those great big conversion vans and Tim would drive, with me and André sitting in the back watching movies and drinking beer. It was a lot of fun.

"He would take me to restaurants and bars that he frequented in New York or wherever we were. One night we worked the Cow Palace in San Francisco. Afterward we went back to the Marriott Hotel there at the airport and André was just in a really good mood. He orders a bottle of Dom Perignon, a hundred-dollar bottle of champagne. Before we got off the bar stool, he had ordered ten. We drank a thousand dollars' worth of champagne that night, just because he felt like it."

TIM WHITE: *"When André was in a bar, and this is old-school, but he's the top guy, and if any of the guys come in the bar, he'd be insulted if they paid for a drink. He just wouldn't hear of it. He bought for everybody."*

With *Saturday Night's Main Event* earning blockbuster ratings, NBC invited World Wrestling Federation to spin off the series with a live prime-time special. Dubbed *The Main Event,* the show would mark the first time professional wrestling had been on live national network television since the 1950s. Of course, only one match could headline such a momentous broadcast—the long-awaited rematch between André and Hogan, with the World Heavyweight Championship on the line.

January 6, 1988: Municipal Auditorium, Nashville, TN

"Wow, do I have some news for you," Craig DeGeorge says, "on Friday night, February 5, live on nationwide television, World Wrestling Federation will present a bout of all bouts. Simply put, one of the greatest ever. For the first time since *WrestleMania III,* the Eighth Wonder of the World, André the Giant, will challenge the World Wrestling Federation Heavyweight Champion, Hulk Hogan."

André takes to the platform, holding on to Ted DiBiase's shoulder for support. Virgil, as ever, counts cash.

"Ted DiBiase, the Million Dollar Man, I know you have an investment in all of this."

"Last year at *WrestleMania III,* all you people saw André the Giant put Hulk Hogan to the mat for a three-count in the first two minutes of the match, and then he was unjustly robbed of the match and the title. And just a couple of weeks ago, once again, you saw André the Giant choke Hogan all the way to the mat. That could've ended it right there. It could've all been over, but he didn't. He didn't.

"Why? Why, because André wants the same thing that the Million Dollar Man wants. And on Friday, February 5, in Indianapolis, Indiana, in front of the whole world, everything will come true. I told you people that I always get what I want, and I want the World Wrestling Federation Heavyweight title.

"And you people thought that you couldn't be bought. You don't believe that the Million Dollar Man can buy everybody. I've had you on your knees, begging me for money, barking like dogs. And yet, each and every time, I've proven to all of you that you do indeed have a price for the Million Dollar Man. But you, Hogan, you thought that you would be the exception. You thought that you would be the exception to that rule. And I told you, Hogan, that by hook or by crook, I would get what I want! Because I always get what I want! And this is the hook! This is the hook that will deliver to me the World Wrestling Federation Heavyweight title.

"André, I know that you're gonna beat Hogan. I know that you're gonna win the match, but please tell me how! How are you gonna do it?"

"DiBiase," replies the Giant, "when I gon' step in that ring, believe me, when I get out of that ring, I will be the World Champion! And the way I will do it, I will *squeeze,* Hogan, and *squeeze* and *squeeze* and *squeeze,* until the belt fell off of your waist, Hogan. And believe me, I'll be more happy because I got millions of reasons to be happy. And I want to make this man happy too! And then when I will pick up that belt, you want I going to do?"

"What are you gonna do, André?"

"Ha ha ha!"

"What are you gonna do then?"

"Ha ha ha! You want to know?"

"Yes, André, I wanna know!"

"I will present you that belt and pronounce you the World Champion, *ha ha ha ha*!"

"Can you see it, Hogan? Can you see it right here? I will be the World Wrestling Federation Heavyweight Champion!"

ROYAL RUMBLE: THE MAIN EVENT TITLE MATCH CONTRACT SIGNING

A table and chairs are set up in the center of the ring. André, DiBiase, and Virgil wait in one corner, Jack Tunney in another. Mean Gene has the mic, and the bell rings.

"All right, ladies and gentlemen, this is the moment that millions of people all over the world, all around the globe, have been waiting for. The official signing for the bout that will be taking place on Friday night, February 5, in Indianapolis, Indiana, for the World Wrestling Federation Heavyweight Championship. I would like to introduce the man who will be defending his title on Friday night, February 5, the current World Wrestling Federation Champion, Hulk Hogan!"

"Real American" plays as the crowd explodes to its collective feet. Hogan, wearing a white T-shirt and boots with sky-adorned tights, comes to the ring as André glares impassively. DiBiase puts his hands to his waist in the universal gesture for "I'm going to win that belt." André, bored, leans back on the ropes as Hogan goes through his listening-to-the-fans ring entrance.

"At this time," Mean Gene resumes, "I would like to introduce the man who on Friday, February 5, will be challenging Hulk Hogan for the title, he is seven-foot-four-and-a-half, 425 pounds, André the Giant!"

André stares at Hogan, hands in his pockets, gently bouncing back on the ropes.

"With André tonight, the bodyguard, Virgil, for the Million Dollar Man, Ted DiBiase!"

DiBiase holds his lapels and soaks in the boos. Hogan rubs his thumb and forefinger together, shaking his head to let DiBiase know that he has no interest in the Million Dollar Man's cash.

"At this time, ladies and gentlemen, I would like to intro-

Making *The Main Event* official.

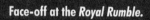
Face-off at the *Royal Rumble*.

duce to you the esteemed president of World Wrestling Federation, the distinguished Jack Tunney. Mr. Tunney . . ."

Okerlund and Tunney shake hands, as Mean Gene holds the mic for the president. "Thank you very much. Gentlemen, your respective representatives have studied thoroughly the contractual material, let's get with it and sit down."

"All right, gentlemen," Okerlund says, "if you'd please be seated, we can get the signatures affixed to the proper documents. President Tunney, with the contract. André, Mr. Rousimoff, if you'd be kind enough, sir, please be seated and we can get along with the business at hand."

Hogan joins Tunney at the table, but André stands stony, hands in his pockets.

"Just a moment," Mean Gene implores. "André the Giant, if you would be kind enough to please sit down. President Tunney?"

"Yes, please. Will you sit down and sign the contract?"

But André just rocks against the ropes, staring at Hogan.

"I get the impression that we are playing mind games in anticipation of this big February 5, date in Indianapolis. I won't ask again, but, André, please."

Finally, the Giant steps toward the table, then stops. After a pause, he proceeds, never letting go of his stare-down with Hogan. He stands at the table and stretches his hands, making fists, rubbing the palms together, and intertwining his thick fingers, as DiBiase chuckles.

The crowd begins to chant the champion's name, "Ho-gan! Ho-gan! Ho-gan!" At last, André pounds a fist upon the table and takes a seat, his eyes constantly on the Hulkster.

"Now I believe we can get down to the business at hand," Mean Gene says. "I believe Mr. Hogan's signature goes on page two. . . ."

DiBiase reaches for the mic. "Go ahead, go ahead, Hogan, sign it. Sign it. Why're you hesitating? What are you waiting for? Are you having second thoughts, Hogan? Are you thinking maybe you should've accepted that generous offer I made? Why do you hesitate? You look a little nervous. This is what you wanted, isn't it? You wanted to prove to all the *Hulkamaniacs* that your pride and your integrity means more to you than money! So why do you hesitate, Hogan? Are you getting cold feet? Are you thinking maybe that's not just a contract for World Wrestling Federation Heavyweight title in front of you? No, Hogan, that's a career-ending contract, and you know it! Because you know this man right here just about a year ago at *WrestleMania III* beat you, in just under three minutes, he beat you, Hogan! That's it, sign it! Go ahead, sign it!"

Shaking his head, Hogan puts pen to paper and signs the contract, shoving it at Tunney as he stares up at a gloating DiBiase. "You just signed your career away, Hogan, because as of February 5, this man will have all the money in the bank! That title will be bought and paid for around my waist! And you, you will be history!"

The Million Dollar Man restores his hands to his lapels as he laughs heartily. Tunney places the contract before André.

"All right," says Mean Gene, attempting to restore order, "André the Giant, yet to affix his signature to the contract that will sign and seal the meeting of these two men for the first time since *Wrestle-Mania III*. André the Giant challenging Hulk Hogan on Friday night, February 5 in Indianapolis, for the World Wrestling Federation Heavyweight Championship."

André studies the contract as Hogan returns the pen to Tunney, who then attempts to pass it to the Giant. "Mr. Rousimoff, please."

André shows something in the document to DiBiase, who laughs. "That's a little extra money. You know me, that's just a little incentive money, ha ha ha!"

"Apparently something in the contract being pointed out to André by the Million Dollar Man, Ted DiBiase," Okerlund explains. Tunney continues to try to get André to sign, but the Giant holds up his hand. "He wants to take his time as he peruses the contractual materials. The preeminent title in all of professional sports today, the World Wrestling Federation Heavyweight Championship."

Hogan seethes with anger, and André further consults with DiBiase. "I don't know what's going on here. Ted DiBiase, you've had an opportunity to read this material through, this contract—"

"Let me tell you something, little man!" the Million Dollar Man replies. "He can take all the time he wants! This man has waited for almost a year for this opportunity. He was robbed of this title just about a year ago, he can take his time, he is savoring the moment! You just hold the mic and shut up!"

"Is there any kind of a problem, Mr. Tunney?"

"There shouldn't be."

"There's nothing here that's gonna prevent us from signing this contract here tonight, live in front of an audience all over the country?"

"I certainly hope not."

André drops the documents onto the table and grins at Hogan. At last, he signs.

"Finally, André the Giant is signing the contract for the big one, February 5, Friday night—"

DiBiase grabs the mic again. "Now that you've signed the contracts, André, put your official stamp of approval on it!"

The Giant rises, as does Hogan, who tosses his chair aside, knowing what is sure to follow. The two competitors lock eyes across the table. "Go ahead, André," rants DiBiase, "put the official stamp of approval on it!"

Hogan lunges for DiBiase, who backs away, giving André the chance to grab the champ's shoulders and plant his face into the tabletop. He then flips the rather flimsy-looking table over onto Hulk, who sells while lying under the overturned furniture.

"Ha, ha, ha! Look at your champion!" brags DiBiase, as André climbs out of the ring. "Look at him! Take a long, hard look! Because that's what you're gonna see on February fifth!"

He tosses the mic to the mat and joins André on the aisle. Hogan sits stunned as the crowd boos its disapproval, and then chants their hero upright.

TED DIBIASE & VIRGIL (W/ANDRÉ)
VS. HULK HOGAN & BAM BAM BIGELOW

Ring announcer Howard Finkel introduces DiBiase and Virgil by noting that "they make their winter residence in the Netherlands Antilles."

Vince McMahon—doing his first commentary in five years, subbing for Gorilla Monsoon, who had suffered a minor heart attack—calls André "the most awesome creature that walks the face of this Earth today."

DiBiase and Virgil put the boots to Hogan and Bigelow immediately, but the babyfaces get up and manage to knock the heels' heads together. DiBiase is sent into the ropes for a double boot. Hogan stands over him, tears off his shirt, and throws the belt to the mat. He takes DiBiase around the ring, smashing his head into the buckles. Bam Bam places his big bald noggin on the buckle, and Hogan slams DiBiase's head into it. The Million Dollar Man finally falls flat on his face. Hogan lifts him up, chops him hard, whips him into the buckle for a clothesline. Again, DiBiase goes face-first to the canvas.

Hogan grabs DiBiase's hair and grinds his face into the canvas. Bigelow is tagged in, and the beatdown on DiBiase continues, with a big clothesline followed by headbutts and elbows. Tag is made, and Hogan comes in with a boot to DiBiase's midsection. The Million Dollar Man goes down, and Hogan walks across him, stepping on his back. He lifts DiBiase up, sends him into the ropes, barely connects with an elbow to the forehead, but DiBiase sells it anyway. He gets up, and Hogan punches him into Bigelow's corner. Their faces ping-pong DiBiase with shots to the forehead, but the Million Dollar Man eventually drops. He rolls back against the corner and begs Hogan for mercy. Hulk stomps his midsection, while André protests from outside.

Hogan suplexes DiBiase, then goes after Virgil, knocking him off the apron. DiBiase is still down, so Hogan drops an elbow, then another. He pauses to taunt André, suggesting he come into the ring for a taste. Hulk pulls DiBiase up by his hair, winds up, and lands a big haymaker. He goes back onto the ropes, but André trips him up and Hogan is, at last, down.

DiBiase takes full advantage, immediately dropping elbows into the back of Hogan's head, then pounds the champ's face into the mat. He rolls him over toward the ropes and chokes Hogan. The ref breaks it up, and as DiBiase argues, André reaches in and pulls Hogan to him by the hair. He grabs hold with both hands and headbutts the Hulkster. DiBiase returns and puts the boots to Hogan. He sends him across the ring, into the ropes for a clothesline, and then raises his arms in triumph. The MSG crowd is hot as hot can be. DiBiase tags Virgil, holds Hogan's arms behind him, and the bodyguard goes up top, landing a fist to the champ's head.

Virgil hammers away, choking Hulk under the ropes. Again, the ref separates them, and as Virgil distracts the official, André pulls down the bottom rope across Hogan's throat. "That's a mean, nasty giant," says Vince.

Virgil makes a tag, picks up Hogan, pins his arms back for Di-Biase to drop an elbow from the second rope. The Million Dollar Man stomps Hogan's forehead, then lands a shot on Bigelow, who barely budges. The punishment on Hogan resumes, with a series of chops, finally sending the champ backward over the top. DiBiase comes over after him and pounds Hulk's head into the apron. He brings Hogan to the steel barricade and drives his forehead into that as well. DiBiase goes back in, leaving André to snatch up the back of the champ's trunks and throw him back into the ring.

DiBiase brings Hogan into the corner and tags Virgil, who pounds away on the champ's back. Virgil spins Hogan around, hits a forearm to the chest, whips him into the ropes for a clothesline. Hogan is on his knees, and the bodyguard chops at his throat. Hogan reaches up and rakes Virgil across the face. Virgil quickly tags back in DiBiase, who puts Hulk back down by dropping fists to the forehead. He covers but only gets two. The Million Dollar Man locks a sleeper on the champ.

From outside, André demands of the ref, "Ring the bell." Hogan manages to get to his feet and drives three elbows into DiBiase's gut to break the hold. Hulk comes off the rope, and a shoulderblock sends DiBiase down. He goes off the rope again, over DiBiase. Di-Biase gets up but misses the clothesline. Hogan comes off the ropes again, and a double clothesline puts both men down. DiBiase reaches Virgil, who tags in just as Hogan tags Bam Bam. Bigelow comes in, and they go toe-to-toe, with Bam Bam taking the advantage. He presses Virgil up over his head, slams him down, and falls into a headbutt. Bam Bam drops an elbow and covers, but DiBiase makes the save. Hogan quickly drops a leg on Virgil as the ref sends DiBiase out. Bam Bam comes off the ropes, and Hogan assists him by shoving his big body down onto Virgil. Bigelow covers and gets the three-count at 9:26.

Everybody is in the ring, including André, as the bell sounds. André grabs the back of Bam Bam's collar and headbutts him—missing him completely—then goes for another, which connects. Hulk goes for the Giant, but André headbutts him as well. The heels put the boots to Hogan, who rolls out and is followed by DiBiase and Virgil. Bobby Heenan, joining McMahon on commentary, notes that they're "softening him up for February 5."

Back in the ring, Bam Bam comes up behind André and drop-kicks him into the ropes. The Giant falls as Hulk starts tossing chairs into the ring. Hogan and Bigelow wave the chairs around as the heels fume outside. André takes off his sports coat, but DiBiase and Virgil prevent him from getting in the ring.

February 5, 1988: Market Square Arena, Indianapolis, IN

ANDRÉ THE GIANT VS. HULK HOGAN

As the live broadcast begins, "Mean" Gene Okerlund interviews André, DiBiase, and Virgil.

"Well, gentlemen, tonight you have the chance at the World Wrestling Federation's Heavyweight Championship. Your comments."

"Chance? André already is champion," declares the Million Dollar Man. "He beat Hogan at *WrestleMania III* until the referee, obviously a Hulkamoron, cheated on the three-count. But this time Virgil will keep an eye on the referee, and Hogan won't squirm loose. That coward has run from André for a year. Tonight, he meets the Giant, and the rest is history!"

"All right, Ted DiBiase, obviously you are very confident, and obviously the Giant is ready."

"Of course he's ready! He's had the finest training at the finest facilities that money could buy. Everyone knows that money makes the man, and it takes big money to match up to a big man like this. That's why André's with me, the Million Dollar Man. And that's why Hulk Hogan is always with those nickel-and-dime *Hulkamaniacs*. Hulk Hogan is small change compared to André the Giant. Your account is overdrawn, Hogan, and André's gonna close it!"

"André the Giant?"

"Once I gonna get my hands on you, I never stop," says André. "Never! I'm going to squeeze and twist and squeeze again and squeeze and never stop!"

"That's it, André," DiBiase encourages. "This one's for the money! Let's go!"

"I'm sure it is for the money, Vince," Okerlund concludes. "After all, André the Giant has millions to become the heavyweight champ."

"These two have waited a long, long time to lock up once again in a rematch," Vince McMahon says as he introduces Okerlund's interview with Hogan.

"Well, apparently, Hulk Hogan, André the Giant has millions of reasons to become the World Wrestling Federation Heavyweight Champion."

"Well, with all the controversy, Mean Gene, from *WrestleMania III,* I've tried to keep an open mind, man. But I've viewed the film a thousand and one times. André the Giant, you only had me down for a two-count. I slammed you and beat you, one-two-three, right in the middle! Maybe the prayers, the vitamins, and the training are small change to you, Multi-Million Dollar Man, but I've invested my three assets wisely in a lifelong profit-sharing plan with all my little Hulksters, brother! Virgil, you watch the referee. That's cool. All my *Hulkamaniacs* are gonna be watching you, Multi-Million Dollar Man. Then, André the Giant, one-on-one, with the whole world watching, I'm gonna prove to you I can beat you and *Hulkamania* will live for-*ever*!"

• • •

Finally, it's time for *The Main Event*.

The participants are introduced. Hogan enters the ring and advances on André, swinging the title belt. But referee Dave Hebner holds him off and snatches the championship belt from his grip. He holds the title belt out for all to see as Hogan seethes.

Jesse Ventura points out that he "feels good" about Hebner serving as referee, as opposed to Joey Marella. Hogan stares at the heels as he tears off his shirt. André doesn't even glance in his direction. Hogan goes though the *Hulkamania* moves, but the Giant is unfazed.

Hogan draws a line on the canvas as the bell sounds, inviting André to cross it. The Giant takes his time entering the ring, then hangs back to confer with DiBiase and Virgil. Hulk comes over and nails André with a right, then hits a noggin knocker on DiBiase and Virgil. He pulls them both over the top and tosses Virgil into the ropes for a big boot, which sends him over and out. He repeats the move on DiBiase, leaving him alone with André.

The Giant advances, but Hogan hammers away with punches and chops. André reels, but doesn't go down. Hogan takes his head and pounds it into the buckle. André staggers, but even an elbow off the ropes won't put him down. A clothesline has little effect, so Hogan stops to knock DiBiase and Virgil off the apron.

Another couple of shots on André, then Hulk goes and stomps on DiBiase's hand, sending a fistful of cash flying. André holds on to the rope for support and backs into the corner, where Hogan rakes his face. A clothesline from across the ring keeps André wobbling. Hogan winds up and lands a Sunday punch, but the Giant stays upright. He rakes André's face again, then goes up top. But André catches the champ by the throat and slams him to the canvas. André attempts a falling headbutt, but Hogan rolls out of the way.

André lies on his back, still loopy, so Hogan goes to cover him. The Giant's arm shoots up and catches Hulk's throat. He squeezes until Hebner counts to four, and then releases the champ. On his knees, he catches Hogan again and resumes choking, always sure to release the grip before being disqualified.

They rise, and André lands a big right, knocking Hogan into the corner. He whips him hard across to the opposite turnbuckle, and Hogan goes down face-first. André stamps on Hogan's fingers, and then scoops him up for a slam. A boot to the midsection doubles Hulk up, opening his back for another kick. A headbutt and a chop keep Hogan down on the mat, where he wraps his arms around André's columnar leg. André stomps hard, sending Hogan flying. The Giant puts Hogan into the corner, chop and headbutt. He grabs Hogan's traps and squeezes, lowering his head for another butt.

André whips Hogan to the ropes for a big foot to the chest, but loses his balance and goes down as well. Hulk rolls outside for a breather, but Virgil is there and tosses him right back in. Hebner is distracted by Virgil, so André throttles Hogan for as long as he can, wrapping his shoulder strap around the champ's neck. Hebner breaks it up, but André soon resumes choking Hogan.

Hogan gets his arms up and breaks the grip and begins hulking up. He gets to his feet and separates André's arms. A kneelift to the Giant's belly and a series of chops reverse the momentum. He hammers André into the corner and rakes the Giant's face. André lurches forward as Hogan goes to the second rope for a clothesline that takes the Giant down, to the crowd's delight. He goes for the legdrop, but Virgil catches an ankle. Hebner reprimands Virgil while Hogan goes to the other side of the ring and successfully drops the leg on André. He covers for at least five counts, but Virgil and Hebner are continuing their debate.

Hogan goes to the ref and complains, giving André time to get up. He comes behind Hogan, takes two handfuls of hair, and pounds two headbutts. A double underhook suplex takes Hogan down. André covers. On two, Hogan lifts his right shoulder . . . but Hebner looks only at the left and completes the count. The bell rings at 9:05, and André is the new World Wrestling Federation Champion.

DiBiase and Virgil run in to celebrate. Hogan is flummoxed as the crowd boos its disapproval. Hebner goes outside to fetch the belt, still dismissing Hogan's complaints. The championship belt is presented to André, and Hebner raises his arm.

Okerlund goes for the postmatch interview. "This is no surprise," says André. "I told you I am going to win the World Heavyweight Championship, and now I surrender the World Heavyweight Championship to Ted DiBiase."

He wraps the belt around DiBiase's waist. "Hold on, André," says Mean Gene. "What are you saying, you surrender the title to Ted DiBiase?"

"Yes sir, and this is the new world champion!" André and Virgil hold up DiBiase's arm. Hogan is POed, but Hebner blocks his path. He lifts up the referee and moves him aside, giving the heels time to clear out.

DiBiase taunts Hogan with the belt. All of a sudden, a second Hebner arrives in the ring. "How can there be two Dave Hebners?" wonders Jesse. Hogan finally turns around and sees double. He grabs them both by the necks and attempts to uncover the truth. Baffled, he lets go and circles the ring. The two Hebners start arguing until one shoves the other down, and then kicks him out of the ring.

"There has to be some chicanery going on around here," says McMahon.

Hogan seemingly agrees and goes after the remaining Hebner, despite his protests of innocence. He tries to escape through the ropes, but Hulk catches him and pulls him back in. André, DiBiase, and Virgil return to see Hogan press Hebner high above his head. Hulk throws the ref out, dropping Virgil and DiBiase to the floor.

Later, in the locker room, Hogan is apoplectic.

"Bedlam and pandemonium," declares Mean Gene. "Things in somewhat of a chaotic state here. Hulk Hogan, I'm sure there's going to be a thorough investigation by World Wrestling Federation into what happened here tonight, and I know you could not be any more disappointed."

Tears are streaming down the Hulkster's face. "How much money did they spend on the plastic surgery, man?" he bawls. "I had all bases covered! I had the *Hulkamaniacs* watching DiBiase; I had Virgil in his place. Never in my wildest dreams, Mean Gene, would I think that I would get ripped off by a penny-pinching, two-timing referee! How much money on the plastic surgery! How much money did he spend to pay the referee off when I turned around, Mean Gene? They were identical! *Identicaaaaaaal!*"

Okerlund shows Hogan the replay.

"Look at the shoulder, brother! The referee is paid off, brother! Look at the hundred-dollar bills falling out of his pocket!

TED DIBIASE: *"It was one of the greatest angles and finishes of all time."*

BRUCE PRICHARD: *"Ted's purchase of the Heavyweight title from André was a history-making event. We kept it real quiet, and nobody knew about it except the talents involved. The goal of the angle was threefold: (1) it was a way to get a Hulk Hogan and André the Giant rematch; (2) it would move the Million Dollar Man character into the spotlight; and (3) it would plant the seed for the introduction of Ted's Million Dollar Belt."*

With a 15.2 rating and a viewing audience of 33 million, André v. Hogan broke every record, standing to this day as the most viewed pro wrestling match in history. At the end of 1988, *Pro Wrestling Illustrated* awarded André vs. Hogan at *The Main Event* its top honor: "Match of the Year."

Though his title reign lasted mere seconds, André's victory marked his one and only World Wrestling Federation Championship. DiBiase's run as the announced "champion" lasted a bit longer—one day, with matches on two cards, a matinee at Boston Garden, and an evening bout at Philadelphia's Spectrum.

February 6, 1988: Boston Garden, Boston, MA

HULK HOGAN & BAM BAM BIGELOW (W/SIR OLIVER HUMPERDINK) VS. TED DIBIASE (W/VIRGIL) & ANDRÉ THE GIANT

André, Virgil, and DiBiase—wearing the title over his silver suit— enter the ring to intense heat. DiBiase is introduced as "the new World Wrestling Federation Heavyweight Champion."

André and DiBiase put the boots to Hogan and Bigelow as they slide under the ropes. André and Hogan go toe-to-toe while DiBiase and Bigelow trade punches. Hogan gets the momentum and grabs André's hair to drive his face into the turnbuckle, but referee Joey

Marella takes hold of the Hulkster's blond locks and pulls him off. As Hogan turns to argue with the official, DiBiase runs at him. Hogan gets the boot up and takes him down. From behind, André turns Hogan around, but a shot to the head sends him over the top rope to the wooden floor.

In the opposite corner, Bigelow is going to work on DiBiase. Marella tells Hogan to get out of the ring, and the Hulkster angrily relents, finally tearing off his T-shirt as he goes to his corner. André, on the outside, slowly climbs the wooden steps to his own corner. Meanwhile, Bigelow hits an atomic drop on the new champion, and then pitches him into the ropes for a clothesline.

The tag is made, and Hogan comes in. DiBiase kneels, imploring his rival to be gentle. The Hulkster is not in a forgiving mood and hammers away at the Million Dollar Man, whipping him into the corner and running in with a clothesline. DiBiase goes down flat, and André climbs in. Hogan is right there, raking the Giant's eyes, then downs him with a clothesline in the corner.

The crowd noise is unrelenting. Still stunned, DiBiase stands up and turns into another big right from Hogan, sending him back to the mat. Hogan kneels over him and pummels away at his head. André crawls over to make the save, and Hogan takes him in a headlock and continues his rain of punches. The Giant rolls out to the apron, but Hogan stays on him, hitting his back and shoulders. Standing outside, André reaches up and pulls Hogan's head down, choking him on the top rope. Marella calls for him to break, so André hits a hard chop on the top of Hogan's head and lets go.

"My word," Lord Alfred Hayes declares on commentary, "I've never seen Hogan so much on fire as he is this evening."

On the other side of the ring, Bigelow is smashing DiBiase into the buckle. Marella heads over to officiate. Hogan, turning away from André, gets caught by the Giant, who pulls him to the apron and starts choking with the bottom rope.

Bigelow gets sent to the corner by the ref. DiBiase takes the opportunity to put the boots to the flailing Hogan. André lets go and pulls himself up the steps. DiBiase pushes Hogan face-first into the turnbuckle, then steers him to André in the corner, smashing Hulk's head into the Giant's. Tag is made, and DiBiase holds Hogan for André's chops. Bigelow runs in to save his partner, but Marella—his back turned to the double-teaming—sends him back out.

DiBiase goes to the apron. André takes Hogan's hair from behind and headbutts him. Hogan goes down. André picks him up and wraps the shoulder strap around his neck, hiding it with his arm. DiBiase tags in and clotheslines Hogan against André from behind. Marella sends André out. DiBiase whips Hogan into a clothesline, and then basks in the heat before dropping a fist into Hulk's head. After three shots, DiBiase covers, but Hogan gets a shoulder up. DiBiase locks a sleeper on Hogan as the announcers discuss the previous night's "extremely controversial" events.

"There's some question about a lookalike referee," says commentator Craig DeGeorge.

"There was a lot of controversy," notes Lord Alfred. "DiBiase paid for everything. He bought everybody. The only man he couldn't buy is the one he's in the ring with right now."

"They're talking plastic surgery perhaps, a look-alike Dave Hebner. Of course, so much happening in terms of that, the controversy, we can't really elaborate on it further until Jack Tunney makes his statement sometime perhaps this coming week."

The crowd goes ape as Hogan finally hulks up, DiBiase shaking his head in disbelief. Elbows break the hold, and a forearm off the ropes drops DiBiase down. Hogan comes over the ropes, skips over DiBiase. Hulk then ducks DiBiase's clothesline, hits the ropes, and springs back into a double clothesline that takes both wrestlers down.

Hogan tags Bigelow, who goes to work on DiBiase, whipping him into the corner for a clothesline. DiBiase falls and bounces to where his head is on the mat and his boot is on the top rope. Bigelow presses him up and slams him down. He attempts a headbutt off the ropes, but Virgil trips him up. DiBiase takes advantage by dropping elbows into the back of the fallen Bam Bam's head. DiBiase goes up top, but Bigelow catches him and slams him. Tag to Hogan.

DiBiase begs off, but Hogan shakes his fist and attacks with a boot. He takes DiBiase's head and runs him across the ring, pummeling him into the buckle. As DiBiase reels, Hogan hits André with a forearm, felling the Giant with an arm tied up in the ropes. A big boot and a legdrop from the Hulkster finishes the match at 7:59. André charges in, but Bigelow chases him off wielding Humperdinck's cane. The heels run off. Hogan pulls in two steel chairs, stands up on them, and gestures to his waist that he is the true champion.

"In my book," Lord Alfred says, "he's *still* the world's greatest athlete."

TED DIBIASE: **"Quite frankly, because of the pain that André was in, I was the guy that had to create the action in the match. There were times when we would walk to the ring and André would keep his hand on my shoulder. The appearance was, well, this is my partner, he's towering over me and we're walking to the ring together. But what he was really doing was steadying himself. I was his crutch. I would go in the ring and do all the selling and the bump-taking to create the excitement in the match. I'd give André the appropriate tags, but they'd always take the falls on me."**

The outrageous happenings at *The Main Event* threw World Wrestling Federation into total mayhem. In addition to ordering an immediate investigation of the affair, President Jack Tunney officially vacated the world title—the first time there was no World Wrestling Federation Champion since Buddy Rogers won the title in 1962. To resolve the matter, Tunney commissioned the company's first-ever championship tournament, to be held, of course, at the upcoming *WrestleMania IV*.

June 1988

"DAVE HEBNER'S SHADOW: AN INVESTIGATIVE REPORT"

On the night of February 5, at the Market Square Arena in Indianapolis, Indiana, Earl Hebner, wearing referee's garb, entered through a side door and waited for a signal from DiBiase. In the dressing room, Dave was removing his shirt from a supply closet. Slam! Virgil closed and locked the door, imprisoning Dave inside.

As Hogan and André battled in the ring, with Earl officiating, Dave pounded on the sealed door. By the time he got someone's attention and was released, it was too late. Earl had done his dirty work, ignoring a Hogan pin of André and counting out Hogan even though his shoulder was off the mat.

[Jack Tunney] had no choice but to let the decision stand. Even though Dave had been slated to officiate, it turns out Earl is licensed as a referee in the state of Indiana, so his decision was official—and final.

February 13, 1988

WORLD WRESTLING FEDERATION PRESIDENT JACK TUNNEY MAKES HIS ANNOUNCEMENT

February 5, 1988 will go down in World Wrestling Federation history as a day of infamy. Never before has there been such controversy to surround a World Wrestling Federation Championship match. Despite having viewed, time and again, videotapes of the Hogan-André match, the decision of the referee is as always, unfortunately, final. Therefore Hulk Hogan is *not* the World Wrestling Federation Champion. However, it clearly states in the rulebook, that in order for a wrestler to be deemed champion, he must either pin the reigning titleholder or make him submit. *That* is the only way a wrestler can become champion.

Therefore, unequivocally [sic] I can state that Ted DiBiase is also *not* the World Wrestling Federation Champion. Furthermore, it also clearly states in the rulebook that a reigning champion may at any time in his tenure end his reign by publicly surrendering the title, which is exactly what happened when André the Giant presented the championship belt to Ted DiBiase. Therefore, André is also *not* the champion either.

It is my decision that to be fair to the last two reigning champions of record, Hogan and André, and to furthermore be fair with the number-one contenders who would have faced either André or Hogan as champion, I now declare the title vacant, and this vacancy to be filled on March 27 of this year during *WrestleMania IV,* in the form of the first ever World Wrestling Federation Championship tournament.

In this championship tournament, the last two title holders of record, Hogan and André, will justifiably be given a bye for the first round of competition. They will not compete in the first round, but will face each other in the opening of the second round of the tournament. The pairings have been completed for the first round of the competition, and they include Jake "The Snake" Roberts meeting "Ravishing" Rick Rude; Don "The Rock" Muraco taking on Dino Bravo; Ricky "The Dragon" Steamboat will wrestle Greg "The Hammer" Valentine; Randy "Macho Man" Savage goes against "The Natural" Butch Reed; Bam Bigelow against the One Man Gang; and "Hacksaw" Jim Duggan will take on the "Million Dollar Man," Ted DiBiase.

It is my sincere wish that all of the participating wrestlers in this historic tournament, and more importantly, all of the fans of World Wrestling Federation, construe my decision as the only just and fair way to determine who will be the new undisputed World Wrestling Federation Champion. Thank you.

April 1988

"A TALK WITH JACK TUNNEY"

Question: You headed the investigation that resulted in findings ruling against André's action. Apparently, the rulebook says that a champion can publicly surrender his title, but that a title cannot be obtained by any other process than winning it in the ring. If the rules were in the book, why was an investigation needed?

Tunney: I certainly knew about the rules. . . . But this was a highly unusual situation. Nothing like it had ever happened before. I asked for an investigation because of the complexity of the issue; and because it was so earth-shaking. After all, the most important athletic title in the world was involved.

The process took time and money. We hired several top attorneys as consultants. I suspected that if the final decision went against him, Mr. DiBiase would not take it well. He supposedly spent a fortune to purchase André the Giant's contract from Bobby Heenan. And it was for nothing. . . . DiBiase may disagree, but the world at large knows we acted in the only way we could. There was no choice.

Question: But André the Giant did not know of the rule. Why didn't you just ask him to recant his surrender of the title and give it back to him?

Tunney: We couldn't if the rule was to be obeyed as written. It says that once the title is surrendered, it no longer belongs to the man who gave it up. Our hands were tied. We had to leave the title vacant.

Question: Why didn't you simply arrange for a rematch between Hulk Hogan and André . . . rather than scheduling the tournament that will take place at *WrestleMania IV*?

Tunney: We decided that, in the spirit of fair competition, we should give Hogan and André a chance to regain the title and at the same time open it up to other deserving athletes. We didn't cut out Hogan and André. We have given them the same chance as everyone else. No, let me rephrase that. We have given them a better chance because they have a bye in the first round of the tournament. I have heard André and DiBiase complain, but Hogan agreed that the next champion should prove he deserves the title by winning a tournament, not just one match.

April 1988

"WRESTLER'S REBUTTAL: I WAS CHEATED!"
by Ted Dibiase

I am the rightful World Champion. I was given the title by André the Giant. I own André the Giant. So I owned the title too. . . . The title was André's. He could do anything he wanted with it. He gave it to me. I am the uncrowned champion.

André worked only sporadically in the weeks after *The Main Event,* usually pairing with DiBiase to do battle with the team of Hogan & Bam Bam Bigelow. Though his wrestling ability was in decline, the Giant's awesome presence ensured his place at the forefront of the World Wrestling Federation's build toward *WrestleMania IV*.

Much of the next year's storyline was foreshadowed on the March 12 installment of *Saturday Night's Main Event*. DiBiase defeated Randy "Macho Man" Savage via countout, largely due to André's show-stealing interference.

The Giant's constant intrusions throughout the match led Savage's manager, the lovely Miss Elizabeth, to leave her ringside position and flee to the locker room. After the bell, as André and DiBiase double-teamed the fallen Macho Man, she returned with help in the form of Hulk Hogan. The champ ran into the ring wielding a steel chair, sending the heels scurrying.

March 27, 1988: Trump Plaza, Atlantic City, NJ

WRESTLEMANIA IV

The Pay-Per-View begins as *Lifestyles of the Rich and Famous* host Robin Leach reads a "Special Proclamation" to introduce the "Battle for the Belt" Championship Tournament: "Whereas World Wrestling Federation has experienced certain extraordinary circumstances concerning the championship, and whereas World Wrestling Federation sought to establish a fair and just way to diligently determine who should be the undisputed champion, and whereas *WrestleMania IV* has been selected as the specific site to determine who will be the undisputed champion by way of an elimination championship tournament, and whereas the top fourteen competitors in World Wrestling Federation have been selected and paired and are present and in readiness to compete, I now proclaim that the Championship Tournament should begin. With champagne wishes and caviar dreams, may the best man win! I'm Robin Leach, and I do know why."

Gorilla Monsoon explains the tourney rules: "First round has a fifteen-minute time limit, second round has twenty-minute time limit, third round has thirty-minute limit, and no limit in the final round."

In the first first-round match, Ted DiBiase (w/Virgil and André) takes on "Hacksaw" Jim Duggan. "André doesn't have to face Hogan until the first match of the second round, so . . . ," Jesse Ventura explains. The announcers ponder the possibility of DiBiase meeting André in the final round.

DiBiase and Duggan trade punches to start, but Hacksaw catches DiBiase and hits an atomic drop that sends the Million Dollar Man over the top rope. Back in, they lock up and DiBiase strikes back, raking Duggan's face, then hitting chops and punches. He shoots him into the ropes, but Duggan ducks the elbow and comes back with a clothesline that has DiBiase going down and bouncing over via his head. Hacksaw gets DiBiase trapped against the turnbuckles and climbs to the second rope to hit ten punches. André yells up at the ref. Hacksaw throws DiBiase across the ring to the opposite corner and tries a tackle, but the Million Dollar Man gets a boot up. DiBiase smashes Duggan's head into the top buckle and hits forearms to the sternum. He whips him into the corner and lands a stiff lariat. DiBiase stomps Duggan before climbing to the second rope for an elbow drop. Duggan goes down, and DiBiase drops a fist right between the eyes. He rolls Duggan over to cover, but Hacksaw kicks out at two.

Toe-to-toe, Duggan throws shots at DiBiase, who responds with a rake that sends Hacksaw to the ropes. DiBiase whips Duggan into the ropes, but Hacksaw reverses the backdrop attempt into a sunset flip. The ref counts to two, but the Million Dollar Man claps Duggan's ears with his boots to break it up.

DiBiase whips him into another lariat and fistdrop combination. Duggan's mouth is busted open. The Million Dollar Man tries for a suplex, but Hacksaw holds on and reverses it for a suplex of his own. DiBiase goes to the second rope and jumps off, only to receive a fist to the belly that somersaults him over. He backs up in a corner and begs off as Duggan approaches. Hacksaw attacks and shoots him across the ring for a clothesline. He whips the Million Dollar Man into ropes, catches him in a bodyslam, and calls for his three-point-stance finishing tackle. He drops into position, but from outside, André yanks his leg out from under him. Duggan turns and tries to grab at André through the ropes. DiBiase comes up from behind and drives a knee into his lower back, while André punches him from the other side. Duggan goes down; DiBiase drops a fist, hooks a leg, and scores the pinfall at 5:02. Hacksaw chases the heels out of the ring with his two-by-four.

Later, Mean Gene interviews Hogan. "Over the last couple of months it has been very difficult for me to introduce this man without using 'World Wrestling Federation Champion' Hulk Hogan. Here at *Wrestle-Mania IV,* this afternoon, you've got the opportunity to change that."

"Oh yeah, it's been hard to live with, man. Fee-fi-fo-fum, André, one long year and your time has come, man. No marks, no scars, no blemishes on the Hulkster, brother. But inside, man, I've been scarred for one long year. Everywhere I go, man, all the little Hulksters ask me, 'Is there any truth to the fact that there was a controversial count? Hulkster, did you really get him over your head? Did you really beat the Giant?'

"Well, today, man, in *WrestleMania IV,* we're gonna wipe all that controversy out. André the Giant, in the second round, when you're fresh as a daisy, with the whole world watching, I'm gonna prove, brother, that I can beat you anywhere, anytime. And all my *Hulka-maniacs,* they're gonna feel it too."

"Speaking of the *Hulkamaniacs,* Hulk Hogan, we have seen them here in Atlantic City, and I know millions others are watching very intently all around the world."

"Yeah, but if you looked in their eyes, man, have you seen the fear in all those little Hulksters? They realize that when I get André the Giant cinched up in the launch position, when I slam him through the Trump Plaza, brother, from New York down to Tampa, Florida, the fault line is gonna break off. And as André the Giant falls into the ocean, as my next two opponents fall to the ocean floor and I pin 'em, so will Donald Trump and all the *Hulkamaniacs.* But as Donald Trump hangs on to the top of the Trump Plaza, with his family under his other arm, as they sink to the bottom of the sea, thank God Donald Trump's a *Hulka-maniac,* he'll know enough to let go of his materialistic possessions, hang on to the wife and kids, dogpaddle with his life all the way to safety. But Donald, if something happens, you run outta gas, and all those little *Hulkamaniacs* run outta gas, just hang on to the largest back in the world, and I'll dogpaddle us, backstroke all of us to safety!"

Hogan poses and backstrokes out of the camera.

• • •

Bob Uecker is looking for Special Guest Timekeeper Vanna White but is surprised by André's large mitt on his shoulder. "Hi, André, hey, my good buddy—"

"Vanna, you get me. You get the Giant, the only professional wrestler who's still undefeated. And Hulk Hogan, I'm proud to be it 'cause now Ted DiBiase is on his way up. That's what he paid me for, to keep you out of the tournament, Hogan, and you are. And I know one thing, and that's what the people gonna know too, and that's what they gonna remember—you are the ex-champion, Hogan, ha ha ha haha!"

"Well, there ya have it. I still haven't found Vanna White—"

"He is the ex-champion. Don't worry about Vanna White. Now, Hulk Hogan, *Hulkamania* is over! Ha ha hahaaaaa!"

"How about getting your foot off my shoulder?"

Rather, André wraps both hands around Mr. Baseball's throat—"Shut up, okay?"—and just as suddenly, smiles wide and leaves.

"Escorted by the bodyguard Virgil and the Million Dollar Man, Ted DiBiase, from Grenoble in the French Alps, weighing 520 pounds—"

"Largest professional athlete in the world today," notes Gorilla.

"—André the Giant!"

André and his entourage walk to the ring, barraged by boos.

"Too many people out there at ringside for my money," says Gorilla. "When you start bringing two or three people down to ringside with you, I dunno, that's a little bit of an edge as far as I'm concerned."

André steps over the top rope, unfazed by the crowd's heat. He's equally unconcerned when "Real American" hits the sound system and Hulk Hogan emerges. The crowd, obviously, erupts. He gets halfway down the long aisle, and then runs to the ring. Hogan slides under the ropes, only to be greeted by a kick from the Giant. He gets up and takes a headbutt as Joey Marella clears DiBiase and Virgil from the ring.

André is pummeling Hogan when the bell rings. A big headbutt downs Hogan, but André brings him to the corner for a turnbuckle smash. A chop and a shot to the ear puts Hogan—still wearing his T-shirt—on one knee. More chops and a headbutt send Hogan into the ropes. He comes off with a flying forearm, but André is barely stunned. Hogan bounces back and hits another to little effect. A third forearm drives the Giant backward into the ropes. Meanwhile, Hulk sees DiBiase up on the apron. He goes over and wraps his hands around the Million Dollar Man's neck, throttling him. André comes over to make the save, but Hogan elbows him in the gut and hits the heels with a noggin knocker.

DiBiase goes to the floor, and Hogan starts chopping at the Giant. At last, André falls, tying his arms in the ropes. With André trapped, Hogan can—finally—tear off his shirt. The crowd, needless to say, explodes. Behind Hogan's back, Virgil and DiBiase frantically try to free André's arms.

André is loose, and Hogan lets fly with rights. The Giant is shaky, but doesn't go down. He slingshots off the ropes for more impact, but the Giant stands tall, if a bit wobbly. Frustrated, he goes back to the ropes, but André has finally dropped down on his back. Hogan drops an elbow on the prone Giant, and another, and another. He covers, but André catches him in a chokehold.

The roles have reversed—André is holding Hogan down, a big mitt on the Hulkster's throat. The ref breaks it up, so André drops a headbutt into Hogan's sternum. Hogan is under the ropes, so André steadies himself and does the big ass splash. He kicks Hogan in the head and then walks to the other side of the ring, shaking the cobwebs out of his head. Focused, he returns and picks up Hogan with his hands around the Hulkster's traps. He breaks at the count of four, and then resumes. André staggers Hogan with a reverse knife edge to break things up a bit, and then back to the choke.

Hogan is fading, collapsing down onto one knee. Marella raises an arm, once it drops; twice, it drops halfway and the hulking up begins. Hogan shakes as he rises to his feet, then muscles André's arms above his head. A knee to the gut drives André back. Hogan swings away, and then clotheslines the Giant into the corner. Hogan signals his plans to slam André, but Virgil is now distracting the referee. As Hogan goes to scoop André up, DiBiase comes from behind with a steel chair. Whack! across Hogan's lower back.

The Hulk turns and chases DiBiase from the ring. He grabs the chair and swings at André, who catches it. They struggle, but Hogan gets a boot into André's belly. He folds, allowing Hogan to at last bring the chair down.

Marella pulls the chair from Hogan's hands. But André has other ideas. He takes the chair and goes for a direct shot on Hogan's head. Hulk catches it, but this time it's André who scores the boot. Hogan doubles over, and André hits the chair hard onto Hogan's cranium. It lands with an audible crack, and Hogan goes down. Marella finally calls for the bell at 5:22.

But Hogan isn't done. He picks up the chair, comes off the ropes, and nails André, planting him onto the canvas. He gets ready for a second shot, but DiBiase and Virgil are there to drag André out of the ring. Hogan goes outside and chases them off. DiBiase places Virgil in front of himself and trash-talks Hogan. Hogan responds, and the Million Dollar Man throws his bodyguard into Hulk and scurries off. Alas, poor Virgil—Hogan suplexes him to the concrete floor and then returns to André in the ring.

A decision is made—both André and Hogan are disqualified. Not pleased at the news, Hogan walks straight up to André, scoops him up, and slams him to the mat, an easier if less historic slam than at the previous year's *WrestleMania*.

As the winner of the Hulk-André match would have met either DiBiase or Muraco, the victor in that bout would receive a bye all the way to the finals. The Million Dollar Man defeated the

MICHAEL KRUGMAN

DiBiase interferes, *WrestleMania IV.*

André and Hogan battle it out, *WrestleMania IV.*

Magnificent One, and then sat back as Randy Savage depleted his strength taking on both Greg Valentine and One Man Gang. The latter match saw Savage winning ugly, scoring a DQ victory after One Man Gang attacked using his manager Slick's trademark cane. Nevertheless, the main event for *WrestleMania IV* was set—Ted "The Million Dollar Man" DiBiase vs. Randy "Macho Man" Savage for the most prestigious title in the sport, the World Wrestling Federation World Heavyweight Championship.

Robin Leach brings out the title belt on a regal red cushion.

The guest ring announcer, Uecker, is accosted by a drunk from the crowd on his way to the ring. He introduces timekeeper Vanna White.

DiBiase is "accompanied by himself . . . uh uh, he's got the big boy with him, André the Giant, here is the Million Dollar Man, Ted DiBiase."

Savage wears white robe, red tights, and yellow boots.

DiBiase forces Macho to the corner, but Savage blocks his blows and deters DiBiase with an elbow. DiBiase reels back, but André grabs Macho's leg and trips him up. Referee Earl Hebner admonishes André, who professes innocence.

Hammerlocks are reversed; Savage gets DiBiase in a side headlock. DiBiase sends Savage into the ropes, who hits a shoulderblock. Savage shoots into the ropes, DiBiase drops flat, and André trips Macho on the other side. DiBiase drops an elbow, but Savage gets up and complains about André. The crowd chants "Hogan!"

Armwringers are exchanged. DiBiase drives Savage's head into the top buckle, then hits forearms and chops. An elbow between the shoulders puts Savage down. DiBiase whips Macho into a lariat. Cover for two.

DiBiase comes off the ropes and shoulderblocks Savage down. Coming off the other side, he tries a sunset flip but can't get Macho over, and Savage drives a fist down into his head. Savage clotheslines DiBiase and hooks the leg for two.

DiBiase rolls to André and confers. DiBiase doubles Savage with a knee to the abdomen, with forearms and chops putting him down. Stomp to the face, whip into an elbow. He lifts Macho up and hits an elbow to the back of the neck before smashing his face into the buckle. Savage is whipped for an elbow, but he avoids it and returns with an elbow of his own. He takes DiBiase's hair and springs over the top, clotheslining DiBiase on the top rope. Back in, Savage hits a high knee into DiBiase's back, sending him over the ropes. Macho goes up top but André stands over DiBiase, blocking the way. "Jump," André says, grinning.

DiBiase and André consult before DiBiase gets back in. Macho talks to Miss Elizabeth, sending her to the back. DiBiase goes to work on Savage, dropping three fists to the head. Cover only gets two, so DiBiase hits a snapmare into a reverse chinlock. Meanwhile, Elizabeth returns to the ring with Hogan in tow. The Hulkster grabs a chair and sits in Macho's corner.

Macho and DiBiase go at it in the corner. Hebner pulls off Di-Biase, so André grabs Savage by the tights. Hogan is there in a hurry, breaking it up with a shot to André's neck. Macho fights DiBiase off with elbows, but DiBiase rakes Savage's eye. A clothesline and elbow set up a pinning attempt, but Macho kicks out at two. DiBiase suplexes Savage and covers again for two. Gutwrench suplex gets two. Scoop and a slam; DiBiase goes up top, but Macho catches him. He slams him down, then goes outside and up. DiBiase rolls away from the flying elbow. Macho favors his elbow as DiBiase locks the sleeper on. Hebner is distracted by André, so Hogan comes in and hits his steel chair across DiBiase's back. Savage doesn't quite know what happened but goes up, drops the elbow, hooks the leg, and wins the championship at 9:27.

Hogan takes the title belt from the cushion, runs in and hands it to Macho, then ducks out between the ropes to fetch his chair. Savage and the lovely Miss Elizabeth celebrate their triumph as Hogan keeps André at bay outside.

"Savage didn't need my help with DiBiase," Hogan told the official publication of World Wrestling Federation after the match. "I just wanted a cheap shot at that nasty Giant."

Though the Hulkster attributed his involvement in *WrestleMania IV*'s finish to purely selfish reasons, his assisting Savage to obtain the World Heavyweight Championship led to the formation of one of the World Wrestling Federation's most renowned storylines—the rise of the Mega Powers.

With "The Million Dollar Man," Ted DiBiase.

12

André was reunited with manager Bobby "The Brain" Heenan soon after *WrestleMania IV*. DiBiase and André would still partner up in the ring, while Heenan would act as adviser and business representative. Heenan was brought into the fold to amplify the heat the faction drew from the fans. ■ Heenan's first order of business was to challenge Randy "Macho Man" Savage for his recently acquired World Wrestling Federation Championship. Another wrestling legacy, Savage was born Randy Poffo, the eldest son of wrestler/promoter/world-record-holder-for-most-consecutive-sit-ups Angelo Poffo. An aspiring baseball player, Poffo got into the family business during the minor league's off season and never looked back. He took on the "Randy Savage" moniker while working in Georgia Championship Wrestling, but his lack of a push soon lead to his leading his dad's International Championship Wrestling promotion. When ICW folded, Savage—along with his younger brother, "Leaping" Lanny Poffo—hit the Memphis territory. There he became a top heel via feuds with Jerry Lawler and the Rock 'n' Roll Express.

In 1985, Savage was brought up to World Wrestling Federation, where he allied on camera and in the ring with his then-wife, Elizabeth Hulette. Under the managerial aegis of the lovely Miss Elizabeth, the Macho Man rose through the heel ranks feuding with Tito Santana, Bruno Sammartino, and a Miss Elizabeth–smitten George "The Animal" Steele.

Though André vs. Hogan captured most of the attention at *Wrestle-Mania III,* Savage's Intercontinental Championship match with Ricky Steamboat is regarded by aficionados as the event's true highlight. A masterpiece of psychology and athleticism, the match was a fifteen-minute nailbiter, with close to twenty breathtaking near-falls before Steamboat took Savage's title away. The match was hailed as an instant classic, going on to be honored as "Match of the Year" in both *Pro Wrestling Illustrated* and the hugely influential *Wrestling Observer.*

Savage's thrilling physicality and outsize personality—not to mention the lovely Miss Elizabeth—made him a perfect Superstar for World Wrestling Federation in the *Hulkmania* Era. He soon turned babyface and began feuding with the Honky Tonk Man. When *WrestleMania IV* arrived, Savage emerged as the top candidate to carry the World Heavyweight title after Hogan's 1,474-day reign.

Of course, there were those who disagreed. "André is the true champion," Heenan said in the official company magazine. "He will prove that when he meets Savage. The title belongs to André, not to Savage or any other humanoid. I'm going to see that André gets the chance to take it for himself."

Randy Savage, the newly crowned champion, hits the stage to the strains of "Pomp and Circumstance," accompanied of course by Miss Elizabeth.

"All right, champ," Craig DeGeorge says, "I think everyone would agree here that the madness has never been madder! But—and there is a 'but' here—there are many, many good contenders on the horizon for you, Macho Man."

"Oooooh yeah! I'm ready for anybody—big, tall, got money, don't got money, challengers come and go."

André—in tights, ready to wrestle—and Heenan emerge from the back. "Wait a minute," says Vince. "What's this? They're not scheduled to be out here."

"Is André gonna challenge the Macho Man?" wonders Ventura, as Savage stands his ground on the stage.

André promises to choke out Randy Savage, June 21, 1988.

The Giant makes good on his promise, June 21, 1988.

MICHAEL KRUGMAN

"You've got something to say to me, say it now," the champion dares. "No way, 'cause Macho Madness surrounds you now!"

André smiles wide, gesturing his intent to wring Savage's neck, while Heenan mimes the wearing of the title belt. All of a sudden, Ted DiBiase leaps onto the stage from behind and Pearl Harbors the Macho Man, sending him hard to the floor.

"From behind, Ted DiBiase, knocking the Macho Man off the platform!" says Vince. André lifts Savage by his bandana and begins strangling him. DiBiase jumps down and throws a series of blows to the trapped champ's midsection. Virgil holds Miss Elizabeth by the shoulders, forcing her to watch as DiBiase puts the boots to Savage. André picks Savage up and continues to throttle him, letting Heenan and DiBiase hammer away on his belly.

"Look at this attack, this double team," exclaims McMahon. "Big, strong tough guys, give me a break! They didn't even have enough guts to come on him head-to-head, face-to-face! They came at him from behind, and that Giant is choking the life out of Savage!"

"But you've got to remember, McMahon, it's not how you play

the game, it's whether you win or lose," philosophizes Ventura as the beatdown continues.

"Come on!" yells Vince. "Get somebody out here!" The crowd agrees, chanting, "Ho-gan! Ho-gan! Ho-gan!"

It matters not to André, who maniacally continues to choke the champ, with DiBiase joining in with punches to the head.

"How much punishment can one man take?" wonders McMahon.

André grabs a virtually unconscious Savage's feet, and DiBiase takes the arms. "One, two, three!" They swing him up onto the platform, dropping him at a crying Elizabeth's feet. Heenan tosses the title belt onto Savage as Elizabeth tends to him.

"DiBiase and André the Giant have fallen to new depths here in World Wrestling Federation," says Vince. "How can they possibly justify what we just saw?"

TED DIBIASE: "I don't think André cared for Randy too much. I don't know why. Of course, Randy is a peculiar guy. His relationship with Elizabeth was like she was a bird in his cage. In the dressing room, if you said hello to her he'd give you a dirty look like, 'What are you doing?' Really suspicious. I don't know, but that might have played into it, but André didn't really care for him much."

JAKE ROBERTS: "Randy Savage hated wrestling [André], 'cause he'd chew Randy up and spit him out."

BLACKJACK LANZA: "He almost kills Savage one night in one of the main events. Savage is laying down and André just kept sitting on him and jumping on him, just beating the hell out of him. He got disqualified, which saved the championship, and afterward Savage said to him, 'This isn't the way to get me over.' André just said 'Thank you' and left."

Despite his antipathy toward the Macho Man, André was willing to tolerate Savage thanks to the new champ's commitment and respect for the wrestling business. Others, however, were not so lucky. Over the years a number of wrestlers incurred André's wrath in the ring, usually due to excessive ego or simple disregard for the time-honored wrestler's code. As the unofficial—but universally acknowledged—head of the locker room, it was André who meted out lessons to disruptive influences. In June 1988, Bam Bam Bigelow was put through André's school of very hard knocks.

TED DIBIASE: "Randy Savage and I were wrestling against each other. It was a double shot day—we were the main event in Baltimore at a matinee show, then they shot us out to a Learjet and flew us into New York City and we were the main event in a cage in Madison Square Garden. The limo takes us right up to the top of the ramp and we're running in, putting our shoes on, and getting ready to go. Bam Bam Bigelow comes in the dressing room, grabs his bag, and goes. Doesn't shower, gets his stuff, and out the door he goes. Turns out André had wrestled him that night, and he made the guy miserable. He didn't hurt him to the point where he was injured, but he let him know he didn't care for him. So Bigelow just quit.

"He came back shortly afterward, but I could tell that the incident changed him. What was wrong with Bigelow, and I noticed it right off the bat, was he came in with an attitude, like 'I'm a star and you're gonna treat me like one.' André just let him know, you know what, we're all the same here. When Bam Bam came back, he really was a different guy. I think if he were still with us, he'd tell you, 'I needed that.'"

TIM WHITE: "I remember what he did to Bam Bam Bigelow in the Garden. Bam Bam got this big push, but he didn't show the proper respect. So André gave him a little dose of reality in that ring. He just rag-dolled him all over the place. It was kinda hard to watch. But he got back into André's good graces because of the fact he learned. Bam Bam turned out to be one hell of a great wrestler, and God rest his soul, as well.

"André was the boss of the locker room. He didn't have to say but two words—all he had to do was look at you, and you knew to shut up. Easy as that. That's the kind of leadership he brought into the locker room. He did it like a father would do to his family. That's what it was, it was his family, and if someone needed discipline or needed to be talked to, André would take care of it."

CRAIG DEGEORGE INTERVIEWS ANDRÉ, HEENAN, DIBIASE, & VIRGIL

"Ladies and gentlemen," introduces Craig DeGeorge, "here are my guests, Bobby 'The Brain' Heenan, Virgil the bodyguard, Ted DiBiase, the Million Dollar Man, and the Eighth Wonder of the World, of course, André the Giant. The moment is here; now it's time to get the response, the response to the challenge, of course, Brain, from Randy 'Macho Man' Savage. He has stated, of course, that he has issued a challenge to meet the tag team to my right, Eighth Wonder of the World, André the Giant, the Million Dollar Man, Ted DiBiase. On Randy 'Macho Man' Savage's team, a partner to be named later, and that is of his choice. The challenge is out, Mr. Heenan—what is your response please?"

"I'll tell you exactly what my response is," the Brain replies. "You know, I've had some lengthy meetings lately with World Wrestling Federation President Jack Tunney. And I have asked for a concession. I have asked for something that needs to be asked for. Now if he, Randy 'Macho Man' Savage, the World Wrestling Federation Champion, wants to go out and scrape up some partner, pay some ham-and-egger to hang with him, to be his partner, that's fine. You want to challenge this team of André the Giant, Million Dollar Man, that's fine. But under one condition and one condition only will that take place. And that's if we get an official, a referee that isn't some namby-pamby sissy that doesn't have the backbone to back up a decision, not like a Dave Hebner or a Dave Hebner look-alike or a Joey Marella that can't count past two. We want somebody, we want a man, a man that can control law and order in that ring. And you ask me, will we sign for that? Read my lips, humanoid—yes, we will!"

André holds DiBiase's arm high, waving to the crowd.

"You know, gentlemen, this might be your lucky day, Mr. Heenan. Because just prior to this interview, the office of the president indicated to me that a referee has in fact been assigned to this matchup, to this challenge by the Macho Man Randy Savage. And that guest referee is none other than Jesse 'The Body' Ventura!"

"What?" exclaims commentator Vince McMahon as Jesse chuckles. DiBiase waves a handful of cash, gesturing not to worry. André, Heenan, and DiBiase all laugh loudly, obviously pleased with the announcement.

CRAIG DEGEORGE INTERVIEWS
RANDY SAVAGE (W/MISS ELIZABETH)

"This is it, McMahon," Jesse Ventura says as the interview gets under way. "This is the announcement we've been waiting for."

"Macho Man," starts DeGeorge, "I know you are well aware, perhaps too well aware, of what happened last time we talked on this very same platform."

"Ooooh, yeah, and that's not gonna happen this time, no," says Savage with confidence. "Last time that I was interviewed out here on this exact same platform Bobby 'The Weasel' Heenan and André the Giant came strolling right out here, and I'm tellin' you, issuing the Macho Man a challenge, and I didn't know that I was being set up. 'Cause the Million Dollar Man and his money set me up so that DiBiase could attack me from behind and knock me off this platform and straight onto the concrete floor. Right over there—airborne, yeah— right inside the concrete, which made me easy pickin's for André the Giant, Ted DiBiase, and Bobby Heenan, and that's not gonna happen this time.

"And I'll tell you something else that's not gonna happen this time, and that is Virgil, the bodyguard of the Million Dollar Man, of the man with the dirty money, because Virgil came out here and put his dirty, slimy hands on my manager Elizabeth's shoulders, and forced her to watch André the Giant, Bobby Heenan, and Ted DiBiase take turns kicking me in the ribs, punching my teeth out, and an almighty choke from the Eighth Wonder of the World, André the Giant. That's not gonna happen this time!

"And the reason that it's not gonna happen this time is 'cause right now, at this very second, I've got somebody watching my back, somebody I can trust, somebody in this building right now, and that somebody is my tag team partner, and I got me a tag team partner. André the Giant and Ted DiBiase have got me a tag team partner, and he's the greatest tag team partner that anybody in the world could ever have. And here he comes right now. . . ."

"Real American" plays as the crowd cheers.

"Well, I'll tell you what, McMahon," Jesse notes. "Now we know why Jack Tunney came to me to referee this, because I'm the only man in the world that could keep law and order with these four."

"Jesse, that's a tall order, even for you, the attempt to maintain law and order between DiBiase and André and these two tag team partners, the Madness and the Mania coming together."

Hogan and Savage pose on the platform, culminating, as ever, in Hulk tearing off his yellow T-shirt.

"You know something, Macho Man," says Hogan, "I like your style, brother. I know where you're coming from, I know where you're going, 'cause I been there. But there's one thing, Macho Man, you only made one mistake and that mistake is, brother, when you're the champion, you should know, whenever you dial on the telephone, they're gonna be trying to wiretap ya, trying to martyr your cause. You shoulda known that the local operator would be the stool pigeon that would make the phone call you made when you asked me to be your tag team partner, the call that would be heard around the world. But that's okay!

"First thing, we don't care about the phone call that André the Giant and the Million Dollar Man know about, we don't care because, number one, you and I are fighting for different things, man. You and I are fighting for the love of all those *Hulkamaniacs,* for the love of all the Madness, yeah. Number two, Macho Man, you and I are fighting for the same lady, brother. She is now *our* manager, and you and I are fighting for her honor, Macho Man. But the third thing, Macho Man, the third thing we're fighting for is the cause. Just like the phone call that was heard around the world, the handshake between you and me that will unite us as one being, the handshake of the Madness and the Mania together will formally be felt around the world. We will make the world stand still, because this is the first public shaking of the Mega Powers, brother."

They clasp hands, and Hogan pulls Savage close to whisper some secret into his ear.

"Hogan, I got one question for ya," Savage says. "During that *SummerSlam*, yeah, on August 29 in Madison Square Garden, yeah, the *SummerSlam*, when the Mega Powers go down that aisle, yeah, what happens when Ted DiBiase and André the Giant are put away and all forms of transportation in New York City, all the limos, all the taxis, all the airplanes, come to a complete *stop*?"

"That's okay," Hogan assures him, "that's okay. Because you and I have given fair warning to my little Hulksters, we've given fair warning to all your Madness Maniacs. They'll be there, they'll be watching, but there's one final point I have to clear up with you, Macho Man. The thing that's on my mind that I want you to know, is that when we step in the ring, man, and the lovely Elizabeth is in *our* corner, she's my lady too, brother. Because from now on, with the Mega Powers united as one, she guides every step of the way, signs every contract, and is our inspirational force that will help us overcome all odds. And what are they gonna do when the Mega Powers come running through?"

They shake hands again, and pose down on the platform.

"I'll guarantee you something right now, McMahon," Ventura says. "I can guarantee you quite simply there will be a clear-cut winner. I'm on the record right now, there will be a positive victory from either this team or the Giant and DiBiase. There will be a winner, because I'm tired of everything that's gone on in between."

André and DiBiase responded to the formation of the Mega Powers by adopting their own mega-moniker—the Mega Bucks. As *SummerSlam* drew near, the Mega Bucks were regular visitors to *The Brother Love Show*. Inspired by the classic *Piper's Pit* format, the interview segment was hosted by Bruce Prichard as Brother Love, an aggressively unctuous televangelist with an exaggeratedly crimson complexion. Unlike real-life contemporaries like Jimmy Swaggart or Jim Bakker, the white-suited Brother Love didn't preach about the Man Upstairs. Rather, he advocated the power of "love," which he regularly relayed through his oily catchphrase, *"I loooooooove yoooooouuuuu!"*

THE BROTHER LOVE SHOW W/ANDRÉ, TED DIBIASE, VIRGIL, AND BOBBY HEENAN

"Y'know, *SummerSlam '88*," oozes Brother Love. "Monday night, August 29, it will be a *looooove* fest, yes, yes indeed, in New York City, Madison Square Garden. And Brother Love will be a part of it, with a very special guest, but I'll tell you about that later. Because what I want to talk about right now is the main event. A Tag Team match, pitting the likes of the World Wrestling Federation Champion 'Macho Man' Randy Savage and his partner, Hulk Hogan. They are calling themselves the Mega Powers. However, they will be facing the team of Brother 'Million Dollar Man' Ted DiBiase and Brother André the Giant, the Mega Bucks."

André, Ted DiBiase, Virgil, and Bobby Heenan come out to furious boos and hugs from Brother Love.

"Brother DiBiase. Brother Brain. Brother Giant, it is an honor." Love reaches to shake André's hand, but the smiling Giant engulfs him in a hug. "Brother Vir-gil, it is good to see ya. Brother DiBiase—"

"Ya know, Brother Love," says the Million Dollar Man, "on August the 29, on a hot summer night in the Big Apple, New York City, in the Arena of Arenas, Madison Square Garden, they're calling it the *SummerSlam*. They're calling it the meeting of the Mega Powers against the Mega Bucks, that's what they're calling it. Well, I'll tell ya right now, we've got all that, right here on this one team. 'Cause there's nothing in the world more powerful than the Eighth Wonder of the World, André the Giant—"

"Nothing!" testifies Brother Love.

"—And the power of the wealth of the Million Dollar Man rolls on and on and on, as we all well know. And you, Macho Man, you never cease to amaze me. You kept the whole wrestling world held captive, holding their breath, anxiously anticipating the big news—who would be your partner to face this unbeatable team? Hulk Hogan. Big deal!"

André punches his fist into his hand as DiBiase continues. "Do you think, for one minute, that we're supposed to be scared? That we're supposed to stand here and tremble in our boots, because you went and got Hogan, because he's gonna crawl back out from underneath the rock where he's been licking his wounds and hiding the last time he faced this man? You're a three-time loser, Hogan, and you're gonna be going down one more time!"

DiBiase takes hold of his purple lapels, letting the world know he's come to the end of his sermon. "Well," says Brother Love, "Brother Giant, I have a question for *you*! What is it that the Giant *loooves*?"

"Brother Love," André grins, "I gonna tell you what Brother André loves. And I know one man who knows much better than me what I love is Brother DiBiase. What I love?"

DiBiase laughs and rubs his thumb and forefinger together. Virgil waves a fan of Benjamin Franklins, and then passes it to the Million Dollar Man, who gives it to the smiling Giant.

"You say they are full of love! They love you!" says Brother Love, the crowd booing intensely. Heenan puts a hand on the host's shoulder.

"We also love Jesse 'The Body,' the referee. He's gonna give us a fair shake. And them too." Heenan and DiBiase throw their heads back in laughter, while André grins, counting his money.

"That's true," Brother Love says, wagging an index finger heavenward. "They love you, Brother Jesse loves you, just like *I* love you. I love *you*."

He shakes hands with DiBiase, who of course slips Love a few bucks.

CRAIG DEGEORGE INTERVIEWS ANDRÉ, DIBIASE, VIRGIL, AND HEENAN

The Mega Bucks take the platform. "Wow. Look how huge André is," says Vince. "Almost like André gets bigger every day."

"He's a *giant*, McMahon," notes Ventura.

"Just about a week away," begins DiBiase. "*SummerSlam*. They call themselves the Mega Powers, and they're gonna come and face the Mega Bucks, well, let me tell you, I've known all along that this would be the ultimate destiny for you, Hulk Hogan and 'Macho Man' Randy Savage. Ultimately, total disgrace, dishonor, and defeat! I've waited a long time, Hogan. All the way back to when I offered you a king's ransom. All you had to do was give me the belt and retire in luxury. But not you! Too much pride, too much concern over a bunch of little Hulkamorons. Too much pride, Hogan. And it's gonna cost you *everything*. Everything in one night. Isn't that right, André? Tell 'em what's gonna happen."

"DiBiase, I tell you one thing," the Giant thunders. "I'm so proud, next week I'm finally gonna be back in the ring with that little kid, Hulk Hogan. Because four times I put him down and I take his toy away. And he's still crying about his toy, ha ha ha ha ha! But Hogan, I want you to know, I'm not Santa Claus. I no will give you the toy back! No way! Hogan, ex-champ and the champ-anzee you got with you, we're gonna come in there next Monday, and believe me, you gonna see who is the *real* professional wrestler, and who is the toughest guy."

He hugs DiBiase as Heenan takes his turn. "Gentlemen, one important thing. One important thing, André, Million Dollar Man, Virgil. We have a special referee, a man that will give us a fair shake, in Jesse 'The Body' Ventura. And as 'The Body' said, there will definitely be a winner and a loser! And you know one thing, Jesse always tells it like it is, ha ha ha ha!"

"That's right," DiBiase agrees. "And he said a long, long time ago

The Mega Bucks interviewed by Craig DeGeorge.

that he had to agree that everybody did indeed have a price for the Million Dollar Man, ha ha ha ha!"

"What do you have to say about that?" questions Vince.

"No comment, McMahon," responds Ventura. "No comment."

THE BROTHER LOVE SHOW W/JESSE VENTURA

"My guest this week is a man who has been appointed special guest referee by President Jack Tunney to officiate the main event in *SummerSlam*, between the Mega Powers and the Mega Bucks," announces Brother Love. "So please welcome my guest at this time, Brother 'Body,' Jesse Ventura.

"Brother 'Body,' it is a pleasure to have you out here. I have a few questions for you, concerning your refereeing the main event at *SummerSlam*. You see, because you are a very controversial member in this matchup, and I would like to ask you, first of all, will your former relationship with your former tag team partner 'Macho Man' Randy Savage have any bearing on the outcome of this match?"

"Well, Brother Love, let me just put it to you this way," says Ventura. "When you use the word 'former,' that's exactly what it is. 'Macho Man' Savage and I have not been together at all since Elizabeth came along."

"Brother Jess, another question that comes to mind is that not long ago, you were quoted on national television as saying that Jesse 'The Body' Ventura did indeed have a price for the Million Dollar Man. Will this have anything to do with your decision in this match?"

"Let me just say this. At that time Jesse 'The Body' Ventura might have had a price for the Million Dollar Man, but now I've done *Predator,* I've done *The Running Man,* and I've made enough money in Hollywood that I don't need the Million Dollar Man's money."

The crowd cheers.

"But Brother Ventura, another question. You, it is common knowledge of your professional jealousy toward one Hulk Hogan. Will this have any bearing on this match?"

"Hey, I can't help it if the Hulk is jealous of the Body. I'm a movie star, Hulk Hogan is just a wrestler."

"Brother Body, there is one more note I would like to address, because I have this from a very good source, that 'The Body,' Jesse Ventura, is deathly afraid of one man, that being the Eighth Wonder of the World, André the Giant. Now, your being deathly afraid of André, will that have any bearing?"

"You see this, Brother Love?" Ventura asks, holding up a clenched fist. "I could step back into the ring tomorrow and probably become the world champion if I wanted to. Do you think I'm afraid of anybody?"

The Mega Bucks come to the set, greeted by furious booing.

"Brother Heenan, Brother Brain, it is good to see you. What are you doing out here?"

"Jesse 'The Body,'" Heenan says, "my good buddy. André the Giant has a little something here he'd like you to listen to."

"Jesse, I just want to say something," André says, waving a pointed finger at Ventura. "You better pay good attention. All right?"

The Giant pulls on Ventura's lapel for emphasis, and then steps behind Heenan.

"And remember," continues DiBiase, "Jesse Ventura, when you pay attention to the Million Dollar Man, it always—and I mean always—pays off."

DiBiase snaps his fingers, and Virgil begins passing him hundred-dollar bills, which the Million Dollar Man places into Ventura's inside breast pocket. Jesse grins as André pats him on the shoulder, congratulating him for his decision. The Mega Bucks leave.

"You see, Brother Jesse, the great benefactor, Brother Million Dollar Man, is continuing to spread the word of love. And he and the Mega Bucks will do it at *SummerSlam*, and what an honor, what a pleasure it will be for *you*, Brother 'Body,' to raise the hands of the victors, the Mega Bucks."

"Let me just say this, Brother Love. It's definitely gonna be my pleasure at *SummerSlam '88*, for Jesse 'The Body' to raise the hand of the victors, 'cause there definitely will be a winner, and I promise you there'll definitely be a loser. And that, my friend, will be the real pay-off! There'll be a winner!"

CRAIG DEGEORGE INTERVIEWS THE MEGA POWERS

Randy Savage, Hulk Hogan, and Miss Elizabeth come to the platform to the strains of "Real American."

"Well, you know something, brother," begins Hogan, "ever since the Mega Powers been together, the whole country's gone crazy, man. But you know something, there's a reason for it. It's the way you're rewarded when you work hard. Look at the Macho Man, Randy Savage. He worked so hard in *WrestleMania*, look how he was rewarded, yeah. And as far as Hulk Hogan goes, man, because I trained so hard and I was so dedicated, I've got a sound mind and a sound body and the largest arms in the world—one heck of a reward! And as far as some of the other rewards go, because I've been walking the straight and narrow, I got a whole generation of little Hulksters following me.

"You know something, Macho Man. Think about the rewards, man. If we win this match—which we will—in Madison Square Garden this Monday night, the *SummerSlam*, we're gonna be rewarded with the fact that the Madness and the Mania is gonna live forever as the Mega Powers. Our lovely manager, Elizabeth, is gonna guide us to heights never before realized, and also all my little generation of Hulksters are gonna live forever with us. Think about the rewards the Multi-Million Dollar Man and André the Giant have got. They've already got the money, man. They've already been rewarded, they've already had the payoff. And you know what happens, brother, when people get paid off before they do the job."

"Ooooh yeah," says the champ. "The big man is right. The big man is right! Hulk Hogan, I understand what you mean. They've already taken the money. That was their motivation, and they've received their reward. But in the *SummerSlam*, when it gets hot and heavy, when the going gets tough, they're not gonna have the heart that the Macho Man and the Hulkster have!"

"You know something, Macho Man? Since they got the money, they might—when the going gets tough—they might quit right in the middle of the job. Then we'll have to drag 'em back and beat 'em anyway. But think about this, brother. If something happens, and things go the other way, if something happens, the Multi-Million Dollar Man has the deck stacked again. If Jack Tunney is at ringside, if he's paid off, if Jesse Ventura's been paid off, if the timekeeper's been paid off, if the dudes who set the ring up put an extra metal bar in there, just so we can crack our heads, we're gonna have to use our secret weapon, brother."

"Ooooh yeah, the secret weapon!"

"The secret weapon, brother. You remember, in Venice Beach, California, when we were hangin' and bangin' with the greatest intensity we've ever had, getting ready for the *SummerSlam*, we had everybody on Venice Beach watching us. And all of a sudden, when our secret weapon came struttin' down the beach, you remember what happened."

"Oooooh yeah, remember, yeah. Elizabeth with her canary yellow high heels, yeah. Uh-huh. In her yellow polka-dot, French high cut, itsy-bitsy string bikini, yeah, everybody turned their eyes and was hypnotized. And they were put into a state of shock. And you know what? Nobody cared how much weight Hulk Hogan and Macho Man had on the bar. In fact, Hulk Hogan, you and me, we were hypnotized also, weren't we?"

"That's right, Macho Man. When we saw Elizabeth in that string bikini, not only were all the people on Venice Beach hypnotized, but you and I were frozen in our tracks. That's why I say, brother, if the tide turns the other way. If we're up against unsurmountable [*sic*] odds in the *SummerSlam* in Madison Square Garden, that's when we'll give Elizabeth the high sign. And when she undoes the Velcro fly on the back of her skirt and takes her skirt off, underneath the skirt, with that French high cut, itsy-bitsy teeny-weeny yellow polka-dot bikini, she'll come up on the apron, man, she'll walk the apron, just like she won the Miss America contest, and as André the Giant turns around and freezes like a big redwood in his tracks, so will the Multi-Million Dollar Man. He'll turn around and freeze. And when that happens, brother, I'm gonna sneak up behind the Giant and I'm gonna chop him down just like Jack and the Beanstalk!"

"Oooooh, yeah. And I'm gonna pickpocket the Million Dollar Man and get a roll of silver dollars out and knock him out!"

"You know something, brother? No matter which way it goes,

we're gonna beat 'em. If we have to use our secret weapon, that's cool. But the payoff, we're gonna be rewarded for working real hard. We can beat 'em that way too. But the last thing, brother, they're gonna see as they're lying frozen in their tracks in the center of the ring, defeated, is our arms raised in victory, brother, in the *Summer-Slam*. And Elizabeth will be giving 'em the kiss of death after we give the Mega Power handshake and leave the ring, brother."

"Ooooh yeah!"

They shake hands as "Real American" plays, and then put their secret weapon up on their shoulders.

Hara Arena, Dayton, OH

THE BROTHER LOVE SHOW W/THE MEGA BUCKS

"My guests this show are the men who are involved in the main event that evening. The men who will demolish the team of 'Macho Man' Randy Savage and his partner, Hulk Hogan. Please welcome my guests, the Mega Bucks, Brother André the Giant, Brother Million Dollar Man Ted DiBiase, Brother Brain Bobby Heenan, and Brother Virgil."

The Mega Bucks come to the stage. "Brother DiBiase, it all comes down to this Monday night."

"That's right, Brother Love," says DiBiase. "This Monday night, Madison Square Garden, the so-called Mega Powers versus the Mega Bucks. It finally comes to a head, it finally comes full circle, Hulk Hogan. You know what I'm talking about. This goes all the way back to an offer, an offer of a lifetime. I offered you a king's ransom, Hogan. All you had to do was hand the title over to me and retire. Live the life of luxury. But no, not you, Hogan. Not you, Hogan. Too much stubborn pride. Too much concern over a bunch of little brats, your little Hulkamorons. Well you know what, Hogan? All the little Hulkamorons are jumping ship. They're jumping off your train, why? Why? Because they don't want to support a loser, and that's what you are now, Hogan, nothing but a loser. A three-time loser . . ."

André grins over DiBiase's shoulder, his fingers intertwined, choking an imaginary neck.

". . . You wanna talk about Mega Power? *This* is Mega Power [pointing at André]. And with the combination of André the Giant's power and my money, we are an unbeatable team. And you crawl out from under a rock to team up with the so-called Macho Man, the so-called undisputed World Wrestling Federation Champion. Let me tell you something, Macho Man. You're too busy looking over your shoulder. You're jumpy now. You're jumpy because you took the dive off the podium. You ate the concrete, and the Giant choked the life out of you. Now you're hiding behind the skirt of a woman. That's right! André? What's it gonna be, André?"

The Giant laughs maniacally. "It be the most beautiful Monday night I ever have, ha ha ha ha!"

The Brain takes the mic, but André pulls it away. "I'm not finished! You know why the most beautiful Monday night I ever have? Because it's easy money! Ha ha ha ha! It's not just easy money, but it'll be easy night. You know why?"

"Why?" says DiBiase.

"Look who we got in the front of us. The ex-champ and the champ-anzee, ha ha ha ha!"

André laughs, displaying his shark teeth. Heenan takes his turn. "And one good thing we all have to take into consideration. There is no team called the Mega Powers, *this* is your Mega Power [pointing at André], *this* is your Mega Bucks [pointing at DiBiase]. They do not exist! So, Elizabeth, you and your discount-store dress and your two-dollar bottle of cologne can go take a hike! Because we're gonna wipe the mat with them and we're gonna get a fair shake, because we have a fair referee in Jesse 'The Body.' And we know we can *trust* him!"

The Mega Bucks all laugh. Brother Love takes back the mic. "You see? Take this as a message, Mega Powers. Because when they get through stomping the mat with you, pulverizing you, and completely demolishing you, remember one thing—they *looooooove* you!"

DiBiase passes a handful of hundreds to André, who puts his arm around the Million Dollar Man's shoulder and plants a kiss on his cheek.

DiBiase and André are the Mega Bucks. . . . Never has a more dangerous duo entered the ring. In André, there is superhuman size and
strength, the frightening might of a true giant. He is the man-
mountain, the colossus that looms over the wrestling ring like a
volcano about to explode. . . . André and DiBiase are especially dangerous now because they are not in *SummerSlam '88* just for victory.
They want much more. They are there in hopes of gaining their final
gratification in the total annihilation of Savage and Hogan. Thus far,
neither DiBiase's millions and ability nor André's mass and power
have been able to bring that end about.

August 29, 1988: Madison Square Garden, New York, NY

SUMMERSLAM: THE MEGA POWERS VS. THE MEGA BUCKS W/SPECIAL GUEST REFEREE JESSE "THE BODY" VENTURA

Jesse Ventura arrives in full-fringed regalia. "What kind of referee
attire is that?" questions Gorilla Monsoon.

"That's Hollywood style, bro-ther," explains Superstar Billy Graham, subbing for the otherwise engaged Ventura.

The Mega Bucks—total combined weight of 780 pounds—enter
first. DiBiase is announced as "making his summer residence in
Hyannis Port, Massachusetts." The crowd is oddly sedate until
Howard Finkel announces the Mega Powers, who enter to "Pomp and
Circumstance."

Savage is resplendent in Hogan's red and yellow, his rhinestoned
cape bearing lightning bolts and the legend "Mega Powers," as do
Hogan's trunks. His T-shirt, however, proclaims "Hulk Rules," just so
no one gets the wrong idea as to who the star of the show is. Miss
Elizabeth, "the First Lady of Wrestling," proves the point with her
canary yellow—with red trim—ensemble.

"What a beautiful robe that is," Graham enthuses. "Probably cost
$10,000."

"At least," agrees Gorilla.

The Mega Bucks.

André stares down Hogan, a sly grin on his face, as the Hulkster rips off his shirt.

Jesse lays down the law. "I want managers—you, you, and you—out on the floor." André reaches out a hand, but Hogan doesn't take the bait. Heenan, however, shakes Ventura's hand before leaving the ring.

Jesse changes the tag ropes to the opposite corners—lower left and upper right—as the teams debate who will start the match. Hogan taps him on the shoulder for an explanation, and Ventura bites his head off—"You get your hands offa me!"

Savage tells Hogan he wants to start. They argue. Savage sits on the middle rope, opening the door for Hulk.

He gets up and into the ring as the bell sounds and turns right into André. Savage and André lock up. The Giant punches him into the corner, chops him hard, then headbutts him before tagging in DiBiase. They circle each other, DiBiase pointing toward Hogan, telling him, "I want *you*." Savage spreads his arms wide, letting him know that he's right there, but DiBiase continues to demand Hulk. Savage decides to oblige and tags in Hogan.

DiBiase breaks the lockup and rakes Hulk's eyes. Blows are exchanged. DiBiase attempts a kick to Hogan's gut, but Hulk catches the boot, spins the Million Dollar Man around, and lifts him up for an atomic drop. DiBiase reels into Savage's corner. Macho Man punches him in the forehead, turning him around into a roundhouse from Hogan. He rotates back to Savage, who pops him right back to Hulk. Another shot sends him back to Macho Man. Jesse tries to intercede, but Savage shoves him out of the way and nails DiBiase, who finally goes down.

Hogan lifts him up and whips him into the ropes for a big clothesline. Basking in the applause, Hulk tags in Savage. Together they whip DiBiase into a double chop, finishing with double elbows. Heenan gets up on the apron to complain, but Ventura is on top of it, making sure Hogan gets out of the ring. Savage pounds DiBiase's head into the neutral turnbuckle, and the Million Dollar Man goes down hard, face-first onto the canvas. A quick tag to Hogan and Savage holds DiBiase's arms behind his back, holding him open to a kick

MICHAEL KRUGMAN

from Hogan. Hulk brings DiBiase to the neutral corner, bounces his head on the turnbuckle, and then crosses the ring to bounce it on the opposite side. Savage extends a leg through the ropes, and Hogan, holding a handful of Million Dollar hair, slams DiBiase into the big yellow boot.

Tag is made, and Hogan locks a full nelson on DiBiase. Savage goes up top and drops a double ax-handle right between the restrained DiBiase's eyes. Macho drops a knee and covers, but DiBiase kicks out after one. Another tag and the Mega Powers whip DiBiase into the ropes for a double boot to the face. Hogan covers, but DiBiase kicks out at two. Hogan bodyslams DiBiase, follows with three elbows, then goes for André in the corner. He swings, but André catches him and bonks Hulk with a headbutt.

Savage gets in the ring to complain. He turns from Ventura to discover André has entered the ring, and he too receives a Giant headbutt. The Mega Powers are down in the middle of the ring, but Ventura is too busy telling Elizabeth to get down off the apron.

DiBiase drops an elbow to the back of Hogan's head and at last tags in André. Hogan rolls to the ropes so André can hold on to the top to land a series of sit-down shots to Hulk's sternum. He then places a massive boot on the bottom rope, crushing Hogan's throat. Ventura starts counting, and André breaks at three. He picks up Hogan by the hair, places a boot on the middle turnbuckle, and smashes Hulk's face into his size-22 foot. Ventura tries to prevent André from keeping his hands around Hulk's throat, but the Giant's not big on following instructions. André squeezes Hogan's traps, keeping things nice and legal. Hulk falls to his knees as the Giant applies more pressure. André gets behind the seated Hogan and grips the neck harder. Savage argues with Jesse, giving André a moment to strangle Hogan with his singlet strap. Macho and the Body jaw as DiBiase comes in to hit a cheap shot to Hogan's gut.

DiBiase tags in and propels himself to hit a thrust kick to Hulk's midsection. Deep in enemy territory, Hogan takes a beating from DiBiase. He whips Hogan into a clothesline and covers for two. He drops a few shots between Hogan's eyes and tries again for a two-count. The Million Dollar Man locks a chokehold around the red-faced

Hogan's throat, but Ventura chooses not to break the hold, much to Macho's chagrin. Hogan rises to his feet, but DiBiase keeps his arm clamped tight around his throat.

Ventura lifts an arm to check Hulk's status, and he keeps it raised, signifying the beginning of his hulking up. DiBiase shakes his head in disbelief, but Hogan is now up. He nails three elbows to DiBiase's gut, finally breaking the hold. He slingshots off the ropes, ducks under DiBiase's clothesline, comes off the opposite ropes, and the two men double-clothesline each other as the crowd goes wild. Hulk eventually crawls to his corner and makes the tag just as DiBiase catches him. Savage unloads with roundhouse rights, whips into the opposite buckle. He bounces off into an elbow and goes down. Savage hits a backdrop, then takes a fistful of hair, runs toward the ropes, and goes up and over, leveraging DiBiase's throat into the top rope. DiBiase goes down as Savage scrambles to the top. Bombs away—a flying ax-handle lays out DiBiase. An elbow sends DiBiase to the corner. Savage attempts a splash, but the Million Dollar Man gets out of the way in time. Savage quickly regains control and tries to whip DiBiase into the ropes. He reverses, sending Savage instead. He ducks under DiBiase's clothesline and slingshots off and hits a high crossbody for a two-count. They get up, and a clothesline drops Savage, giving DiBiase time to tag in André.

The Giant throws Savage into the corner. A big right is followed by shoulderblocks and a couple of back splashes. Savage falls down, but André lifts him by the throat. He punches the Macho Man back to the mat and sits on his head, pinning his neck against the rope. He pulls him up, brings him to DiBiase, and headbutts him down before making the tag.

DiBiase suplexes Savage over, hooks the leg, but only gets two. He lifts up Savage for a backbreaker, goes to the second rope, and tries a reverse elbow, only to have Savage roll out of the way. Macho Man searches for his corner and at last makes the hot tag to Hogan.

Hulk points an angry finger at DiBiase, who shakes his head, begging as he backs into the corner. Six big rights, whip across to the opposite turnbuckle, clothesline, suplex. André comes in, but Hogan is on fire and clotheslines the Giant, sending him to the mat. Hogan locks the sleeper on DiBiase while Savage goes to the top. He tries the flying elbow, but the Giant gets his boot up. Savage rolls out to the floor. André grabs two handfuls of thinning blond hair and pulls Hogan off DiBiase from behind. A headbutt knocks Hogan loopy, and André pitches him out to the floor.

Ventura starts to count as the Mega Powers reel on the floor. Miss Elizabeth gets up on the apron, and Jesse goes over to tell her that she has to get down. Across the ring, Heenan and Virgil climb onto the apron, and Jesse tells them to get down as well. The count is stopped as Jesse stands in the middle of the ring between both managers. Elizabeth removes her skirt, revealing bright red bikini bottoms. She strolls along the apron as Jesse and the Mega Bucks stare. No one seems quite sure how to respond to this new development.

Meanwhile, the Mega Powers climb back to the apron. Elizabeth throws her skirt into DiBiase's face as Savage goes to the top and nails André from behind, sending the Giant across the ring and over the ropes. Macho goes after Heenan and Virgil, while Hogan slams DiBiase. He places a boot on the Million Dollar throat and signals for the flying elbow. Savage goes up and hits his finishing mover perfectly. Hogan then drops the leg and covers—one-two . . . Ventura pauses, but Savage grabs his arm and slams his palm onto the mat for three at 13:57.

Monsoon explains what occurred as Hogan tosses Elizabeth's skirt into the crowd. "They were bewildered, befuddled, and bewitched."

"And so were we," Superstar adds. "And so were the millions of people around this nation watching this telecast."

André prepares to headbutt Jake "The Snake" Roberts.

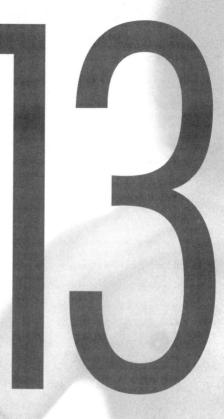

13

Not only was it a huge popular success, *SummerSlam* proved

historic—if nothing else, it marked the first time a Diva disrobed

on a wrestling Pay-Per-View. ■ In the fall, World Wrestling

Federation went on its annual tour of Europe, playing to SRO

crowds in Milan, Italy, and Paris, France. As wrestling's most

famous European, the mammoth Frenchman was among the trip's

biggest attractions. He played up his heel role, demanding to be called "André the Giant" after being introduced to Parisian wrestling fans as "André le Giant." André and Tim White also took advantage of being on foreign soil to engage in some banned-in-America in-ring hijinks.

TIM WHITE: "We took some liberty when we were in Europe and I refereed a couple of his matches. It was a no-no at home, but André said, 'Timber, we're in Europe, I think we'll have some fun.'

"It was the most fun I ever had. We had such a blast in the ring. One match was with Tito Santana, who André loved. They could play cards together forever. When André got along with a guy, they had some unbelievable matches. Other times it was just business.

"On another trip, I refereed André's match with Bret Hart. The finish is André squashes Bret and gets the one-two-three. After the match, Bret, with his sense of humor, goes, 'Timmy, what the fuck was that one-two-three? I kicked out!'

" 'You kicked out? Well, here's what I saw.' I said, 'You ever see *The Wizard of Oz?*' 'Yeah.' I said, 'Remember when the house landed on the Witch and all you saw was two little feet dangling out? That's all I could see when André was on top of you. There was no kicking out!'

"He goes, 'You son of a bitch,' and then we all started laughing."

Upon his return, André was forced to confront the effect his physical weakness was having on his role in World Wrestling Federation. After nearly three years, André, with manager Bobby Heenan, was done with the promotion's biggest star, Hulk Hogan. The feud, in its many permutations, was one of the most successful programs in wrestling history, but after the big blow-off at *SummerSlam,* it was time for the players to move on.

For André, that meant that he was no longer going to be in the promotion's main program. Rather, he would be used as a featured attraction, his sheer star power serving to keep him in the forefront of World Wrestling Federation storylines. His new feud would pit him against a rising fan favorite, Jake "The Snake" Roberts.

Like DiBiase and Savage and so many other Superstars, Roberts was born into the wrestling business. The son of NWA/AWA/WWA grappler Grizzly Smith, Jake entered the ring in the Louisiana territory of the early 1970s. He moved on to Mid-South, where he was mentored by the legendary

Mr. Wrestling II. From there, he went to Georgia Championship Wrestling and joined "Precious" Paul Ellering's original Legion of Doom stable alongside King Kong Bundy, Buzz Sawyer, the Spoiler, and of course, the Road Warriors Hawk & Animal.

Roberts then joined NWA, where he had an intense NWA World Television Championship feud with the great Ronnie Garvin and perfected his trademark finishing move, the DDT. Jake returned to Mid-South for a television title feud with Dick Slater, but was soon invited up to New York to become a featured World Wrestling Federation wrestler.

He shocked Federation fans by nailing a DDT against his former NWA tag partner, Ricky "The Dragon" Steamboat, on the concrete floor outside the ring. Before long, Roberts found himself drawing more cheers than heat and turned babyface. He hosted his own segment, *The Snake Pit,* which saw him unleashing streams of darkly philosophical consciousness while interviewing his fellow superstars.

André's entanglement with Roberts began at *SummerSlam,* when André's fellow Heenan Family member, "Ravishing" Rick Rude, came to the ring wearing tights airbrushed with a painting of Jake's wife, Cheryl. Later, Rude wore the offending garb to another match, prompting Roberts to run in and remove them, leaving Rude nude. The Giant officially entered the picture on the October 1988 installment of *Saturday Night's Main Event.*

October 25, 1988: Baltimore Arena, Baltimore, MD

SATURDAY NIGHT'S MAIN EVENT: "RAVISHING" RICK RUDE (W/BOBBY HEENAN) VS. JAKE "THE SNAKE" ROBERTS

Bobby Heenan and Rick Rude enter the ring, with the Ravishing One wearing the provocative ring attire that kickstarted this rivalry. Backstage, Mr. and Mrs. "The Snake" (accompanied by Damien, of course) are interviewed by Mean Gene. First and foremost on Okerlund's mind are Rude's "insulting tights."

"The whole Heenan Family are just like flies," Jake hisses, "flies buzzin' around our garden. And I've got the DDT."

Roberts comes to the ring with wife and snake in tow. Rude

taunts them with his patented pelvis-pumping and hip-thrusting. Jake seems cool but finally reaches his limit. He grits his teeth in anger and attacks Rude. They tie up, and soon Rude has the advantage, shoulderblocking Jake in the corner. Roberts counters with a forearm to the back and soon has Rude dancing around the ring in a wrist-lock. Rude counters by sending Jake into the ropes.

Roberts slingshots over Rude, off the ropes again, Rude leapfrogs, turns around, and gets a right to the belly. A DDT is attempted, and Rude slips out of the ring to confer with Heenan. Roberts reaches down and pulls Rude up by his hair. On the apron, Rick rakes the Snake's eyes. Roberts tries the wristlock and short-arm clothesline, misses, and receives a short arm from Rude. Forearm smash sends Jake into the corner; Rude smashes his face into the buckle. Roberts misses a round-house right, but Rude connects. Jake swings wildly, but Rude lands another. Roberts goes down, Rude drops an elbow.

As Jake sells, Rick visits Cheryl in the corner. Roberts gets up, but Rude is there with a kidney punch and whips him into the opposite buckle. Rude returns to Cheryl and gives her a bit of the pelvic thrust.

"She's loving every minute of it," says Jesse Ventura.

Rude drives another fist into the small of Jake's back, turning him into a forearm smash. Whip to the far side. Rude turns to Cheryl, not seeing Jake's quick return, and spins around into a clothesline. A series of lefts followed by a right to the throat knocks Rude to the mat, his head hitting the canvas hard. An inverted atomic drop is followed by a face plant onto the mat. Jake puts Rick's neck on the bottom rope and pulls his arms back, giving Cheryl the opportunity to slap him.

"That is sickening, McMahon!" fumes Ventura. "She is acting as a manager and is interfering in the match!"

Heenan agrees and demands Cheryl be barred from ringside. Roberts argues with the ref, but Cheryl is sent back.

After the break, Jake and Rude are battling outside. Rick sends Roberts into the post. He takes Jake's wrist and pulls him face-first into the pole, not once but twice, then gets back into the ring, beating the count. Jake is outside as Rude does his happy dance.

Jake gets in and drives a fist into Rude's breadbasket. A hard right drops Rude. Roberts signals for the DDT, hooks it, but Rude reverses into a back bodydrop and elbows to the chest. Rude goes up top, tries to drive a fist into Roberts's head, but Jake slithers away. Still, Rude covers for two. He rises and shakes his package over the prone Roberts.

Rick lifts Roberts and sets up the Rude Awakening, but Jake breaks it by biting Rick's wrist. He sends Roberts to the ropes, telegraphs a back bodydrop, but Jake catches the top rope and catches Rick with a fast DDT.

Heenan gets up on the ringpost and signals to the back for help as Roberts tries to pull the tights off the fallen Rude. The Brain comes from behind, kicking at Jake's back—the bell rings at 6:06.

André lumbers out as Heenan continues to kick away on Roberts. Jake catches the Brain's ankle, but André is there. He hammers at Jake's back, and then grabs the hair for a crushing headbutt that sends Jake rolling out of the ring to the floor. André and Bobby tend to Rude. Jake brings the sack holding Damien to the apron, then takes the snake out of the bag. Heenan slides out of the ring, leaving André to face Roberts and his pet. They stare each other down, André seemingly frozen. Jake points Damien's head at André, who holds out a hand, backing away. He turns to Heenan—"I don't like that at all! Bobby!"—yelling for help as he backs around the ropes.

"I didn't think the Giant was afraid of anything," Vince says.

André shakes his head, terrified, as Jake taunts him with the snake. Finally, Roberts tosses the python onto the Giant. André goes down, leaving the snake slung over the top rope. Jake quickly reaches out and pulls Damien off, dropping him onto André, who clutches his chest. The snake slithers off, but Jake returns him to his place atop André. Damien slithers around what McMahon refers to as the now-unconscious Giant's "crotch area."

Jake takes Damien and stands over the horizontal Giant, holding the snake over his head in triumph. He leaves, and Heenan rushes to André's aid. He rips open André's sport shirt and tries to resuscitate, pounding on his chest.

André's heart-stopping—literally!—fear of snakes was revealed as his only weakness, the key to beating the hitherto invulnerable Giant. Over the months, Roberts used his snake to gain the edge over the ophidiophobic André, effectively nullifying the size and strength advantage.

The Giant's ophidiophobia is revealed on *Saturday Night's Main Event.*

"BATTLE OF THE TITANS: JAKE 'THE SNAKE' ROBERTS DESTROYS 'RAVISHING' RICK RUDE AND EXPOSES ANDRÉ'S HIDDEN FEAR; THE HEENAN FAMILY IN TURMOIL"

Colossus toppled. André the Giant, the awesome man-mountain who fears no man, fell to pieces at the touch of Jake's python, Damien. Wrapped in the coils of Damien, André crashed to the canvas in a faint so dead that a news bulletin declared he had suffered a heart attack. . . . The news was out. There is a chink in André's armor of invincibility. The Eighth Wonder of the World is deathly afraid of snakes. . . . André has always been Heenan's ultimate weapon, not just because of his immense size and strength but because of his reputation as a man without fear. Now the world knows that André quakes over serpents—which makes him very vulnerable to one Jake "The Snake" Roberts.

Every man, even André, has his own personal devil.

JAKE ROBERTS: "I'd met André years before, and driven him around Louisiana. He was bigger than life, no doubt.

"First time I wrestled him, it was in Los Angeles and it was an ugly, ugly day. 'Cause he tested me. André had a way, sometimes he did that. If you didn't respond to the test, he was gonna make your life a miserable hell.

"To be in the ring with him, to me, that was probably one of my greatest moments. Even in the old days, whenever he toured different territories, your top guy got André. Well, to me, that was saying, 'Jake, you might be a top guy now.'

"There was a lot of great times out there with him. To me that was one of my crowning moments. A fine, fine man."

TED DIBIASE: "André wasn't bosom buddies with Jake, but André respected his ability. One night they were wrestling, Jake's lying down in the corner, selling it, and André walks over and steps on his long hair. Then he reaches down, grabs him, and starts to pull him up. Jake's going, 'Ahhhh!' 'Get up,' André says, 'Get up.' 'Ahhhhhh! My hair!' André stepped off Jake's hair and goes, 'Oh, excuse me.' I was outside on the apron, just laughing."

VINCE MCMAHON: "André didn't like Jake because Jake was a big-time drug user. They were in the ring, and Jake was scared to death. He just wanted to do whatever it was André called, never questioned anything.

"So Jake is on his back, André steps on Jake's hair, and then takes Jake's arms and pulls him up, literally pulls his entire body off the mat. Meanwhile he's stepping on Jake's hair, pulling it out by the roots.

"I admit, I enjoyed it. You know, no one outside of our business would ever understand what we enjoy and why, or why we behave like we do. We're all kids. And some of that has not changed."

GENE OKERLUND INTERVIEWS ANDRÉ AND BOBBY HEENAN

"Obviously, what we've seen in the past few weeks," Mean Gene phi-losophizes, "no man is an island. Some men have feet of clay. That's quite obvious to me, Mr. Heenan."

"I beg your pardon. Repeat that."

"Well, I'm just trying to point out that everybody's got an Achilles' heel. Apparently André the Giant has a phobia."

"You're talking about Jake 'The Snake' Roberts, aren't you?" Heenan says angrily, pointing a finger in Okerlund's face. André grabs his manager's shoulder at the sound of Roberts's name, seem-ingly shaken up by even the possibility of confronting his serpent. "Don't use that word in the presence of this man or in the presence of me! There's no place in the great sport of professional wrestling for something as low as Jake Roberts. Period!"

"Wait a minute. André, and Bobby Heenan, I'm just trying to point out, this man's only human. It could happen to anybody. I'm afraid of getting in an elevator!"

"You're trying to point out the fact that André the Giant is afraid of that thing that Jake Roberts drags around with him."

"Damien," Okerlund reminds the audience.

"I'm not afraid!" argues André. "I'm not afraid, and I'm proud to say it!"

The Giant turns to face the camera. "But Jake, when you come in that ring, don't ever take that thing with you. Because you will pay for it."

André's eyes widen as he raises a huge, clenched fist.

"You will pay for what you take, Jake. Believe me, you think you are tough. But you should to ask to the ex-world champion . . . ask for any other wrestler that you want to, they will tell you, because I'm the only undisputed wrestler in the wrestler in the world! And put that in your mind, Jake, you'll get it. But if you are to step in the ring with me, come on and you're welcome *anytime*! [speaking softly] But don't take that thing with you."

"This man is obviously beside himself, Bobby Heenan," observes Mean Gene.

"I'm gonna tell ya, very, very quiet and plain, so even your small little mind understands it. I will not be responsible for what André the Giant has in mind or what he does to Jake Roberts. And if you people keep chanting that word 'snake,' he's going to pay!"

André gestures choking out Roberts, grinning hungrily. The crowd hisses "Snake! Snake! Snake!"

"Obviously we have not heard the end of this one between André the Giant and Jake 'The Snake' Roberts."

André turns and menaces Mean Gene. "I told you not to say it," Heenan growls.

"I didn't say anything!"

"You said it!" snarls the Giant.

"No, I didn't," Okerlund says, backing away as the camera fades to black.

Roberts and his python began haunting the anxious André, making surprise appearances in the Giant's matches with other wrestlers. Having uncovered André's weakness, the Snake was determined to exploit it.

November 16, 1988: Arco Arena, Sacramento, CA

SATURDAY NIGHT'S MAIN EVENT
ANDRÉ VS. RANDY "MACHO MAN" SAVAGE

André and Heenan enter the ring to huge heat. Meanwhile, "Mean" Gene Okerlund interviews Randy Savage backstage.

"André the Giant is the Eighth Wonder of the World," Macho Man says, "and he's the largest man ever to enter the squared circle, yeah. And to be a great champion, I've got to beat the Giant. Hulk Hogan was a great champion and *he* beat the Giant, oh yeah. And if the Hulkster—my partner in the Mega Powers—could do it, then *I* will do it, ooh yeah. I owe it to the fans; I owe it to the title; I owe it to Hulk Hogan; and I owe it to Elizabeth, the manager of the Mega Powers, yeah."

"What about Bobby 'The Brain' Heenan?" asks Okerlund.

"Ooh yeah, I know him. I know him to be a two-legged snake and

I'd be real real real surprised if André the Giant isn't afraid of him too. Isn't that funny, Elizabeth? Isn't that something? The time is now! Down that aisle yeah to beat the Giant yeah!"

The bell sounds and Savage attacks, only to receive André's grip around his throat. André chops and headbutts the champion in the corner. Savage responds by taking it to the Giant with elbows and forearm smashes. Unperturbed, André chops Savage to the mat. He cinches his arms around him and squeezes, ramming him into the corner. A series of knees to the midsection is followed by a shoulderblock. He leans onto the champ, pushing back with his full weight, smiling wide. Savage surprises him with a knee to the back, then pounds with a double ax-handle.

André chops him away and applies a front facelock. Savage tries to maneuver André's massive leg, but the Giant gets his singlet strap around the Macho Man's throat. Heenan distracts referee Earl Hebner so André can choke the champ.

Huge heat from the crowd as André blocks the ref's view of the illegal move with his massive body. Savage tries to fight his way free, but the Giant keeps the facelock and strap around his neck. He takes Savage's arms and holds them behind his back, the leverage choking him further with the strap.

Miss Elizabeth protests, but only serves to distract Hebner from seeing André headbutting Savage from behind. Eventually, the Giant removes the strap and paintbrushes the champ, who shoulderblocks André into the corner. He survives a kneelift and continues to charge. André grabs Savage's wrist and pulls him close, leaning his forearm onto Macho Man's face, stretching his arm by putting his weight onto the champ. Savage reaches up for some hair, but Hebner pulls it off. A headbutt plants Savage. André goes back to the choke, pushing Macho back up against the ropes with a one hand throttle. He breaks when the referee reaches the count of four, then regains the choke. He takes hold of the top rope and pulls it forward, bouncing Savage face-first onto the canvas.

There's massive heat from the fans. Heenan is gleeful, saying "I love it, I love it, I love it," as André manhandles Macho. The Giant squeezes Savage's traps. Savage fights back, but André cinches the underhook. Savage breaks it with a jawjacker, the bounce smashing the top of his head up into André's chin. André grabs his mouth in pain, allowing Savage to double-ax-handle him into the corner. He hammers at André, which only enrages the Giant, who immediately returns to the choke. Savage breaks free and tries a double ax-handle off the ropes. The Giant reels, Savage pounds his head into the buckle and goes to the second rope for an ax-handle smash across the back of André's head. The Giant goes down and Savage kicks away at him, reveling in the shift in momentum.

Jake the Snake, wearing his leathers, arrives at ringside and puts his sack under the ring. André pulls away from Savage and asks Hebner, "What's he doing here?" Hebner tries to take control by ejecting Roberts. Savage hops over the top to talk it out with Jake, who finally complies.

He returns to the ring and hits a running ax-handle on André, who was busy talking to Heenan, telling him to find the snake. André fights off Savage but is preoccupied by Damien's presence. Savage keeps up the attack while Heenan searches for the snake, lifting up the apron, removing Finkel and Mike McGuirk from their chairs. André is distracted, but Savage fails to take him down, though one of his blows draws blood from the Giant's brow. A headbutt puts the champ onto the mat, and André goes back to demanding Heenan find the snake.

Savage wisely rolls outside and chases Heenan. He gets up on the apron and is caught. André pulls him back onto the ropes and chops him over the top into the ring. Heenan finally finds the bag and heads to the back, but Jake returns and chases the Brain into the ring, forcing Hebner to call the double DQ at 8:42.

Savage whips Heenan into André, tying him up in the ropes. Macho continues to assault Heenan, tossing him up and over and out. Macho invites Roberts to join him in the ring. Hebner frees the terrified André just as Jake unleashes Damien and gets ready to pitch the python onto the Giant. André rolls out and escapes up the aisle. Savage and Roberts and Damien pose in the ring, as Heenan helps the Giant toward the back. André collapses halfway, but Jake merely taunts him from the ring.

"THE GIANT'S MORTAL FEAR: ANDRÉ'S SNAKE PHOBIA
IMPACTS ON TITLE MATCH"

by Ed Ricciuti

Jake issued a challenge. . . . "Everyone has something they fear, Giant, even you. Some people are afraid of the dark. Some of their own thoughts. I know what your fear is, André, and I'm looking forward to meeting you again."

In November, the second *Survivor Series* saw the program continue, though unlike the Pay-Per-View's initial installment, André was no longer the headliner. Teams formed around the two protagonists, with the Giant supported by Rick Rude, Dino Bravo, Curt "Mr. Perfect" Hennig, and Harley Race, with the managerial assistance of Frenchie Martin and Bobby Heenan. The Snake was joined by "Hacksaw" Jim Duggan, Ken Patera, Scott Casey, and Tito Santana.

Survivor Series **1988 program**

"ANDRÉ THE GIANT HAS A PHOBIA"

André the Giant, the gargantua who fears no other man, has a phobia—of snakes.

The truth is out. The sight of a snake totally unnerves the huge Giant. He absolutely dreads serpents. Fear spreads through his mammoth body and grips his brain with icy claws.

Bobby "The Brain" Heenan has protested Jake's carrying of Damien to the officials. "It's not fair," Heenan says. "It's a travesty. It's dangerous."

Heenan's words are not all bluff. If the one thing André fears is eliminated, Heenan's cunning mind reasons, the Giant can be unleashed to do the Brain's will. So Roberts must expect that Heenan is hatching all sorts of crafty—and dangerous—schemes against the Snake and Damien. Roberts cannot count on André's fear of snakes to eliminate the danger posed by Heenan and his brutal behemoth. The threat to Roberts is as real as the fear inside André's mammoth breast.

SURVIVOR SERIES: ANDRÉ THE GIANT, RICK RUDE, DINO BRAVO, MR. PERFECT & HARLEY RACE (W/FRENCHIE MARTIN & BOBBY HEENAN) VS. JAKE ROBERTS, "HACKSAW" JIM DUGGAN, KEN PATERA, SCOTT CASEY & TITO SANTANA

"What a piece of humanity," says Gorilla Monsoon of André. "A condominium with feet."

André interferes briefly, reaching in to grab Duggan from the apron after Hacksaw pitched Perfect over the post with a roundhouse right. . . . Later, Casey gets trapped in the enemy corner by Rude. André holds him there for Race, who tags in and goes to work. As he pounds Casey into the buckle, André reaches in and chops Casey's back. . . . Duggan struts in enemy territory as he battles Perfect. This time André catches him and pulls him into the corner for Perfect to punch away at his midsection. André headbutts Duggan down, then leans over to grab him by the hair for another. . . . Race takes Tito into the corner and rams him directly into André's head, which, Ventura notes, "is worse than hitting the turnbuckle."

André enters when Santana pins Race, surprising Tito by grabbing a fistful of hair as he rises from the mat. The Giant stays close to the ropes, holding the top while choking Santana with his right hand. As ever, he makes sure to keep it legal, breaking the grip just before getting disqualified. He bounces Santana against the ropes, then lets go, sending Tito face-first to the canvas. A massive chop is followed by a pair of buttdrops. Santana tries to fight back but is throttled to his knees. André sends him into the ropes, setting up a sunset flip that fails to pull André over. Rather, André sits down on Tito and scores the pinfall at 14:40.

Hacksaw enters and immediately clotheslines the Giant, trapping him in the ropes. Referee Joey Marella and Rude try to untie him, but Duggan takes the opportunity to land a series of punches to André's head. Roberts jumps in and continues the assault, also managing to deck Rude and Perfect before choking the trapped Giant. Freed from the ropes, André headbutts Jake away and tags Rude in. . . . Later, Perfect gets Roberts under the ropes, allowing André to stand on the bottom rope to choke the Snake. . . . Duggan is DQed for using his two-by-four on Bravo, setting up Roberts in a four-on-one situation. He takes on Perfect, who tags in Bravo, who brings in Rude. Rick rakes Jake's eyes, pummels him into the buckle, lands a big round-house right. Roberts wanders into the enemy corner, where Bravo takes a shot, knocking him to the mat. Inverted atomic drop keeps Jake down as Rude keeps up the attack. Eventually Rude decides to end it by dropping a fist from the top. Rick stands over Jake and swivels his hips before heading into his corner to tag in André. Roberts gets up and surprises Rude with a DDT at 28:45.

André climbs in and picks up Roberts from the pin position, pummeling him with punches before choking him mercilessly against the turnbuckle. He is enraged to the point where he leans in and bites the Snake's throat, before returning to the vicious choke. At 29:39, referees Marella and Earl Hebner call for the bell, DQing the mad Giant. André headbutts the barely conscious Snake to the canvas before leaving. Perfect hooks the leg and gets the three-count, ending the match at 30:03. Sole Survivors Perfect and Bravo celebrate with Frenchie Martin, while André and Heenan confab outside.

Meanwhile, Roberts is on the floor, bringing Damien out from under the ring. He pitches the python into the ring, then taunts André, who quickly leads his team up the aisle.

ANDRÉ VS. JAKE "THE SNAKE" ROBERTS

Bobby Heenan takes the mic before the bell. "I'm gonna make it very simple for you, Jake. If you wanna have a match, and don't wanna disappoint all your humanoid fans, then I suggest that snake goes back to the dressing room or there is no match!"

Roberts argues with referee Earl Hebner, then relents and puts the sack under the ring. Jake goes on the attack, wrapping an arm around André's chest and beating on his back with a forearm. Clothesline ties André up in the ropes, though Jake seems to have injured his upper arm in the process. Hebner tries to free him, but Roberts, still favoring his right arm, starts choking the Giant. He breaks at the count of four, then grips André's throat for more. André gets loose and leans on the ropes for support. Roberts attacks but is caught in André's grip.

The Giant leans Roberts on the ropes and alternatively chops and chokes. He pushes Jake down on the ropes. "C'mon, André," Hebner yells, "let him up!"

André grits his teeth and chokes Roberts harder. "I'm gonna dis-qualify you in a minute," Hebner promises.

Finally André lets go, springing Roberts face-first off the ropes. He rolls all the way across the ring, his head under the bottom rope. André wraps his arms around the top for leverage and stands hard on the bottom, choking Roberts.

André stands Jake up and immobilizes him with a wristlock, then goes to work on his injured shoulder and arm with headbutts and punches. A front facelock disguises the strap around Roberts's throat.

Jake fights out and leads André into the corner. The Giant coun-ters with a headbutt and they reverse. André shoulderblocks Jake against the buckles. Hebner breaks it up, and when André goes in for another, Roberts chops him hard across the shoulders. André reels backward and drops to one knee, holding on to the top rope.

Behind him, Roberts calls for the DDT. He tries to catch André as the Giant rises, but is pushed away, favoring his upper arm. André reaches down and chokes him. "C'mon, André, you're gonna kill him," says Hebner between counts of four.

"That's what I'm here for," André says, grinning, then hits a pair of big butts on Jake's chest. "Ha ha ha ha!"

André pulls Jake up by his hair and sets him up in the corner for more chops and choking, then leans back to squash the Snake. He turns away and Jake gets up on the second rope. He jumps and just barely hits André across the shoulder with his injured arm. André goes down anyway, giving Jake time to go outside to retrieve Damien from under the ring. He tosses the python in just as André turns to face him. "Ahhhhhhh!"

André bolts as Heenan runs in after the sack. Roberts hits him with a knee, and Heenan bumps over the top. André lies against the bottom rope in terror as Jake takes Damien out of the bag. Hebner calls for the bell, DQing Roberts at 6:20. André rolls out and up the aisle before Jake can place Damien atop him.

THE BROTHER LOVE SHOW W/ANDRÉ AND BOBBY HEENAN

André is casual in sports shirt and slacks. "Now, several weeks ago, brothers and sisters," begins the red-faced televangelist, "Brother Love told each and every one of you that we were on a crusade, to rid the company of its serpents. And here is the man who is going to do it, Brother Eighth Wonder of the World, André the Giant. But you see, a lot of people out here said that Brother Giant was afraid of snakes. But that indeed is not the case at all, is it, Brother Brain?"

"No, he's not afraid of snakes," replies Heenan. "I'll guarantee you that."

"What?" asks an indignant André, but Heenan reassures him, mouthing, "You're not afraid of snakes."

"No, no, Brother Giant is not afraid of snakes, isn't that right, Brother Brain?"

"Hey!" says André, making sure Brother Love isn't alleging any ophidiophobia on the Giant's part.

From left: Brother Eighth Wonder of the World, Brother Love, Brother Brain.

"Like I said before," Heenan explains, "he just does not like to be surprised. And what I've done is, I've taken this man and I've hired the best hypnotist in the world just to prove to myself and this man *and the world* that André the Giant fears no man, let alone no snake!"

"Y'know, Brother Brain, to prove it, why do you know that right back here in this bag right here is a gigantic fifteen-foot snake."

André quickly backs away to the far edge of the stage. Heenan is clearly angered as Brother Love continues. "I brought it out here just to prove to everybody that the Giant is—"

"No, no, no, no," Heenan interrupts, stopping Brother Love from opening the bag. "There's nothing to prove to anybody. You can take my word for it. This man, the Eighth Wonder of the World, fears nothing."

But Brother Love is determined, and again reaches down to open the sack. "But let's show everybody that he's not—"

André grabs Brother Love's arm to stop him, his eyes never leaving the bag. "It's obvious these people don't need to know how he or myself feel about whatever you brought in that bag," says Heenan. "It's not necessary."

"But we will prove it to everyone!" Brother Love declares, bending to reveal the bag's contents. "We'll bring it out—"

Both André and Heenan grab an arm and yank Brother Love away. Heenan and Brother Love exchange a few heated words off-mic as André takes a few steps backward, always keeping a close watch on the sack. He keeps going, winding up safely behind Brother Love's pulpit.

"Well, you see, ladies and gentlemen," the crimson preacher declares at last, finally having been shown the light, "you have witnessed a miracle! A miracle! Brother Giant fears no man! He fears no serpent! He's not afraid of some snake in the bag! And he certainly is not afraid of *you,* Jake 'The Snake' Roberts!"

Brother Love returns the mic to its holder and hugs Heenan while André maintains a safe distance from the bag.

"Well, I guess they proved it, huh, McMahon?" notes Jesse Ventura.

"Yeah, I don't think so," says a still-skeptical Vince. "Not to me. Not to me at all."

The *Royal Rumble* kicked off 1989—the latest installment in the ever-increasing slate of World Wrestling Federation Pay-Per-View, and the starting point for *WrestleMania* buildup. The event was and remains headlined by the *Royal Rumble* itself—a thirty-man, over-the-top Battle Royal, with wrestlers entering the ring at two-minute intervals. With André the undisputed king of Battle Royals, the *Rumble* made an ideal match to light the fuse of his upcoming match with Roberts at *WrestleMania V.*

ROYAL RUMBLE: PARTICIPATING WRESTLERS: AX, SMASH, ANDRÉ THE GIANT, MR. PERFECT, RON GARVIN, GREG VALENTINE, JAKE ROBERTS, RON BASS, SHAWN MICHAELS, BUSHWHACKER BUTCH, HONKY TONK MAN, TITO SANTANA, BAD NEWS BROWN, MARTY JANNETTY, RANDY SAVAGE, ARN ANDERSON, TULLY BLANCHARD, HULK HOGAN, BUSHWHACKER LUKE, KOKO B. WARE, THE WARLORD, BIG BOSS MAN, AKEEM, BRUTUS BEEFCAKE, THE RED ROOSTER, THE BARBARIAN, BIG JOHN STUDD, HERCULES, RICK MARTEL, & TED DIBIASE

André enters the *Royal Rumble* at number 3, following Ax & Smash—World Wrestling Federation Tag Team Champions Demolition. The Giant gingerly climbs on the apron and enters, immediately on the receiving end of a double clothesline from Demolition. He goes down, and the tag team begins pummeling him with double ax-handles. Back up against the ropes, Ax and Smash put the boots to André, literally placing their boots on his throat. He gradually gets to his feet, but is pushed into the corner. He manages to get free, but Demolition continues their assault.

As the buzzer goes off, signaling the entry of number 4, André is on the offensive, banging Ax and Smash's heads together. Mr. Perfect saunters to the ring as André has his arms held behind his back by Ax, allowing Smash to rain punches. Smash goes to drive a shoulder into the Giant, but André puts up a big boot and takes him down. Perfect finally runs in, punches Smash, then starts hitting André, who is now crushing Ax into the corner. Smash gets back into it, throwing blows at Perfect as André chops Ax. As Ax drops to his knees, André grabs Smash by the hair and tosses him over the top rope. Perfect tries to shift André's balance by taking hold of his leg. Ax takes André's boot, the Giant bent face first into the turnbuckle, allowing Perfect to kick up into his midsection. Ax and Perfect double-team André, now down in the corner, choking him as they put the boots to him. Two boots in the throat, André's head on the bottom rope. Perfect takes his foot off André, and Ax turns on him. The two trade blows as André catches his breath. Ax sends Perfect face-first into the opposite turnbuckle, and then quickly returns to the now-standing Giant. But André gets his hands around Ax's neck, choking him down to his knees. Perfect breaks the choke with forearms to André's back, but gets a huge headbutt for his efforts and comes very close to elimination. Back against the corner, André chops and punches Perfect and Ax as the capacity crowd counts down the entry of number 5, "Rugged" Ronnie Garvin.

Garvin runs down the aisle as André beats on Ax. Perfect goes for André's gut and is joined by Garvin, dropping André again to the mat, his back up on the ropes. André is tied up in the top two ropes as Perfect and Garvin each grab a leg in an attempt to eliminate the Giant. Ax turns his attention to Perfect. Garvin stupidly frees one of the Giant's arms, but pays for it with a punch. André gets back up and goes at it with Ax, who falls into the corner, setting up André to crush him with his big butt. With Ax trapped under André's behind, Perfect and Garvin team up on André. He butts their heads together, sending them both down to the mat. André gets to center ring and punches Perfect three feet off the canvas. Before long, all three men are again beating on André. Ax and André begin battling in the corner, while Garvin and Perfect exchange chops.

The buzzer sounds, sending in Greg "The Hammer" Valentine, as André gets triple-teamed against the ropes. Valentine runs in and drives an elbow into André's forehead, making it a four-on-one battle. Somehow André pushes them off and, with a mighty forearm, sends Garvin out over the top.

MICHAEL KRUGMAN

André destroys Demolition, *Royal Rumble 1989.*

Valentine chops at André's chest in the corner, but the Giant gets his hands up and starts choking the Hammer. Ax clotheslines Perfect, and then breaks up André's choke with an ax-handle to his shoulders. Holding on to the rope for support, André starts choking Ax, a hungry grin sweeping across his face for the first time in the match. Perfect comes from behind and takes two handfuls of André's hair, turning him around for a series of chops.

The buzzer goes off, and Jake Roberts runs in. André turns away from Perfect and catches his nemesis with a big boot. André holds Roberts's head as the Snake punches away at André's midsection. André chokes the Snake down onto the top rope. The Hammer, sensing an opportunity, whips himself off the ropes and clotheslines the Giant's back, but is shrugged away. He tries it again, but André refuses to be distracted from his assault on Roberts. Jake goes down, allowing André to place a big boot on his throat. He then sits down on Jake's chest, then steps right on the Snake's belly, placing his weight on Roberts's guts. André then shoulderblocks Roberts into the corner. Ax tries to intervene but takes a big chop to the chest. The Hammer tries it, and gets a headbutt for his efforts. André wraps his shoulder strap around Roberts's throat, choking him into the turnbuckle.

"The Outlaw" Ron Bass enters at number 8, considers attacking André, but thinks better of it. André grabs the back of Jake's tights and tosses him up and over. He turns and decides to enact payback on Valentine, who backs himself into the corner. André grabs his throat and squeezes. Perfect pulls André off, and then finds his own neck in the Giant's grip. Hammer tries to help, but André piles Perfect and Valentine into the corner, driving his shoulder into Perfect's midsection. He chops Perfect away, then resumes choking Valentine.

Shawn Michaels runs in and takes on Bass, André now crushing Valentine's throat with a boot. André turns to face Bass as Michaels and Perfect go at it. Maintaining a grip on the top rope for balance, André chokes Bass into the corner. He puts the Outlaw into a bearhug, the Hammer now up and attacking André's back with blows.

The buzzer sounds, and Butch Bushwhacker comes in as Bass and Valentine double-team André. All of a sudden Roberts returns, holding Damien in his sack. He slides the snake into the ring. André's eyes pop out in fear at the sight of it and he quickly climbs out over the top, eliminating himself. André leaves as the ref chews out the Snake, who takes Damien and leaves.

"André bailed outta there in a hurry," says Gorilla Monsoon, "which proves only one thing, Jess."

"He's still deathly afraid of snakes," Jesse Ventura agrees.

The ultimate winner of the *Royal Rumble 1989* was none other than André's old nemesis Big John Studd, who had returned to the World Wrestling Federation roster some weeks earlier. When Heenan attempted to welcome Studd back into the folds of the Heenan Family, Big John rejected the offer. The stage was set for a return to the classic André vs. Studd feud, only with the roles reversed—it was now André as the heel in the war of the gargantuas.

May 1989

"ANDRÉ VS. STUDD: WHO'S THE REAL GIANT?"
by Keith Elliot Greenberg

André the Giant gripped the dressing room curtain and pried it open just enough to peer down the aisle at the action in the ring. The date was January 15, and the Giant—who had earlier quit the *Royal Rumble* when a python-waving Jake "The Snake" Roberts approached the ring—wanted to size up a man he hadn't seen in two years: Big John Studd.

"André can be a very introverted character," says a source close to the wrestling family of manager Bobby "The Brain" Heenan. "He's very secretive about his inner feelings. But he makes it clear that John Studd occupies a good deal of his thoughts. I don't know if it's Studd's size, his reputation as a brawler who never quits, or the simple fact that they're so often compared with each other. All I can tell you is that André sees Studd as a pretender who must be put down hard."

As Studd stood in the center of the ring, André slowly closed the curtain and lumbered down the dressing room corridor. A reporter approached to ask him about his earlier run-in with Jake the Snake. A morose André took a wide step around the journalist, but before disappearing behind a changing room door, the Giant uttered a phrase indicating Studd, not Roberts, was on his mind: "I am still the *real* giant."

Big John Studd had only made his return to World Wrestling Federation a few days earlier when he visited the screening room of the television production facility. . . . Although Studd spent several hours reviewing matches of the top stars, the majority of his time was devoted to studying André.

"He wanted to see everything the Giant had done lately—Singles matches, Tag Team matches, Battle Royals—you name it," the technician says. "And he wouldn't watch the matches once, but five or six times. I can't remember him saying a lot during the screening. A few times, he pressed the stop button, rewound the tape for a few seconds, looked at André executing a move in slow motion and muttered, 'Interesting.'"

"Ever since Big John Studd returned, he and André the Giant have been on a collision course." The words were spoken by commentator Jesse "The Body" Ventura during a break between television matches. "It's just so obvious to me. When Studd was in the ring before, it seemed he was wrestling for a one-man audience: André. Studd spent his hiatus from wrestling perfecting new techniques, and he wanted André to know it. When the referee raised Big John's hand, I thought he was going to grab the microphone and say, 'Look who the giant *really* is.'"

Gorilla Monsoon agrees: "André and Studd both have their concepts of what a giant should be. Although size plays a part of it, the word 'giant' to them means totally domination. André and Studd both have the power, the talent, and the experience to rise to that position. Each sees the other as the biggest obstacle to gaining that achievement."

André claims otherwise. "Big John Studd does not stand in my way," insists the man-mountain from the French Alps. "He is just another wrestler, and I am the giant of professional wrestling." He thrusts his arms forward, intertwines his fingers and shakes, choking an imaginary foe. "This is what I would do to Big John Studd." His eyes pop out, and a grimace sweeps across his face. "I would leave him lying in the ring, knowing what it is like to lose to a real giant."

Heenan, the Giant's manager, says he is uncertain that Studd is even qualified to wrestle André. "A member of the Heenan Family does not just sign on the dotted line to go against some slouch. You have to prove yourself to get in the ring with one of my men. And I'm not so sure that Big John Studd has proved anything. He just burst onto the scene, making these outlandish claims about who he is and what he's done. He was so busy lying, I'm surprised he didn't say that he invented the cure for polio. André is a legend of professional wrestling—the one and only true giant—and he might not want to dirty his hands with this untested scrub."

"Untested?" Studd rages. "Heenan must be living in fantasy land! If I recall correctly, you didn't see André's arm raised at the *Royal Rumble*. Millions of people watched me win the match—long after André was eliminated. That's a giant? To me, it sounds like a fraud."

"With the type of animosity that exists between these two, I think the rulebook would be left at home," Monsoon states. "I expect André and Studd to fly at each other from the opening bell, with putting the opponent out of action taking precedence over a clean victory. Remember, a lot is at stake here. Whoever comes out on top wins bragging rights to the term 'giant.'"

"I'll be watching this one very closely," Hulk Hogan admits. "The Hulkster's wrestled both men and knows how deadly each can be. When either grabs hold of you, it feels like you're about to split in half. They're that strong! When André the Giant and Big John Studd lock horns, it'll be a nuclear explosion. Only one man will walk out of the mushroom cloud after it's all over. And everyone will call him 'giant.'"

Tensions mounted in February as Studd was named special guest referee for André and Roberts's match at *WrestleMania V,* making it the first official confrontation between the two men vying to be recognized as the true giant of World Wrestling Federation. With Studd wearing stripes and Damien slithering in his sack outside the ring, the deck would be undeniably stacked against the indestructible Giant at the annual extravaganza.

ANDRÉ VS. TITO SANTANA & JIM POWERS

The unlucky babyface team enters first, seeming unaware that they are the victims of this two-on-one Handicap match. "What a match this is gonna be," says Jesse Ventura as André comes to the ring. "Yes, it's gonna be a great one," agrees Vince.

Santana and Powers go right for André, but receive a noggin knocker almost instantly. André begins choking Santana, as Powers tries to break it by hitting his huge back with a series of ax-handles. André tosses Tito aside and grabs Powers in a bearhug.

Vince McMahon notes, "There's someone out there in the wings looking forward to being a guest referee."

"André," says Big John Studd via remote, "I understand you're very concerned that I'm the special referee in your match with Jake 'The Snake' Roberts in *WrestleMania V*. Well, you can count on one thing, I can't be pushed around, and I won't be intimidated, and I guarantee you there will be a winner!"

Meanwhile, the Handicap match continues, with Santana and Powers double-teaming André into the corner. André headbutts Santana to the mat. Powers throws an ax-handle to the Giant's chest, followed by punches to the midsection. For his trouble, he receives a headbutt of his own.

"That's the Eighth Wonder of the World in there," says Jesse Ventura. "The master of the Battle Royals. You think he ain't ever been double-teamed before?"

"He's been double-teamed, triple-teamed, and every other kind of teamed," McMahon acknowledges.

André is taking the double-team efforts with a grain of salt, getting in his offense when he can. He takes Powers's arms and pulls them back, and then drives a headbutt between his shoulders. Santana flies in, throws a few punches, and hits a dropkick, almost sending André over the ropes. Powers nails a dropkick of his own, and now André is reeling on the ropes. But André quickly regains his momentum and stacks Santana and Powers into the corner, crushing into them with a series of shoulders.

Suddenly, Jake Roberts's music hits, and his voice is heard in the arena. *"André. Damien and I are watching you! Come on, André. Where am I? You never know where we're gonna be."*

Heenan searches around the ring while André continues working on his opponents.

"But sooner or later, André," Roberts's disembodied voice continues, *"Damien will strike. Just like I will."*

Heenan accuses Howard Finkel of having something to do with Roberts's presence, but the ring announcer shakes his head, denying any knowledge. Santana and Powers take advantage of the moment, coming at a distracted André from behind. He turns and grabs them both in a double bearhug. He lets go, tosses Santana into the ropes. A sunset flip fails, but a clothesline from Powers knocks the Giant backward. Santana takes a leg as Powers covers, but André tosses him off at one. André gets up, headbutts Powers, and whips into Santana, sending Tito rolling out through the ropes. André—gingerly—drops an elbow on Powers, and three seconds later, it's over at 3:32.

Heenan holds André's arm up as Roberts's voice is heard again. *"André, be careful where you step, my man. You never know where Damien might be."*

André looks around, disconcerted by the possibility of confronting Damien.

"We're watching you, André," the Snake goes on. *"Both of us are watching you, all the time."*

January 25, 1989: Veterans Memorial Coliseum, Phoenix, AZ

LORD ALFRED HAYES INTERVIEWS ANDRÉ AND BOBBY HEENAN

"I want to show you all," the Brain begins, "just how much fear Jake 'The Snake' Roberts has for this man. When they asked us to sign the contract for *WrestleMania V*, against Jake 'The Snake,' they asked for a stipulation about a special referee. I said, 'Sure, we'll have a special referee. You can throw whoever you want in there!' but I never thought for one moment it would be six-foot-ten, 390-pound Big John Studd! Now this man, and I use that term loosely, is nothing but a

backstabbing, ungrateful lowlife! I took him to the heights of professional wrestling, I made him exactly what he is today, but that's all
right! Because I'm a bigger man, and I'll tell ya something, Lord
Alfred Hayes, André the Giant is definitely a bigger—"

The crowd pops as Studd comes to the platform. "Uh-oh," notes
Gorilla Monsoon. "Big John is on his way. Take a look at that bohe-
moth [sic]."

Studd stands on the bottom step and stares eye-to-eye with
Heenan. As he climbs up to the platform, the Brain scurries to safety
behind André. The Giant and his old rival stare each other down, with
André still the bigger man. André sucks on his teeth, showing no fear
and slight boredom at the thought of facing Studd once more. He
grins as Monsoon wraps the segment, saying, "Not a whole lot of dif-
ference in size between these two guys. What a referee Big John
Studd is gonna make."

January 29, 1989: Los Angeles Sports Arena, Los Angeles, CA

ANDRÉ VS. JAKE "THE SNAKE" ROBERTS

André refuses to get in the ring as long as Damien is in the corner.
"No way," he says, shaking his head as he walks back up the aisle.
After some discussion with Roberts, referee Joey Marella trots toward
the locker room to settle the issue. André comes halfway to the ring,
and Marella explains to Roberts that his snake will have to go. Jake
stomps his foot but ultimately places Damien under the ring.

André comes to the ring, lifts up the apron, and demands Damien
be farther away. "All the way," he tells officials, gesturing his desire
for the snake to be far out of Roberts's reach.

André climbs between the top ropes, and before he can stand up,
Jake hits him with a knee to the face. The Giant reels back and gets
his arms tied up in the ropes. Roberts begins choking André. Marella
breaks the choke, but Jake throws a series of shots to the seated
Giant's forehead. Jake goes to the apron, planning to fetch Damien,
but the ref stops him. Meanwhile André sits on the mat, trapped in

the ropes, terrified of Damien. Prevented from getting his snake, Jake goes back to choking André. He then quickly goes out to the floor, but the ref promises to disqualify him if he brings Damien into the ring.

Jake comes back in. Marella frees André from the ropes, and the Giant immediately wraps a big hand around Roberts's throat. Holding on the top rope for support, André—on his knees—brings Jake down to the canvas, putting all his weight on Roberts's neck. He then stands erect on Roberts's solar plexus, though he keeps a grip on the ropes for balance. André steps off, but clamps a big boot down on Roberts's hand. Holding his hand down, the Giant grabs a fistful of Roberts's hair and pulls him up, stretching his arm. He removes his foot, allowing Jake to stand up, and then hits a hard chop before wrapping both hands around Jake's throat.

Jake breaks the choke with shots to André's midsection, and then forces André into the corner with a series of rights. The Giant—holding himself up by gripping the rope—pulls Roberts's hair, but Jake gets loose and starts pummeling André with lefts and rights. Roberts turns away for a split second, and André grabs his hair, pulling it around and in for a headbutt. Roberts goes down, his head on the apron under the bottom rope. André sees the opportunity and steps on the bottom rope, strangling Roberts under it.

Marella breaks the choke, and as André argues, Roberts rolls toward the center of the ring and catches his breath. He gets up, but André is right there. He grabs Roberts's throat and pushes him back against the top rope. He chokes him repeatedly, then jerks Roberts back so he slingshots forward across the ring. Jake is still on his back, giving André time to come to the other side of the ring.

Holding the top rope with both hands, the Giant drops a sit-down splash onto Jake's chest, his face nonchalant. Roberts gasps for breath, holding his battered ribs. André stands over him, gesturing for Roberts to get up and face him. He wipes sweat from his huge brow and flicks it down on the squirming Snake. Roberts reaches up for help and André assists, only to headbutt him as soon as Jake is on his feet. A chop sends Roberts to the corner, setting up André's back-splash and series of shoulders to the midsection.

André jaws a bit with the ref, and when he goes back, Roberts

manages to land a forearm across the Giant's shoulders. André reels, stung, down to one knee. Roberts attempts the DDT, but André shoves him away, pulling himself up with the rope. Still maintaining his hold on the top rope, André drops to a knee and chokes Roberts. The ref counts to four repeatedly, but André keeps returning to the

Jake Roberts and Damien keep the Giant at bay.

choke. Eventually he decides to lift Roberts up by his hair, chopping him into the corner for another backsplash. André crushes his weight back on Roberts.

Marella and André debate the legality of the move, giving Roberts time to climb up on the middle rope. He leaps, barely hitting

André with a forearm. Nevertheless the Giant goes down, flat on his back. Jake rolls out and goes for Damien. As André gets to his feet, Roberts opens the sack and tosses the serpent into the ring. André howls and falls back. Jake takes Damien and winds it around the flailing Giant. André rolls out and onto his feet, the snake wrapped tight around his wrist. André jerks himself free and stumbles away up the aisle as the bell rings, the winner of the match via DQ at 7:32. Roberts is in the ring, his hand bleeding profusely from a snakebite.

FACE TO FACE W/ANDRÉ, BOBBY HEENAN, JAKE ROBERTS, AND BIG JOHN STUDD

Vince McMahon moderates a *Face to Face* debate between the *WrestleMania V* protagonists. Two podiums are arranged in classic debate fashion.

"With me at this time, Bobby 'The Brain' Heenan [furious boos from the crowd, prompting André to clap for his manager] along with the Eighth Wonder of the World, André the Giant [more boos].

"At *WrestleMania V*, with Big John Studd as the guest referee, André the Giant will meet *Jake 'The Snake' Roberts*!"

"He better not have that snake with him," Heenan says, as André grabs Vince by the shoulder. "He better not have a bag with him!"

Roberts is indeed carrying his sack. André is enraged and points a finger in McMahon's face. As Jake approaches the platform, André steps behind Heenan. "You tell him that bag goes back right now!"

Jake places his bag on the platform. Vince backs away, as does André.

"You better back up," Heenan says to McMahon. "You better get somebody out here. Somebody to control this man!"

"Gentlemen, gentlemen," Vince says in an attempt to restore order.

André is howling "No! No!" while pointing at Jake's sack.

"You're safe, André," McMahon says. "The snake is next to a police officer and is fine. May we please have ninety seconds for Jake 'The Snake' Roberts? Go ahead, please."

Jake leans on his podium like a politician. "In any contest, in any physical matchup, we have comparisons. I do not match up with this man's size. In fact, the last time he was my size, he was a fetus. You understand that?"

André begins to interrupt, but Heenan manages to back him away from the mic.

"Hey, come on. I've got my time. I got my time. But you know something, every man, every woman, every child, has something inside that makes them snap. Whether it be deep water, dark rooms, or whatever's in the closet, or maybe what's underneath the bed. Your problem is in that bag. I know that. In *WrestleMania V*, John Studd will be the special referee. The reason he is that special referee is because we need somebody in there that can keep the rules down the middle. I don't like John Studd, you don't like John Studd. There's no favoritism. All I want is a fair shot at you, my man, because you use the same style every time. You put those big hands around some-body's neck and you choke the life out of them."

Though André has been bellowing unintelligibly throughout, it is Heenan who rebuts. "You want a fair shot?"

"Wait just one moment, please," interrupts moderator McMahon. "We would like to hear from André the Giant. Your rebuttal?"

Heenan ignores Vince and proceeds. "You want a fair shot? It's simple. We don't need no John Studd. We don't need anybody! If you are man enough, scum, if you are man enough, you wouldn't have to bring a bag! You wouldn't have to bring some poisonous reptile to the ring! If you had one little bit of wrestling ability, if you had it down here, you'd get in the ring with this athlete! But no, you wanna bring some poisonous snake into the ring! So fine! Then we're gonna have to handle matters our way! And you know our way is the only way we handle things!"

"Mr. Heenan," says Vince, "Big John Studd is the guest referee. He will be impartial—"

"Oh, yeah, McMahon. He'll be impartial. He used to be a member of the Family, until he got stupid! You think he's gonna give me a fair shake? You think he's gonna give him a fair shake?"

"That's not fair," André rants. "It's two against one!"

"Intimidation has always been the key," notes Roberts as Studd comes to the platform. "You intimidate by size, and I intimidate by the snake."

Studd stands between the podiums, and Heenan lights into him. "You don't belong out here! Get outta here and leave now! You hear me!"

"A comment, please, from the guest official, the guest referee in this matchup. John Studd."

"I'm Big John Studd! I can't be pushed, I can't be shoved, and I can't be intimidated! And when I step over that top rope, the referee in one of the most important matches in the world, I will be impartial! You won't shove me—"

"I will tell you one thing," André says, getting into his longtime nemesis's face. "You come in that ring and you better do your job! Because I come down that way to put him down, and you better count one, two, and three!"

"When I step in that ring, I'll do my job and both of you do your job, and I'll be the referee and I'll *raise*, I'll *raise* the winner's hand! Do you understand?"

"A parting word from Jake 'The Snake,' please," asks Vince.

"I'm gonna have one helluva night come Sunday, April 2, my man. All I want is you!"

"*WrestleMania V* will be the last time you put your feet in that ring," growls the Giant. "That be your *last time!*"

"Gentlemen, thank you very much. Thank you very much. Best of luck to André the Giant, Bobby 'The Brain' Heenan—"

"Tell you what, André," Roberts says. "Don't leave just yet, okay. I wanna give you a little good-bye present."

He reaches for the snake. André grabs the podium to protect himself and walks off the platform, escaping just as Damien is loosed.

SATURDAY NIGHT'S MAIN EVENT: RICK RUDE VS. BRUTUS "THE BARBER" BEEFCAKE

"Ravishing Rick" Rude and his manager Bobby Heenan take on Brutus "The Barber" Beefcake in a match to establish Beefcake as the official barber of World Wrestling Federation. "Will that position be permanent," asks Mean Gene, "or will Booby Heenan and Rick Rude see that it's a washout?"

Beefcake and Rude battle back and forth until at 4:10, André arrives. He chats with Heenan. Though Beefcake is distracted by the Giant, he catches Rude in an inverted atomic drop, his knee right in the chin of the Ultimate Warrior (emblazoned on the rear of Rude's tights). He whips Rude into the corner, but the Ravishing One gets a boot up, and Beefcake goes down.

"I don't know why André the Giant is out at ringside," wonders Vince McMahon. "He has no business being there."

"Why?" responds Jesse Ventura. "He's a member of the Heenan Family. That gives him business to be at ringside. The Heenan Family is very close. Lookit, he's not doing anything."

Rude tosses Beefcake through the ropes to the floor. André smiles and hits three sit-downs on Beefcake's back, then lifts him erect to choke him out. Heenan watches from the steel steps, grinning and clapping gleefully. Rude distracts referee Dave Hebner as André squeezes Beefcake's breath out.

The crowd pops for Jake "The Snake" Roberts's arrival with Damien. André sees Roberts and his sack and releases Beefcake. Rude drops an elbow from the apron, directly between Roberts's shoulders as Jake tries to free Damien. Rude rolls Jake into the ring and begins punching away. Hebner calls for the bell at 5:45.

André climbs in and catches Roberts, holding his arms wide open for a beatdown by Rude. He turns him around and headbutts him, Rude now taking hold of the Snake's arms. André chops and chokes, Rude punching at Roberts's midsection. André grips the Snake's throat while Rude rakes his eyes. Beefcake gets back in and pulls Rude off, though André keeps pushing Roberts's throat into the top rope.

Beefcake clotheslines Rude over the top, and then tries to stop André with shots to his big back. An annoyed André turns and chops at Beefcake, taking him down with a headbutt. With a boot, he rolls Roberts off the apron and chops and chokes Beefcake, a wide grin across his face.

Heenan's jaw drops as Big John Studd saunters down the aisle. Studd enters the ring. André lets go of Beefcake and turns to face him. The two giants stare each other down. From the outside, Jake pitches Damien between the two big men. André bolts out of the ring, grabbing onto Rude for support.

February 16, 1989: Hershey Park Arena, Hershey, PA

"MEAN" GENE OKERLUND INTERVIEWS ANDRÉ AND HEENAN

Mean Gene begins by saying, "Bobby Heenan, as manager for André, I've got to tell you, Big John Studd is going to be the special guest referee."

"Well, I don't like the idea of Big John Studd being involved in anything to do with Family business," the Brain says, resplendent in a gold-sequined bow tie. "He's a deserter, he's a turncoat, and he's an ingrate."

"He fired you," Okerlund notes.

"He didn't fire me—mind your own business. And if he gets out of line in any way, just like Jake 'The Snake,' they're gonna have to answer to André the Giant."

The Giant wraps his ham hocks around the Snake.

"André, I know it's a sensitive subject with you. Many say that you suffer from the fear of snakes."

"'Scuse me?" glowers André.

"A-a-are you afraid of snakes?" rephrases Mean Gene as André threatens him backward. "Ophidiophobia?"

André points a big finger in the face of the tuxedoed announcer. "I'm gonna tell you, don't mention that word! But just one thing I want to talk about. If John Studd gonna be in that ring as referee, they gonna try to hurt me, but believe me, I never lost a match in my life, I'm still undefeated, and that's the way *WrestleMania V*'s gonna be! For me, I will stay undefeated, because Jake, I will put you down. You maybe need the help from John Studd, but he don't scare me at all. Because I will choke the you-know-what outta him, ha ha ha ha!"

"Now wait a minute. John Studd's gonna be the referee. He's not gonna help Jake Roberts."

"I don't trust John Studd," Heenan says. "I don't trust anybody. And he better not try to help him. But Mr. Roberts, you're gonna need all the help you can find. You better bring five hundred bags, 'cause, pal, you get in the way of André the Giant, you come to the ring with that serpent in the bag, and if John Studd gets in our way at *Wrestle-Mania V*, I cannot be responsible for any of 'em."

"What happens, gentlemen, if that snake, Damien, gets out of the bag?" asks Mean Gene, cowering as André raises a huge hand at the mention of his slithering bête noir.

"I just promise you one thing," avows André, turning to the camera. "Jake, that will be your last match. *WrestleMania V* will be your last match!"

April 1989

"A GIANT PROBLEM: JAKE MUST PLAN A STRATEGY TO DEAL WITH ANDRÉ THE GIANT"

Since Jake and André are fated to meet in a confrontation in *Wrestle-Mania V*, the Giant and his manager, Bobby "The Brain" Heenan, have a problem. Just the fact that Damien is there in the bag, lying in

Jake Roberts feels André's wrath.

Jake's corner, could so unnerve André he might end up being easy pickings for Roberts. If Jake actually produced Damien out of the bag, André would be finished.

So, what are Heenan and André to do? Jesse "The Body" Ventura recently had some advice for them. "If Bobby Heenan can take care of Damien, then André will take care of Jake."

The prospect delights André and Heenan. "Oh, it would be good, Roberts," bellows André. "No Damien means no Jake Roberts."

"You see, Jake Roberts," spits the Brain, "all that it would take is for Damien to be missing for a while, and you'd be finished. You wouldn't be man enough to face André, the biggest, most destructive person in the world. Without Damien, peon, you'd just slither away like the creep you are."

"Ya see, André," says the Snake, "some people are afraid of things like empty houses. Some people are afraid of hard work. And some people, like you, are afraid of snakes. But you are more afraid than most. You pass out cold. I think your fear goes deeper than Damien. Because, deep down in your gut, you know I can take you out, big man."

The DDT is what Roberts relies on to finish off opponents. But applying it on André is not like applying it on any other wrestler. To make the maneuver work, Jake would have to get André in a front facelock. Given the Giant's overwhelming advantage in bulk and height, plus his awesome strength, facelocking him is a nearly impossible task.

All the while, moreover, Jake would have to keep out of the Giant's gargantuan grasp and stay away from his sledgehammer blows. If André managed to corner Jake, he would be battered by mighty fists and could end up in the crush of a titanic bearhug. Roberts could also be nailed by a Giant headbutt, which would certainly mean lights out.

"I would love to see the look on Jake Roberts's face if he were to meet André the Giant in the ring without that miserable serpent, Damien," shouts Heenan. "If President Jack Tunney weren't such a pushover, maybe Damien wouldn't even be around in the first place. But, Roberts, I have to say it. I am not going to be held responsible for what André the Giant does to you. I refuse to pay any of your medical bills. In other words, Roberts, you have just dug your own grave, pal!"

WRESTLEMANIA V: THE MEGA POWERS EXPLODE
ANDRÉ VS. JAKE "THE SNAKE" ROBERTS W/SPECIAL
GUEST REFEREE BIG JOHN STUDD

Studd comes to the ring, followed by André and Heenan. "No love lost between these two," notes Gorilla Monsoon as the two big men point angry fingers in each other's faces.

Jake comes out and places Damien in the corner. André grabs Roberts immediately, pounding his head into the buckle as the bell sounds. Jake grabs his head in pain, and it is revealed that the turnbuckle pad has been removed. André punches and chops, driving Jake down to the mat. Standing over the Snake, André drives his knee into Roberts's chest.

Lifting Jake by his hair, André wraps his big arms around for a facelock. Jake elbows his way out and forces André back against the ropes. He stuns the Giant with blows to the breadbasket, then rushes across the ring for Damien.

André is right behind him. He gets his arms around Roberts's neck and begins choking. Jake reaches up and back, gripping André's hair hard enough to make the Giant wince. André releases his hold, hitting a forearm to Jake's kidneys. Roberts returns fire, punching away at André's big belly, to little effect. After a big right from André, Jake swings wildly and falls backward toward his snake sack.

The Giant catches him by the hair and chops him toward the far corner, where he leans back and squashes the Snake. When Studd demands a break, André pulls a few inches away, and then laughingly falls back against Roberts. Studd counts, but André just drives his butt back into his flattened foe. He turns and wraps what Gorilla lovingly calls his "two ham hocks" around Roberts's throat, releasing the choke as Studd's count reaches four. He repeats the choke three times, finally chopping Roberts hard, and then goes to the ropes to confer with Heenan.

He returns to Roberts, who is down on the canvas, and drops a big butt on the Snake's chest. Jake reels toward the apron. André takes hold of the top rope and stands his full weight on Roberts's rib cage. The Giant laughs as Jake reaches up, begging off. André takes the wrist and lifts Roberts up, pushing him back against the exposed metal where the buckle pad should be.

Jake fires back, with chops, kicks, and punches. He shoots off the ropes and nails a clothesline, felling André, who gets tied up in the ropes. Studd, incidentally, doesn't even try to free him, as is the referee's role. Jake wraps his hand around André's throat, choking him as he springs back and forth in the ropes. He points toward Damien, but Studd tells him no, blocking his path. Roberts punches away at the trapped Giant's head, injuring his fist on André's epic skull.

At last Heenan frees one of André's arms, and he reaches out and catches Roberts by the throat. He powers Jake down, pushing him into his knee. A headbutt drops the Snake, and André demands that Studd begins to count him out. Jake gets to his knees and André grabs him by the traps. Jake gets to his feet, but André headbutts him between the shoulders, putting him right back down.

André chops him to the corner with the exposed turnbuckle and shoulderblocks him repeatedly. A knee catches the Giant in the sternum, and he rocks backward, falling to one knee against the ropes. The Snake gets some momentum, chopping and punching, then smashing André's head into the steel.

Though André is down, he still has enough left to drive a fist into Roberts's gut, doubling him over before he can get any offense going. André pulls himself up by the ropes and chops at the Snake, sending him out through the ropes.

Studd begins to count. Roberts climbs up to the apron, but André knocks him back down with his huge chest. Jake returns to the apron, where André headbutts him. Roberts grabs the top rope, but can't regain his balance and falls down to the mats. Studd reprimands André for not letting Jake into the ring, but André puts his hands on his hips and argues.

Meanwhile, Roberts is heading toward Damien. Heenan tries to get André's attention, but the Giant is deep in debate with Studd. Roberts comes up the steps holding the bag, but Studd is there to stop him. André shoves the ref from behind. Studd turns and shoves back, rocking André toward the other side of the ring. Heenan waves toward the back, and Ted DiBiase and Virgil run in to make the assist. DiBiase sucker-punches Roberts off the steps and steals away up the aisle with Damien. Roberts pursues, leaving André and Studd alone in the ring. Roberts and DiBiase go at it in the aisle, while André tries to choke out Studd, headbutting him between the shoulders over and over.

In the interim, Jake has retrieved Damien, and he unties the sack as he approaches the ring. André is choking Studd with his singlet strap when Damien is tossed into the ring. With a look of horror, André lets Studd free and escapes the ring. Studd calls for the bell, DQing André at 9:44.

TED DIBIASE: "Me coming out and stealing the snake, that was what set up my program with Jake. And then I wrestled him a year later at the next WrestleMania. It was a lot simpler then. I come out and steal a snake at WrestleMania V, and we have a program for a year."

The Brain and the Giant.

14

WrestleMania V marked the blow-off of André's program with Jake "The Snake" Roberts, while kickstarting the Giant's feud with Big John Studd. ■ André's limitations often precluded him from regular wrestling. As a result, he became a featured player in his own storyline. This is where André's membership in the Heenan Family proved most useful. The manager's stable of heels—

including Rick Rude and the Brain Busters, Arn Anderson & Tully Blanchard—provided a ready roster of wrestlers who could give cover to the Giant's diminishing role in the ring. In turn, it united André into lower-card storylines, giving high-profile bump to a second angle.

BOBBY HEENAN: *"André was pretty much crippled up by the end. I used to help him to the ring, he would put his hands on my shoulders to get up the stairs to the ring—I used to be six foot nine, you know, until he put his hands on me. At the end of the match, if André was down and couldn't get up quickly, I would take bumps from whomever—'Hacksaw' Jim Duggan, Jake 'The Snake' Roberts, Warrior—and get the crowd pumped."*

While they had few televised one-on-one matches, André and Studd wrestled frequently at house shows, usually culminating in a DQ finish thanks to interference from Heenan Family member Haku. Once part of the Heenan-managed tag team the Islanders, Haku had earlier crowned himself "King" of World Wrestling Federation, adopting the crown vacated by an injured Harley Race. However, Jim Duggan—an erstwhile rival of André's—had his eye on the throne as well.

The storylines collided in the weeks after *WrestleMania V,* as André and Heenan fumed about their mistreatment at the hands of Special Referee Studd.

March 7, 1989: Convention Center, El Paso, TX

"André the Giant," begins Studd, "when we met in *WrestleMania V,* in the center of the ring, and our eyes locked, the whole world could see that Big John Studd is every bit of a giant as you are. And when I looked in your eyes, André, I saw you flicker. I saw you start to flinch. I saw you feel that the legend of André the Giant is *threatened.* And when I turned my back and you grabbed me and you choked me down, that told me what kind of giant you are. That told me you're a giant with a real big yellow streak running down the center of your back. And when we meet, André—and we will meet in the center of the ring—I will pick you up, all five hundred pounds of you, and slam you to the center of the ring, André. And then I'll cover you, and it will be one-two-three! That's the end of the legend of André the Giant!"

"MEAN" GENE OKERLUND INTERVIEWS ANDRÉ & HEENAN

"Gentleman," Mean Gene Okerlund begins, "I've heard nothing but complaining and griping. You, Bobby Heenan, saying that Big John Studd is responsible for what happened to André the Giant—"

André angrily grabs Mean Gene by the lapels. "You're right, he's responsible," the Giant rages. "He is the worst referee I ever have. I know what I did in that ring and everything was legal! He disqualify me. So don't say he is a good referee."

He lets Okerlund down, and as the announcer regroups, Heenan takes over. "Y'know, it's pretty sad when a little pipsqueak like you stands here and thinks he can talk to this man like he's nothin'! I don't care and he don't care if you're three feet tall or you're six-foot-ten like John Studd. Now Studd was assigned to be a referee. Because he can't do a good job, that's not our fault. He wanted to stick his nose where it didn't belong, and you saw what happened! Okay, he disqualified this man. Fine. We can take that. But when he put those hands around the neck of John Studd, one thing went into Studd's mind. He knew that he was in the ring with a *giant*!"

"All right. André, where do we go from here with you and Mr. Studd?"

"Where do we go from here? I will tell you one thing," André says, pointing a finger in Okerlund's face. "I'm the only giant in the professional wrestling. And I will show him that, and he is going to find what kind of giant I am, because I'm coming in that ring, and John Studd, you are going to have a giant receipt. That's all I have to say."

André cuts off all further questioning, and the camera goes to black.

BIG JOHN STUDD VS. KING HAKU

Bobby Heenan takes the mic from a sky-blue-tuxedoed Mike McGuirk. "At this time, I want everybody to get out of their seats. I want you to get down on one knee and show a proper respect for the King of World Wrestling Federation, King Haku!"

Cue Big John Studd's entrance. The bell rings, and Haku tries to take Studd down with a barrage of chops and kicks. He even attempts a bodyslam, but Studd overpowers him and goes on the offense. A clothesline brings Haku down, followed by a big fist into the breadbasket. Studd whips Haku into the ropes, slingshotting him into an elbow. A big slam plants Haku on the canvas. Studd picks Haku up in a bearhug, tying his arms tight. Haku refuses to submit as André arrives. Studd flings Haku down and stares down André, challenging him to come into the ring.

Haku takes advantage of the distraction by nailing a crescent kick to the back of Big John's head, though he barely reached it due to the huge height differential. Studd drops face-first into the ropes, perfectly setting André up to choke his archrival on the middle rope. Haku kicks and chops at Studd's back as the ref counts, despite the obvious infringement. Finally, he calls for the bell at 2:19, awarding the match to Studd via DQ.

The beatdown continues until "Hacksaw" Jim Duggan arrives, two-by-four in hand. He cracks the wood across André's back, releasing Studd from the choke, and then gets into the ring to whack Haku. Duggan stomps around the ring—"Hooooooo!"—as Studd gets to his feet. Though still woozy, he calls out to André, demanding he return to face him. Nevertheless, the Heenan Family departs, reeling from the lumber attack.

KING DUGGAN VS. DAVE WAGNER

King Duggan—recently crowned after defeating Haku—enters with crown, cape, flag, and two-by-four.

"Finally we have a king we can be proud of," gushes Vince McMahon. "A king that we can look up to. A king who exemplifies sportsmanship."

Duggan takes out Dave Wagner in an instant, scoring the pinfall at 1:49—down, set, running clothesline.

As the bell rings, Heenan comes out and tries to steal Duggan's crown. Duggan comes down, grabs the Brain, and tosses him into the ring. Heenan begs for mercy as Haku arrives and runs into the ring. Duggan whips the Brain into the former King, and the manager rolls out between the middle ropes. Haku and Duggan begin trading blows.

André comes down and pulls himself up on the apron as Duggan gloats over beating Haku to the mat. He turns, sees the Giant, and attempts a clothesline, only to be caught in one of André's patented chokes. A headbutt knocks the King to the canvas. He lifts Duggan up, holds his arms behind his back, and Haku hits a crescent kick to the head. The official rings the bell to stop the mayhem.

Big John Studd comes down and takes out Haku. André head-butts Duggan, landing him in the corner for a Giant boot to the throat. Studd comes up behind André and readies a double ax-handle. André turns and hits a series of chops, but when he gets cocky, Studd drives his right fist right into his ample labonza. André doubles over and rolls out.

"I have never, ever seen André the Giant dropped with one single punch," says a shocked Jesse Ventura. "He caught him lucky, it has to be, McMahon. Has to be a lucky shot."

"Studd would not be chopped down by André," Vince McMahon says. "Just when André was gonna let him have another one, Big John Studd leveled the Giant."

"Must've been a low blow."

"It was not."

MICHAEL KRUGMAN

The two behemoths meet in the ring.

"Had to be," reiterates Ventura.

"It was not," argues Vince.

Duggan and Studd pose in the ring as André gets his breath back. He decides to go for Studd again, but as he climbs up onto the apron, he is stopped by the ref. Studd pushes the ref aside and clotheslines André, who rolls over the rope into the ring. André goes down, and Studd hits him with a forearm to the back. As André rises, he takes another clothesline that sends him down and out of the ring.

"I think André's had enough," says Vince.

THE BROTHER LOVE SHOW WITH BIG JOHN STUDD

"My guest this week is a man who has a giant problem," Brother Love says. "staring him in the face. He is Big John Studd. Brother Studd, you have stuck your nose into other people's business. Perhaps maybe where your nose does not belong."

"All right, hold it right there," Studd growls. "Not the way I saw it. I saw Haku and André the Giant stick their nose into King Duggan's business."

"Well, let me tell you one thing. People who stick their nose into André the Giant's business often end up with *broken noses*."

"Well, let's take a good look at this nose. Does it look broken? Let's take a good look at André the Giant. I saw him get tossed around like he's never been tossed around before, in his whole career!"

"I-I-I'll tell you something, I have never seen André the Giant manhandled the way that he was. But-but-but, he must've been sick! As a matter of fact, I know for a *fact* that André the Giant had a fever! He had a hundred-and-five-degree fever!"

"Well, he was sick, you're right," Studd yells. "He was sick of fear, of Big John Studd! And then he was sick of pain, when he felt this giant fist driven right into his ribs and dropped him to the floor!"

"I'll tell you one thing, you may have done it once, but I promise you, you will never manhandle André the Giant like that again!"

"I'll tell you what. Every time I step in the ring with André the Giant, I will chop him down like the giant oak tree that he is! And there'll be only one giant oak standing, and that's the Giant, Big John Studd!"

In June, the showdown came to a surprising conclusion at a TV taping in Madison, Wisconsin. The card saw André working two matches that day, first with Hillbilly Jim and later in a Tag Team match alongside Rick Rude against Jim Duggan & Ultimate Warrior. However, the real action was behind the curtain.

VINCE McMAHON: "Studd came to me because André was beating the shit out of him every night. Maybe not *beating the shit* out of him, but he was definitely roughing him up a little bit. Studd was scared to death that one day he's going to really piss André off and that's going to be it. He's going to die.

"We were doing television in Madison, Wisconsin. There was a rumor going around—the boys were stirring shit, that's part of the fun we have on the road—about how André was really going to beat the shit out of Studd because he had said something bad about André. And of course he hadn't said anything—André was working him. He had no intention of beating John up that night, although he didn't like him.

"Here's this six-foot-ten, 350-pound guy in my office, literally shaking. 'Vince, I can't do it, I just can't get in there. I'm scared to death of this man, he's going to kill me.'

" 'No, he's not. He's just working you, he's playing with you.'

" 'No, you don't understand, I heard it from the boys, he's really going to kill me. I can't do it. I'm quitting. I'm quitting the business.'

"And he walked out. He quit the business. It was the last I ever saw the guy."

After Studd's surprise departure, André agreed to help put over the World Wrestling Federation's rising star, Ultimate Warrior. Born Jim Hellwig—and now legally known as Warrior—he started out in Mid-South and Bill Watts's UWF before moving on to the Von Erichs' World Class Championship Wrestling in 1986. It was there that he took on the first incarnation of his character, performing as the Dingo Warrior. One year later he went to work for World Wrestling Federation, which refined his role and renamed him the Ultimate Warrior. His pastel-painted face, tasseled ring attire, incomprehensible promos, and perfect physical condition set him apart, masking his actual in-ring skill, which was mediocre at best. Regardless, Warrior became a fan favorite, moving quickly through the ranks until attaining the Intercontinental Championship from the Honky Tonk Man at *SummerSlam 1988.*

But before Warrior could make it to the main event, he needed one final crash course in the business, the kind of schooling only the Giant could provide.

BRUCE PRICHARD: "I don't think that André really cared too much for the human being Jim Hellwig. And he wasn't too keen on Hellwig's in-ring skills, which were very limited at best."

BOBBY HEENAN: "To me, the man had no idea about wrestling. Didn't care about the history of this business. Didn't care about anything. It was like the guy had just come out of a Gold's Gym and had a can of tuna and a raw egg and said, 'Hey. I just saw a WWE truck go by. I'm gonna call them, and I'm a wrestler.' He knew nothing. Nothing."

JIM "J.R." ROSS: "I don't think André liked him. I don't think André wanted to be in the ring with Warrior any longer than absolutely necessary."

Fortunately for André, his matches with Warrior tended not to last very long. The fast-paced encounters were seemingly more about Warrior's dramatic ring entrance than actual wrestling matches. Despite his open dislike of Warrior, the Giant accepted his role and allowed himself to be squashed in order to take the new star to the next level.

VINCE McMAHON: "Jim Hellwig learned how to treat the Boss, every night coming in the locker room with a nice bottle of wine. That was his way of showing respect for André so that André didn't kill him one night.

"The Boss was trying to teach Hellwig how to work. 'Slow down,' he told him, because if you get too fast during a match, the audience can't digest what you've just done. André told him a second time, 'Slow down.' Third time, Hellwig was going to tackle André, and of course he's going full speed, he had not slowed down. André didn't really hit him, he just stuck up an arm, and boom! Knocked Jim right out. 'Now slow down,' André said."

MICHAEL KRUGMAN

ANDRÉ (W/HEENAN) VS. ULTIMATE WARRIOR
FOR THE INTERCONTINENTAL TITLE

André and Heenan enter to huge heat. Howard Finkel, making the ring announcements, accidentally introduces "André the Ultimate Giant," which in many ways, he was. Within seconds, Heenan is jawing with referee Danny Davis. "Ladies and gentlemen, your attention, please," says Finkel. "I've been informed by the referee that unless Bobby Heenan leaves the arena [the crowd cheers], he must leave the arena at the count of ten [Heenan rants at Finkel], if he is not out of the arena, Mr. Heenan will be suspended!"

The crowd counts to ten as Heenan makes his way back up the aisle. "Good riddance to bad rubbish there, I'll tell you right now," says Hillbilly Jim, joining Gorilla Monsoon on commentary.

Finkel begins announcing Warrior, but the crowd noise nearly overwhelms him. The entrance music hits, and Warrior comes tearing out of the back, circling the ring as the Garden explodes. He goes through his usual gimmick, climbing onto the apron and shaking the ropes as André awaits. The Giant seems bemused by Warrior's hijinks, gesturing with a finger that this guy might be crazy. André takes hold of the top rope and mocks the ultimate entrance as Warrior climbs in and runs the ropes. Warrior sees and nails André from behind with a clothesline. The Giant reels and receives a second clothesline, which drops him to one knee.

Warrior runs the ropes as André rises and gets ready to attack. Unfortunately, he lumbers smack into a third clothesline, which fells him in the center of the ring. Warrior comes off the ropes and hits a big splash. Referee Davis counts to three, and it's all over in nineteen short seconds.

"It's unbelievable," says Gorilla. "This place is going bananas. André doesn't know what hit him."

Warrior, who has yet to stop running, skedaddles back to the locker room. The Giant, still in the ring, demands the microphone. "Stop the music!" he bellows, then turns to Danny Davis. "Wait a minute, what, why you count one-two-three? Why? Did anyone ring the bell to start a match? How come you count one-two . . . he don't even ring the bell! He don't even ring the bell to start a match, you don't have the right to count one-two-three!"

The Giant throws down the mic and heads for Davis, who wisely slips out and runs to the back. André, moving gingerly, follows as the fans boo mercilessly.

Perhaps the most memorable occurrence of the program happened outside the ring after a thirty-second match in Cedar Rapids, Iowa. Immediately following the match, André was arrested by the Linn Country, Iowa, Sheriff's Department on assault charges for his attack on local cameraman Ben Hildebrand, who had broken his promise not to shoot any of the in-ring action. A furious André had grabbed the camera cables and put a headlock on Hildebrand, who later went to the hospital with bruises. Though he didn't spend any time in jail, the Giant was required to post a $1,200 bond before being freed.

André and Warrior battled through late in the year, including a main event at *Survivor Series* that saw Ultimate Warrior clotheslining the Giant over the top rope, where he was counted out just twenty-seven seconds into the match. Though André and Warrior's matches were far from classics, the program fulfilled its mission. The feud with André gave Warrior the bona fides to move into the big leagues—he would confront Hulk Hogan at the *Royal Rumble 1990*, and the two went on to headline *WrestleMania VI*. André might not have entirely approved, but once again the Giant had done right by McMahon, doing his part to create what would be wrestling's hottest attraction for much of the early 1990s.

JIM "J.R." ROSS: "I think his series of matches with André around the country was truly what solidified Warrior in those markets. André the Giant was, and always will be, a legend in our business, and when some young guy comes in that has a unique look and a unique ring presentation and entrance and music and the whole presentation, and this new guy wins, and wins often and convincingly, it can't do anything but help André's opponent, in this case, the Warrior."

"MEAN" GENE OKERLUND: "The Ultimate Warrior's feud with André the Giant was something I thought that the office was gonna probably put on their list of real money-making projects. I don't think it made quite as much as they wanted it to, and to tell you the truth, I think André might have got up to here with the Ultimate Warrior."

TED DIBIASE: "I'm sure that that was one feud that he was glad that came to an end. Because André was so big that you had to be especially talented to be able to make people believe that anybody could beat you up. But André could do it. And he's asked to go out there and make this guy. From a business point of view, I understood. From a personal point of view, it made me sick. Absolutely sick. For one reason: I knew he [Warrior] didn't appreciate it."

The Giant raises high the Tag Team Championship, December 13, 1989.

15

Some celebrities are able to escape the spotlight with a pair of
dark glasses and a baseball cap. Unfortunately, those kinds of disguises were simply never feasible in André's case—it'd take much
more than just sunglasses to conceal the seven-foot-four Eighth
Wonder of the World. ■ While many of his wrestling peers would
avoid attention by slipping into the airport lounge, André had

been taught a valuable lesson from Vincent J. McMahon. A star attraction such as André the Giant was his own best advertising and should always be in a position where he could be seen by the paying customers.

Of course, the fans were always thrilled to meet and greet the one-and-only Giant, and André tried to oblige with a smile. But as his physical discomfort developed into constant pain and agony, André's ability to grin and bear the pressures of stardom began to fade and his disposition grew dark.

ARNOLD SKAALAND: "André was one of a kind. You would walk with him and everyone would look at him. It was hard for him, because he was always looked at."

DON MURACO: "André couldn't go anywhere. Everyone else, except for maybe Hulk, could at times be inconspicuous. But not the Giant. A giant is always a giant."

TED DIBIASE: "When you're seven-foot-four, 450 pounds, I don't care where you go, every eye is on you. It's like, 'Oh my gosh, look at this guy.' You add fame to that, and it just multiplies. Where's André gonna hide? How is he gonna disguise himself? He couldn't. And so everywhere he went there was a barrage of people constantly coming at him. Ultimately it got to where he couldn't take it."

RIC FLAIR: "When André got older, he got grumpy. He never got any peace. André was the most well-known sports celebrity in the world. Everyone knew him. He never had any peace, and that's what killed him. Never a day off."

By mid-1989, André was in very bad shape, barely walking other than when in the ring. He used a wheelchair to get from hotel to car to arena. His balance was so poor, he was forced to hold on to the ropes just to stay standing.

"The worse he got, the more he drank," Hulk Hogan wrote in his autobiography. "You could tell because he smelled of alcohol, and he was always unhappy when you talked to him. He was in a lot of pain. There was just nowhere the guy could be comfortable, especially now that he was crippled and hurt. His life was just miserable."

JACK BRISCO: "It was hard for me to watch him. I just felt so bad for him. It was so hard to see him in that kind of pain, the way he was struggling to get around. He tried to cover it all he could. He never would admit that it was bothering him. He didn't want anybody feeling sorry for him."

MICHAEL KRUGMAN

TIM WHITE: "Just from refereeing, I've had both knees done, six shoulder operations. Now magnify that by ten or twenty times because of his size. Doing it as many years as he did, the body just breaks down. But the main thing was, he kept growing, so his spinal canal started closing as his girth got bigger and he got thicker and wider. It just started putting a lot of pressure on the spine, it was killing nerves and stuff all the way to his feet.

"At the very end, I was pushing him in a wheelchair through the airport, and I felt bad for him. He shouldn't be seen like this. I love the guy so much, I just felt bad that he was in so much pain and people were seeing him being wheeled by in a wheelchair."

Nevertheless, André was not yet ready to retire, so he paired up with Haku as the Heenan-managed Colossal Connection.

Haku—born Tonga Fifita on the South Pacific island of Tonga—began his career by studying sumo in Japan, but eventually turned to *puroresu* and All Japan Pro Wrestling. He spent the early 1980s wrestling in Montreal for Frank Valois before joining World Wrestling Federation in 1985. Upon teaming with the Tonga Kid as the Islanders, he adopted the name Haku. The Islanders split up after failing repeatedly to win the Tag Team titles, and Haku embarked on a singles career. As managed by Heenan, he usurped the crown from King Harley Race and feuded briefly with Jim Duggan and Hulk Hogan.

With a reputation as one of the toughest men in the business—he once bit the nose off a bar patron who mocked wrestling as "fake"—Haku was an ideal tag team partner for André.

HOWARD FINKEL: "André certainly was on the decline, so he needed Haku badly as a partner. I think by that time fans might have sensed that André's skills were starting to decline and deteriorate. His in-ring presence was always there, but his skills were limited at best."

The Colossal Connection was in part created to fill the void in the Heenan Family left by the departing Brain Busters, Arn Anderson & Tully Blanchard. As the stable's official tag team, André & Haku were in the championship hunt from the start, feuding immediately with the current title holders, Demolition.

The hottest tag team in the division, Demolition was comprised of Barry

"Smash" Darsow and Bill "Ax" Eadie, André's former partner in the Machines. Blackclad and facepainted, Demolition had been dominant figures in World Wrestling Federation since their debut in 1987, known for their aggressive style and bombastic personas.

The team won the Tag Team Championships at *WrestleMania IV,* titles they retained for a record-setting 478 days. Demolition may have started out as hard-edged heels, but they proved so popular with the fans they turned babyface by late 1988. Ax & Smash tangled with André at *Summer-Slam 1989,* as he joined forces with the Twin Towers—Big Boss Man & Akeem (formerly One Man Gang)—in a Six Man Tag match against Demolition & "Hacksaw" Jim Duggan.

André also contributed to the ultimate end of Ax & Smash's remarkable championship reign, throwing a steel chair into the ring to assist in Heenan's Brain Busters Three-Out-of-Five-Falls victory against Demolition on the July 1989 *Saturday Night's Main Event.* The program continued, with Demolition regaining the Tag Team titles just a few short months later. When both Anderson and Blanchard left World Wrestling Federation in November, the Colossal Connection essentially picked up right where the Brain Busters left off.

October 2, 1989: Civic Center, Wheeling, WV

THE BROTHER LOVE SHOW W/THE COLOSSAL CONNECTION

"You know, brothers and sisters, there are few men who are rougher or tougher than Brothers Ax and Smash of Demolition. And there are even fewer men who Ax and Smash have ever had to look up to. However, my guests this week are certainly rougher, without a doubt are tougher, and indeed, Brothers Demolition, you will look up to the Eighth Wonder of the World, André the Giant, and Haku!"

The Colossal Connection takes to the stage and is warmly greeted by Brother Love. "Welcome, Brother Brain."

"I've got a simple, simple statement to make," Heenan says with no preamble. "Maybe Ax and Smash, Demolition, are walking around right now with those Tag Team Championships of World Wrestling Federation, which belong to the Heenan Family! But I'm gonna guarantee you something, the titles are coming back, they're coming back to where they belong! Because with over eight hundred pounds, over seven-foot-five [pointing at André], and this man's ability [pointing at Haku], there's no way—no way!—that I can lose!"

"Yes, indeed, Brother Haku," Love says, giving Haku the chance to speak to his Samoan fans in his native tongue.

"And Brother Giant, they *will* look up to you."

"I will tell you something, Demolition. We will see who's going to be *demolished,* ha-ha-ha-ha!"

Brother Love starts to speak, but the Giant pulls the mic back. "I'm not finished! Because right now, Bobby Heenan put the best team in the world ever, and Demolition, you may be strong, you may be tough guys, you show that to everybody, but show that to us. Tell us how strong you are. We love to hear you! We *loooooove* to hear you, ha-ha-ha-ha!"

January 1990

"HEENAN SEEKS THE TAG TEAM BELTS AGAIN: CAN DEMOLITION COPE WITH THE COLOSSAL CONNECTION?"
by Keith Elliot Greenberg,

Although [Heenan] is convinced that André and Haku, known as the Colossal Connection, are the most brutal team, the World Wrestling Federation Tag Team belts remain firmly around the waists of Ax and Smash of Demolition.

"Yes, Ax and Smash happen to be the champions now. But when the Brain tells you that's only temporary, you'd be wise to take what he says at face value. There isn't a person alive who knows the company better than I do. I don't make idle predictions. I know that André and Haku are going to be the next champions. And I know this because they're the most deadly team around.

"The reason I paired up two wrestlers as vicious as André and Haku is Demolition's reputation. I don't take back any of the negative things I ever said about Ax and Smash, but they're two tough men to have survived at the top for so long. André and Haku, though—

fortunately for me—are tougher. If it weren't for biased refereeing in his matches against Hogan, André would unquestionably be the champion today. You show me any wrestler he's ever faced, and I'll show you a wrestler who knows what it feels like to be squashed into the mat. Haku is an expert in the martial arts and has no taste for sissies in professional wrestling. As rough as Ax and Smash are, they're two wimps compared with Haku. He could defeat both of them with one hand, while playing Ping-Pong with the other."

Supporters of Heenan's squad say the duo has the advantage due to one seven-foot-four-inch factor: André. "When you go into the ring against André, it's anything but one-on-one," says a wrestler who has both teamed with and fought against the Giant and wished to remain anonymous. "You are in a Handicap match. André's so big and so strong that it's as if you're fighting two or three men. And that's before he loses his temper. When André's angry, there's no safe haven. If you're unfortunate enough to be in there with him, your only defense is to close your eyes and pray."

However, both Ax and Smash have squared off against André before, in singles, tag team bouts, and Battle Royals. They believe he's as vulnerable as any other contender. "Everyone has his Achilles' heel," Ax claims, "and André has several. I think the biggest thing in his favor is intimidation. Some wrestlers just look at him and shiver. Well, you probably know that Smash and I are not just any two wrestlers. When we look at André the Giant, all we see is another victim."

Insiders say that Demolition realizes that André is a difficult man for an individual to fell. Therefore, Ax and Smash have been perfecting their brutal and unique teamwork maneuvers, the plan being to quickly overwhelm and vanquish the Giant.

If too much attention is placed on André, though, Demolition could be conquered by Haku. The coldhearted Polynesian executes his thrust kicks, chops, and flying headbutts deliberately; his goal is not only to strike at will but to maximize the amount of pain. . . .

Haku has no reservations about taking a firm stance in center ring and duking it out with both of his foes at once. One rumor coming out of the Heenan Family camp is that André plans to wear down both opponents for a fresh and pumped-up Haku, who will step through the ropes and put on a display of devastation.

"You think André can wear us down?" asks Smash. "We'll bust him open like a Christmas present. And when Haku starts trying his kicks and other fancy martial arts stuff, we'll bury him with an all-American beating!"

In their preoccupation with preparing for men as menacing as André and Haku, Ax and Smash could forget about the threat to their title posed by the smaller, weaker Heenan. While the manager's athletic abilities are questionable at best, his mind games are notorious. By distracting an opposing wrestler or referee, or slipping a foreign object into the ring, Heenan is an expert at creating a situation that can spell doom for his rivals.

THE COLOSSAL CONNECTION (W/BOBBY "THE BRAIN" HEENAN) VS. DEMOLITION FOR THE TAG TEAM CHAMPIONSHIPS

The Colossal Connection is billed as a total weight of 793 pounds. Haku and Smash go at it; Ax goes for André but gets a headbutt to the mat before André goes out to the apron. Smash goes to his corner, leaving Haku in the ring with Ax. Haku kicks and karate chops on Ax's neck, then lifts him up and chokes him on the top rope. He jerks the rope, popping it into Ax's throat, bouncing him backward. Haku whips Ax into the ropes and hits an elbow. He picks up the still-reeling Ax, drags him into the corner, and drives his head into André's.

"Oh, look at that!" shouts Vince McMahon.

"Drove him right into the skull, right into the cranium of the Giant," enthuses Jesse Ventura.

Ax is loopy, on all fours. A karate chop to the neck and a Haku kick force him closer to the ropes, allowing André to kick him with a big boot while Haku distracts the ref. A forearm to the neck puts Ax into the enemy corner. Haku follows with a chop to the throat. The ref tells Haku that those kinds of shots are off-limits, giving André a moment or two of unfettered choking. Smash runs in to make sure the ref is aware of the double-team efforts, but he is sent back outside.

The Colossal Connection victorious, December 13, 1989.

Amid the chaos, André climbs in and throttles Ax in the corner. Smash protests, but the ref doesn't turn to look. By the time the ref is paying attention, André's back outside and Haku has taken his place, choking Ax. The ref breaks the choke, and again, André takes advantage with an illegal kick right between Ax's shoulders. Haku goes back to work. Ax gets a couple of shots in, but Haku rakes his eyes, pulls him in for a backbreaker, and covers for two when Ax kicks out.

Haku pummels Ax's back with chops and kicks, stopping occasionally to taunt Smash. André tags in; a big right keeps Ax from gaining his feet. André picks him up and starts choking him from behind, and Ax's tongue lolls out. He shoves Ax into a corner and batters his belly with shoulderblocks.

André tags Haku and then leans back onto Ax, crushing him. Haku gets set to charge, André moves, but Ax manages to quickly slip away. Haku goes belly into the post, then down. André pays a visit to Smash's corner as Ax and Haku crawl on the canvas. Ax reaches for Smash, but Haku gets up and kicks him in the ribs. Haku hits a couple of forearms, and then whips Ax into the turnbuckle. He charges, but Ax gets his elbow up and takes Haku down hard. He tries to reach Smash, but Haku gets up and punches him in the gut. He pushes Ax back toward André. He hits a straight-finger jab to the throat, then attempts a karate chop. Ax ducks and catches the spinning Haku from behind. He lifts Haku for an inverted atomic drop, but in doing so, allows Haku to tag the Giant in.

André grabs Ax from behind with two fistfuls of hair, then headbutts the back of Ax's skull. A second butt, and then back to the choking. Smash runs in to make the save. Haku goes after him, but Smash battles him into the corner. The ref breaks it up and brings Smash back to his corner, as André holds Ax's arms behind his back. Haku plants a crescent kick to Ax's throat, André drops an elbow, covers for three. Smash tries to pull André off at two, but it's too late. The Colossal Connection wins the World Wrestling Federation Tag Team Championships at 4:35.

André and Haku pose with the title belts, drawing major

heat. Smash tends to his fallen partner, but André splits them up with a whack from the title belt. Smash runs out and returns with a chair, nailing André's back as he climbs out between the ropes.

"I told ya! I told ya! I told ya!" gloats Heenan, surrounded by the new Tag Team Champions. "New World Wrestling Federation Champions, the Colossal Connection!"

"What a way to start the year!" declares André.

"What a way to start the year!" agrees Heenan.

"Happy New Year!" celebrates Haku.

"Happy New Year!" repeats André, gifting Heenan with the Tag Team Championship belt.

"Oh, thank you," says the manager. "Let me take this one too!"

"We did it!" brags André. "We did it!"

Winning the Tag Team titles marked a rare event in the Giant's storied history, his second-ever title victory in World Wrestling Federation. Of course, the purpose of titles is for them to be defended, and a rematch was slated for the upcoming *WrestleMania VI*. But first, André & Haku and Ax & Smash would meet up in the ring during the annual free-for-all at the *Royal Rumble*.

ROYAL RUMBLE

André, accompanied by Heenan, enters at number 11. The Warlord goes after him immediately, punching the Giant in the chest, leading him back toward the ropes. Backed up on the ropes, André headbutts the Warlord and tosses him over the top. As André walks around the ring, holding on to the ropes, Warlord's manager Mr. Fuji gets up on the apron to complain, but Heenan yanks him down. The two argue, with the Brain making clear that his man has taken down Fuji's man.

Meanwhile, André is giving Dusty Rhodes and Roddy Piper a noggin knocker, and then pushes his back against a polka-dotted Rhodes in the corner. The Giant grabs Piper and stacks him on top of Dusty. Four shoulderblocks are followed by a brief comeback from Dusty and Roddy, but André quickly gets them both into headlocks. Another noggin knocker sends Dusty reeling to the opposite corner, while André chokes Piper against the turnbuckle. Piper digs his thumbs into André's eyes as Rhodes returns to the fray, throwing punches at the Giant as the buzzer sounds.

The Red Rooster runs down, right into Dusty, while André takes a breather in the corner. He then goes for Bret Hart. Meanwhile, Piper eliminates Bad News Brown, who then reaches into the ring and pulls out Piper. They battle up the aisle as André, the Hitman, and the Red Rooster continue in the ring. The buzzer sounds, and Ax runs in, hitting the ring just as André pitches the Rooster over the top. The Giant turns around and is immediately set upon by Ax, who pummels him in the corner. Double ax-handles drop André to his knees, allowing Ax to choke him against the middle rope. André gets free and stands in the corner. He kicks a big boot to Ax's belly. Ax goes down, but André is assaulted by Dusty. Ax and Dusty double-team the Giant, who falls and gets tied up in the ropes. They hit double elbows to the top of André's head, then a series of straight shots. They signal to the crowd their intent to send the Giant over the top. They free his arms, which turns out to be a strategic mistake. André pops both of his opponents in the midsection, doubling them over and sending them to the corners.

The clocks ticks down, and Haku comes down and goes right after Ax. He whips him across the ring, slingshotting him into a clothesline. André holds on to the ropes for support, but is able to kick the fallen Ax, then crushing him with a sit-down. He then stands on Ax's chest, accidentally stepping on Ax's left hand as he dismounts. Ax gets up, and he and André choke each other in the corner. André gets Ax's arms behind his back, and Haku throws chops and a crescent kick. Hart grabs Haku and tries a headbutt, but is instead stunned himself by the Samoan's skull.

One hand on the ropes, André chops at Ax, leading him to the corner for some shoulderblock as Smash arrives. He, of course, heads right for André, and Demolition begin to double-team the Giant, dropping him to the mat. Haku tries to make the save, but instead receives the wrath of Demolition. They whip him into the ropes and a double clothesline, allowing André a moment or two of rest against the post. Demolition goes for him, but gets a pair of noggin knockers. Dusty tries to get Haku over, but André breaks it up and starts choking the Dream. Dusty pokes André's eyes to break it up, and the Hitman takes his turn, choking André against the turnbuckle.

Akeem is the next to enter, and he goes right to André with double ax-handles to the back. André pauses against the ropes but is then the victim of a Demolition clothesline. Haku tries to interfere but receives the same treatment. André gets up, holding the ropes, his back to the ring. Demolition sees their opportunity and together shove the Giant over the top to the apron and then the floor. They then try to throw Haku over, but André reaches over from the floor and breaks it up. The ref sends André to the back as Haku fights both Ax and Smash on his own.

The battle continues, with Haku ultimately eliminating Smash before being disposed of by the *Rumble*'s eventual winner, Hulk Hogan.

BOBBY HEENAN: "Demolition, you guys proved a lot to me and to André and Haku. You've shown us that you're two tough, well-conditioned athletes who never take a step backward. You've shown us that you have a great amount of courage and strength. But you've also shown us that you possess greater amounts of stupidity. Seriously, do you two humanoids think for one second that you can beat the

André demolishes Ax.

Colossal Connection? Well, if you think you can, then come on down, because I guarantee you that at *WrestleMania VI* you guys won't walk out of the ring. You'll be carried out! Demolition, you're done for."

THE BROTHER LOVE SHOW W/THE COLOSSAL CONNECTION

"Thank you, brothers and sisters," Love says, flanked by Heenan and the Colossal Connection. "It is an honor to introduce to you the Tag Team Champions, André the Giant and Haku, the Colossal Connection! Brother Brain, at *WrestleMania*, the Colossal Connection will be defending the titles against a very determined Demolition."

"Brother Love, we have a problem here. And the problem is Demolition. It seems we have what they want. Well, it belongs to the Family. It belongs to the Colossal Connection. And I have right here, the problem solvers. I guarantee it."

"Brother Haku?"

"I have to say, dream on! Because this is belong to the Colossal and will stay with us!"

"And Brother Giant, I'm sure you're going to *looooooove* destroying those painted-up pansies."

"Anytime," agrees André. "And just like Bobby Heenan said, the Colossal Connection belong to the Bobby Heenan Family. . . . To remind you, Demolition, you will be the *ex*-champion, and you will *stay* the ex-champion."

"One more thing," adds Heenan. "I know you love love, Brother Love. But there is no love right now in the Heenan Family. There's nothing but *hatred* and *disgust* for Demolition. So it's simple—if you want, you come and get it! And if you think you can get it, it belongs to you! But like I said before, we have a problem and we're going to solve that problem at *WrestleMania VI*, I guarantee it!"

André grabs the mic. "It's only a small problem, Bobby. Don't worry about it, ha-ha-ha-ha!"

He puts his big hand on Heenan's shoulder, consoling his angry manager, and they leave.

For the first time ever, *WrestleMania* was held at a building outside the United States—Toronto's SkyDome. In attendance for the event were 67,678 fans, setting an arena attendance record that has yet to be broken.

WRESTLEMANIA VI: THE COLOSSAL CONNECTION VS. DEMOLITION

Before the match, Mean Gene interviews the Colossal Connection. Heenan holds André's title belt. "I'm standing here with the World Wrestling Federation Tag Team Champions, the awesome force of the Colostomy Connection."

André and Heenan, who had been smiling, turn angrily to Okerlund.

"Hey! Hey! Hey, Baldy," the Brain says, "what did you call them?"

"The Colossal Connection."

"No, you didn't."

"What did I say?"

"Never mind," decides Heenan, and then turns to the business at hand. "But if you wanna talk evacuation, fine. Because that's exactly where Demolition is headed."

"That's right," agrees André.

"They're headed straight to the treatment plant," the Brain continues. "And gentlemen, we know how we're going to treat them, don't we?"

In unison, the Connection answer, "We're going to eliminate them."

André laughs his booming "Ha, ha ha, ha!"

"C'mon," Heenan says, "let's get moving."

"All right," wraps up Okerlund, "the Colossal Connection. They're anything but regular guys."

In the locker room, Sean Mooney interviews Demolition.

"Eliminate us?" yells Ax. "Well, let me tell ya why they call me the

Ax. Because I can cut down the biggest redwood there is. Even if he is seven-feet-four, 500 pounds. And I'll shear the limbs off that Polynesian oak. But just before I finish chopping 'em down, I'm gonna stand back, look at 'em, and yell, 'Timber!'"

"That sounds pretty good," screams Smash. "But let me tell ya what I'd like to do to André the Giant and Haku. I'd like to throw 'em in the back of a semi tractor trailer, get behind that wheel, push the pedal to the metal, and drive 'em straight off a cliff and watch 'em smash into smithereens."

"Gentlemen, this is beginning to sound like a demolition derby," notes Mooney.

"Now you're catching on," snarls Ax as Smash grins. "Because that's exactly what happens every time Demolition's in the ring. And this match is no different. We're out to demolish and destroy!"

"And after the match is all over," adds Smash, "the only thing that's gonna be salvageable from that scrap heap will be the metal we're gonna use to forge our new Tag Team Championship belts, *haaaaaaaa*!"

In the ring, the Colossal Connection is introduced—total combined weight, 793 pounds.

Demolition enters via cart and removes their leathers. The masks come off, and the Connection attack, André on Ax, Haku on Smash. The bell rings. André headbutts Ax to the floor, then joins Haku in putting the boots—though in Haku's case, bare feet—to Smash. André goes to the corner. Haku shoots Smash, who avoids the chop and starts throwing punches. He drives Haku face-first into Ax's raised boot in the corner and makes the tag. Ax beats Haku down to his knees, then turns to taunt André. The Giant decides to enter the ring. He comes in and hits one big blow to Ax's shoulders before lumbering back out. The ref reprimands him, while Demolition double-team Haku.

Ax and Haku go toe-to-toe. Haku falls to his knees, and Ax claps his ears. Tag is made, and Smash comes in, driving a fist to Haku's midsection. Haku responds with a thumb to the eye. Haku shoots him into the ropes, but Smash blocks the hipblock attempt. He tries a backslide, but Haku counters, and the two wrestlers engage in a test of strength. Smash gets to his knees, and Haku's shoulders hit the canvas. Fortunately, André is there to make the save, kicking Smash to break the hold.

André goes back out. Smash brings Haku to the corner and tags in Ax. He whips Haku, who ducks and thrusts his fingers into Ax's throat. Karate chops and a backbreaker give the momentum to Haku, while André laughs at the ropes. Haku puts Ax down and gets a two-count. A thrust kick to Ax's chest sends him down again. Haku takes Ax's boots, spreads him wide, and kicks a shot downstairs. Ax crawls toward the apron, and Haku chokes him against the bottom rope. The ref calls for a break. Haku argues, so Heenan comes over and slaps Ax across the face.

Ax attacks André in the corner, but André headbutts him down. Haku hooks the leg and covers, but the ref arrives only in time for a two-count. On his feet, Ax tries to fight off Haku, but André reaches in and wraps an arm around his neck, holding him for Haku's gut punches.

Haku covers, but Ax gets his hand under the ropes. Haku drives Ax into André's head—barely—and Ax goes down. Hook of the leg gets two before Smash makes the save. A kick to the throat keeps Ax in trouble. Haku chokes him against the ropes. On his knees, Ax punches Haku below the belt but gets a thumb in his eye in return.

Haku keeps at it, going to work on Ax's traps with chops and a grip. Smash extends into the ring, but Haku chases him away with a kick. Smash comes in, and Haku chops Ax toward André as the ref is distracted. André chokes Ax with the tag rope while Haku goes to the ref to keep him busy. André throttles Ax, Haku making sure the ref continues to debate with Smash.

Haku comes back over, and Ax fires back to little effect as Haku chops him across the thigh and sends him to the canvas. He goes to work on Ax's leg with kicks and chops. He lifts Ax and hits a shoulder-breaker, hooks the leg, but Smash saves at two. Haku whips Ax to the far corner, but Ax gets a boot up. Clothesline gets him closer to Smash, and the hot tag is made.

Smash rams Haku into the turnbuckle, shoots him into an elbow, followed by a big back bodydrop. André comes in, but Smash punches him away. He shoots Haku into the ropes, drops down, and Haku runs straight into a clothesline from Ax. Demolition hit André

MICHAEL KRUGMAN

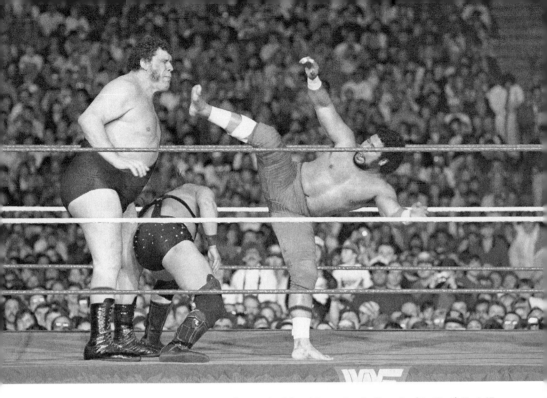

Haku costs the Colossal Connection the Championship, *WrestleMania VI*.

with a double clothesline, sending him down against the turnbuckles. They return to Haku, double-teaming him. The ref breaks it up, allowing André to grab Smash, holding him for Haku. Smash ducks, and Haku's kick hits André, sending him backward to get tied up in the ropes. A clothesline takes down Haku. Demolition lifts him and drops him, throat-first, onto the ropes. Decapitation finishes Haku, Ax covers, and the ref counts three at 9:15.

Heenan gets in the ring as Demolition leave with the titles. The Brain is furious, yelling at the ref. Fuming, he goes to André, shoving him in the shoulder, complaining and pointing at the Giant. André shakes his head, defending himself, pointing out how Haku kicked him in the face. Heenan chews him out, poking him in his chest.

"Do you hear me? I'm the boss!"

Heenan slaps André across the face, and André gets the cold face. He grabs Heenan's lapel and explains that Haku kicked him once again. Heenan keeps arguing, so André slaps him, a big right sending Heenan reeling. André kicks Heenan out through the ropes. Haku gets into position behind him, ready to kick as André turns. But the Giant catches Haku's foot and steers him back against the ropes. Chops and a headbutt drop Haku, and a kick sends him to the floor. Heenan and Haku rush toward the cart to escape, but André catches Heenan. A punch sends the Brain face-first into the steel steps. André gets into the cart and headbutts Haku out. He demands the cart leave, and André rides out of the arena to a tremendous ovation.

Later, Mean Gene interviews Heenan. "Family members, falling like the Berlin Wall. Bobby Heenan, I find that you're tougher to get along than a mother-in-law on a weekend visit to my house."

"Don't you concern yourself about getting along with me. I'm the easiest guy in the world to get along with. But when you're 540 pounds and you're seven-feet-four, and it takes two-and-a-half hours for the blood to reach the brain, you don't think real right—"

"Wait a minute, Bobby Heenan, where do you have the ball . . . the *nerve* to hit André the Giant in the face?"

"I'll tell you where I got the ba—the nerve to hit André in the face. You take orders from me! I'm the head of the Family! You listen to me, you go to the top! You don't listen to me, you're never heard from again. You have just committed, pal . . ."

Heenan pauses.

"What, are you lost for words for the first time?"

"No, I'm not! We lost the championship 'cause he stood on the apron, wouldn't get in the ring, wouldn't help Haku! Haku had to carry the load! Is he lazy? Is he incompetent? What? I'm through with him! I'm starting a *new* Family! I'm bringing in *new* members! Ones that will listen! Ones that will care about me!"

André tells the Brain who's boss, *WrestleMania VI.*

16

WrestleMania VI would be André's last televised match. He continued wrestling, just outside the World Wrestling Federation spotlight.
He teamed with Haku for a match against Demolition in Honolulu,
and then traveled to Japan where he partnered up with Giant Baba
against Ax & Smash in the main event of the World Wrestling Fed-
eration/All Japan/New Japan Wrestling Summit at the Tokyo Dome.

He returned to TV one year later at *WrestleMania VII,* assisting Big Boss Man in the melee that followed his match with "Mr. Perfect" Curt Hennig and Bobby Heenan. André's interference reignited the rift that had developed between the Giant and the Brain after *WrestleMania VI.* The Giant humiliated his manager on a *Prime Time Wrestling* segment in which André discussed winemaking with Vince McMahon, then forced Heenan to roll around in a tub of grapes. The story—never fully resolved after the events of the previous year—soon came to a head, with André finally severing his relationship with the Heenan Family.

March 12, 1991: Coast Coliseum, Biloxi, MS

MEAN GENE INTERVIEWS BOBBY HEENAN

"What about the state of the Bobby Heenan Family?" Okerlund questions.

"The Bobby Heenan Family has never been tighter," declares the Brain. "We've never been more united. We've never been happier."

"Well, that's not the impression that I've been getting as of late."

"Uh . . . like what?"

"Recently, on the World Wrestling Federation's prime-time television, I happen to think that André the Giant was expressing some negative feelings toward you."

"No, no way."

"What about the grapes?"

"You gotta understand something. André the Giant is the biggest member of the Family. We're like this. What happened with the grapes, that was just a little, kind of a put-on, to you and the people. Matter of fact, rolling around in grapes is very therapeutic. It's great for the elbows, it's great for the back, great for the skin! André and I, we don't have any trouble. We're just like *that!*"

"Y'know, I'm getting mixed signals, Bobby Heenan. I get the distinct feeling André the Giant doesn't particularly care for you."

"No, you get—"

"Look!" says Okerlund as André enters. Heenan looks sheepish, then waves at his longtime associate.

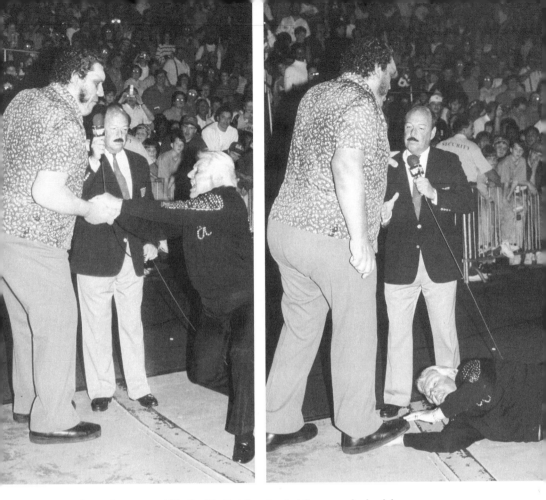

"Put 'er there, pal . . . *aaaaaaah!*" Bobby "The Brain" receives André's message loud and clear.

"I'll be with you in a minute," he says, getting behind Mean Gene. "I'm doing an interview."

André signals that he'd like Heenan to come over and talk to him.

"You want him, right?" asks Okerlund, who then turns to Heenan. "He wants to talk to you."

"I'll show you," the Brain says. "I'll show you how tight we are."

Heenan, accompanied by Mean Gene, comes off the interview platform and approaches André. "You seem to be a little tentative, Bobby Heenan."

"No, no, no. André, how you doing? I want you to show all these hicks, all these hillbillies, h-h-how tight the Family is, how every-thing's okay. Hunky-dory."

He extends his hand to André, but the Giant just stares at him.

"Put 'er there, pal," Heenan says. André finally reaches out and shakes the Brain's hand. "There you go . . . *aaaaaaah*!"

André squeezes his manager's hand with all his substantial might, dropping Heenan to his knees in pain.

"Bobby Heenan, that's the way I am," says André. "I like to laugh at people I don't like. And it look like I don't like you anymore! It look like I'm sick and tired of you and your Family and I hope you get that message! I hope you get that message clear and loud!"

He lets go of the writhing Heenan, then plants his foot down on the Brain's hand.

"Thank you, André," says Mean Gene as Heenan howls in agony. "I'm glad you cleared the air on that."

André shakes Okerlund's hand, puts his arm around the interviewer's shoulder, and the two walk off, leaving Heenan on the floor, tending to his crushed mitt.

With Heenan out of the picture, the World Wrestling Federation's many colorful and conniving managers came out to woo the Giant. Over a series of vignettes, André listened to pitches from such advisers as Mr. Fuji, Slick, and "Sensational" Sherri Martel. At the end of each segment, André rejected the petitioner with manhandling and some thunderous laughter.

March 26, 1991: Thomas & Mack Center, Las Vegas, NV

"Once again, André the Giant is front-page news in World Wrestling Federation," reports Mean Gene. "Recently our cameras were on hand when Sensational Sherri met with the seven-foot-four-inch, 520-pound giant. This should be interesting. . . ."

Cut to: André and Arnold Skaaland holding up a bar, chatting over a couple of beers. "Ahhhh! André the Giant! André the Giant!" shrieks Sherri, in full makeup. She shoves Skaaland out of the way. "I'm so glad to see you! My God, you're bigger than I thought you'd be. What a man! Oh, God, I can't believe it! André, I want to be your manager."

The Giant looks at the camera, incredulous. With a purple-gloved hand, Sherri turns him back to face her. "No, no, please. Anything. Anything. I promise. Anything."

André leers lasciviously, an eyebrow raised. "Anything?" he says, his eyes wide, a lusty grin spreading across his face.

"Anything, André. Anything."

"Anything I want," he says, wrapping his arms around her. He pulls one arm behind her back, and bends her over the bar. "Ahhhhhh!"

He spits on his hand and begins spanking her bottom, to the applause and cheers of the middle-aged businessmen congregating at the bar.

"You big lunk," Sherri says, fuming as she walks out.

"Anything I want," he yells at her, toasting with a laughing Skaaland.

Cut to: Okerlund, a bemused finger on his lips. "My. Sensational Sherri, being told no for the second time in 1991, this time by André the Giant. With *Update*, I'm Gene Okerlund."

April 24, 1991: Docklands Arena, London, UK

UK RAMPAGE '91: THE ROCKERS VS. THE ORIENT EXPRESS

The Rockers, Shawn Michaels & Marty Janetty, bring out André before their match with Mr. Fuji's insidious Orient Express in order to counter Fuji's managerial interference. Later, Mean Gene interviews André, who keeps a hand on Okerlund's shoulder for support.

"I was just visiting my parents in France," says André, "so I come over. And I'm glad I come over, since the Rockers, they want me, if they want, and Fuji, if you want too, you get me for the rest of the tour. I will be all over, I'll be in the ring, and I'll be watching for you. Believe me, Fuji."

"I'm certain the Rockers are very, very appreciative of the fact, André the Giant, that you were here tonight to help them out. And of course, I know it is a homecoming of sorts for you, and this tour of World Wrestling Federation is going to be covering part of Western Europe."

"Thank you. I'm very glad to be back here, see all my friends again."

When André declined the advances of Jimmy Hart—manager of such champions as Honky Tonk Man, the Hart Foundation, and the Nasty Boys—the "Mouth of the South" was not pleased, to say the least. Hart sicced the four-hundred-pound Earthquake on the Giant in what was meant to be the beginning of a new feud.

May 6, 1991: Metro Center, Rockford, IL

"MEAN" GENE OKERLUND INTERVIEWS JIMMY HART (W/EARTHQUAKE)

"Now then, Jimmy Hart," says Mean Gene in the ring, "you got me here to witness this big announcement that you're gonna make. You said it's of such magnitude that it's gonna shock the world and World Wrestling Federation. Jimmy Hart, what is that announcement?"

"Well, first of all, Mean Gene, by now the world knows that the World Wrestling Federation Tag Team Champions is Jimmy Hart's Nasty Boys. And I wanna make sure that the Nasty Boys will stay the World Wrestling Federation Tag Team Champions forever! If anybody wants another shot at the World Wrestling Federation Tag Team Championship belts that the Nasty Boys hold, they're gonna have to go through this next team that I have assembled. So joining forces with the Earthquake—"

"Wait a minute. Who's gonna join forces with Earthquake?"

"I'm gonna tell you who's gonna join forces with the Earthquake. It's going to be none other than—are you ready, Mean Gene?—none other than André the Giant!"

"Wait a minute, Jimmy Hart. You have gotta be kidding me. I don't believe that for a minute. I don't think you signed a contract with André the Giant. As a matter of fact, I know he is in the arena this week. I am going to ask him to come out. I wanna hear it from the man himself. Please welcome the Eighth Wonder of the World, André the Giant!"

André comes out and is greeted in the aisle by an ecstatic Hart. He puts his arm around the manager, but in all likelihood, it is to keep his balance as he walks to the ring. In the ring, André stares down and sizes up his putative partner. Earthquake grimaces as they shake hands.

"I find this all so very hard to believe," says Okerlund. "Is it true that you signed a contract with the Mouth of the South, Jimmy Hart?"

"Look at that smile on his face," says Hart. "Whattaya mean, is it true? Look at that smile, baby!"

"André, I wanna hear it from you. Have you signed a contract with this man, Jimmy Hart?"

"The deal is done, Mean Gene! Look at him! Look at the smile! The deal is done, baby!"

"Just a second, Jimmy Hart. Get the springs outta your shoes! André, you have flat turned down a number of other managers in World Wrestling Federation. First of all, you took Slick, the Doctor of Style, and stuffed him in the truck of his very own limousine. And that was nothing—Mr. Fuji was wining and dining you at one of the great restaurants in the world, and you took Mr. Fuji and you shoved his face in the plate of food. And ya know, Sensational Queen Sherri had you in a hotel, she tried to proposition . . . wait a minute, I beg your pardon. She tried to *entice* you, and she ended up getting a spanking. And Bobby Heenan, Bobby Heenan wouldn't get within ten miles of you, André. Keeping that in mind, again I ask you, yes or no? Have you signed a contract with this man? André, yes?"

"No!"

"Jimmy Hart, he said no!"

Hart is obviously upset as André grins. "You don't humiliate me in front of millions of people! Who do you think you are? You made a deal with me! You made a deal with me, man!"

"I never sign anything from you," André explains as Earthquake sets up behind him.

"Whattaya mean you didn't sign it? You are a liar, man! You signed up with me!"

André grabs Hart's wrist and throws down his megaphone. "Don't call me a liar, okay? Don't ever call me a liar!"

All of a sudden, Earthquake drives his shoulder and the mega-phone into André's left knee, sending him down to the canvas. Earthquake takes the Giant's ankle, drags him into the center of the ring, and drops an elbow into the injured knee. André grabs Earthquake's hair as he twists the Giant's leg. Earthquake gets up and drops another elbow, resuming his hold upon landing. He rises and splashes down onto the knee as André bellows in pain.

"I've never seen the Giant felled like this before," says Vince McMahon.

"I think we're seein' an end to a great career," adds guest commentator Randy Savage. "I have to say, it was a great career."

Earthquake splashes onto André's knee again as the officials try to clear the ring. Earthquake splashes down once more, and then leaves with Hart. André uses the ropes to get to his feet, but goes down just as he gets to his full height. He rolls outside and falls against the steel barricade.

"I don't think he wants anybody to help him up," says Vince. "André, unquestionably as proud as he is large."

André uses the railing to support himself up the aisle.

"You're talking about intestinal fortitude," says Vince. "You're talking about guts. *Giant-sized guts!*"

May 29, 1991: ASU Activity Center, Tempe, AZ

THE BARBER SHOP W/ANDRÉ

Brutus "the Barber" Beefcake—wearing pink and yellow pastel—introduces his guest on *The Barber Shop*. "This week I've got a man, he's the Eighth Wonder of the World. He's André the Giant."

André limps out, supported by a cane, selling Earthquake's assault. Brutus helps the Giant up to the *Barber Shop* stage.

"Y'know, André, it's really a wonder to me that you're standing here right now after what happened to you. We all saw that Jimmy Hart was trying to recruit you, and we all watched as you stood there and you gave the world your answer—No!"

André, holding Beefcake's shoulder, nods in agreement.

"And we also watched as the dastardly deeds were done, as the

Earthquake jumped you from behind and proceeded to try to destroy your knee, to take it on upon himself to totally take you out and end your career once and for all, André."

"It's not once and for all," says the Giant, shaking his huge head.

"Well, we all know that your knee is gonna require a lot of reconstructive surgery, that you're facing a lot of rehabilitation, and y'know, I know all about what it takes to go through a lot of rehabilitation. But what all these people, and what I want to know, was what does the future hold for André the Giant?"

"Well, what it is, the doctor say that you supposed to put a new knees in there," he says, grinning. "But he said I'm too young for it, ho ho. And I really appreciate that. So now I ask him what he can do, and he told me, he said only I could rebuild your knee and you'll be better than ever."

The crowd roars its approval, and André continues. "I don't care about Earthquake, I just care about my knee. And believe me, I'm going to let that doctor to rebuild that knee, and then Earthquake, you start something I have to finish. That may be the last thing I have to do, we never know, but Earthquake, you start some trouble that can be, in the end of that, your worst nightmare you ever had. I promise you that!"

"Y'know, Earthquake, you call yourself 'the Natural Disaster,' but when you come face-to-face with an angry André the Giant, it can only spell disaster for you!"

André drapes his arm over Beefcake's shoulder, who assists him down the platform stairs.

After two months off for "rehab" on his knee, André returned for *Summer-Slam*, where he teamed with the Bushwhackers, Butch & Luke, against Jimmy Hart's Natural Disasters, Earthquake & Typhoon.

SUMMERSLAM

"Mean" Gene Okerlund interviews the Bushwhackers and, on crutches, André.

"André," begins Okerlund as Butch and Luke do their trademark stomp, "I recall a few months back, during an interview I was conducting with you, Jimmy Hart had led us to believe that he was gonna be your manager. But here's what took place at the conclusion of that interview."

Cut to clip of Earthquake coming up behind André and taking his knee out from under him.

"Well, André the Giant—"

"Cousin Luke, are you ready?"

"Boy, am I ready!"

"Oh boy, in a few minutes we're gonna crush that Earthquake and wipe that Typhoon all over the ring!"

"That's right, Cousin Butch. We're gonna lick those Natural Disasters all over the place!"

"And when we're finished lickin' 'em, and when we're finished eatin' 'em, oh boy, we're gonna feed 'em to *you*, André!"

The Giant raises his crutch. "And that will be my chance to get even!"

André accompanies the Bushwhackers to the ring, slowly following them up the aisle using forearm crutches. Despite his pain, he grins broadly as Butch and Luke march toward the ring.

As the 'Whackers do their bit in the ring, Earthquake and Typhoon go outside to confront André. "Let's get him outta here right now," says Earthquake, but the Disasters are surprised from behind by Butch and Luke, who poke them in the eyes and scoot into the ring as the bell sounds. The Disasters follow, but the Bushwhackers go back out to pose with André, who laughingly raises his crutch. They muss with his hair and place one of their hats on his giant head.

André's involvement in the match is minimal. He cheers the 'Whackers on, hoisting his crutch up to keep the crowd's attention. At one point, Earthquake is knocked out of the ring and comes face-to-face with the Giant, who pointedly aims a crutch in his face, sending him scurrying backward. Luke comes out to assist, but Earthquake catches him and hits a backbreaker. André, holding himself up on his crutches, can only watch. Earthquake goes back into the rings, tags in, and finishes Butch off with his Earthquake Splash seated senton for the three-count at 6:27.

Jimmy Hart and the Disasters celebrate. André prepares for battle by getting his crutch ready to use as a club. The Disasters come out and stalk the Giant, who swings the crutch over his head while using the other to hold himself upright. Before the Disasters can make their move, the Legion of Doom come down the aisle and position themselves in front of André. Unsurprisingly, the Disasters back away and roll into the ring. L.O.D. follows, and of course, Earthquake and Typhoon slip back out. André whacks them with a cane as they scurry to the dressing room.

Though André officially "retired" after *SummerSlam,* he continued to work regularly for Giant Baba's All Japan Pro Wrestling. Mostly tagging with Giant Baba, his actual time wrestling was very short. New Japan's Seiji Sakaguchi—a former North American Heavyweight Champion—suggested Baba bring André over to work with Baba in a guaranteed crowd-pleasing match on the All Japan tours. André toured with All Japan three times per year, from September 1990 to 1992. Though the shows were already huge draws, Baba paid André an exorbitant $15,000 per week, a huge sum for essentially a mid-card attraction. But by 1992, André's condition had declined to the point where he was unable to team with Baba in All Japan's annual Tag Team tournament.

JOHNNY ACE (JOHN LAURINAITIS): "People loved him like a god over in Japan. Near the end he and Baba were tagging up, and they loved that. It was an attraction. Baba was not in good shape either, but the sight of the two of them in the ring and the history about what they both brought to the business—André from the American side and Baba from the Japanese side—you put those together, and it

didn't matter. The fans had such an appreciation and respect for what they did in the business, it wasn't about what they actually could do in the ring today.

"Stan Hansen and I wrestled against André and Baba a few times, which were fun matches to be in. Baba and Stan started, Stan tagged me in, and I went right over and chopped André—bam! He looked at me and laughed, 'Ho, ho, ho, ho.' Baba tagged André in, and he just beat the shit out of me."

On September 2, 1992, André made his final television appearance at WCW's *Clash of the Champions XX* at Atlanta's Center Stage Theater. The show—which commemorated twenty years of wrestling on Ted Turner's TBS—opened on the red carpet with hosts Tony Schiavone and Missy Hyatt introducing Gordon Solie and André. André, holding himself up with two canes, was greeted by Schiavone: "André, it's great to have you with us."

"Thank you," replied the Giant. "I'm very happy to be back here to see all my TBS old wrestling stars."

However brief, André's appearance on the World Wrestling Federation's most hated rival struck like a dagger into the McMahon family's heart.

SHANE McMAHON: "When André showed up on Ted Turner's broadcast, it was just such a shock. At that time we were pretty much at war, and my dad specifically was extremely hurt. I don't know why André did it. Maybe he was unhappy being out of the limelight and it was just a nice little thing to be back among the boys. I definitely think he was coaxed into it.

"I remember my dad called André and said, 'Boss, I've just gotta say that you really hurt my feelings. After everything, to see you with a competitor really hurt.' I think André apologized. I don't think he fully realized what he'd done. At that point his health was definitely deteriorating. I think he was upset at the fact that he couldn't do what he used to do. He was on crutches, and that was another thing that upset my dad—why would he ever show that to anybody?"

VINCE McMAHON: "In the later days, André drank even more and internalized even more. He wasn't on the road anymore, so he felt like he had no value. I think that really got to him. André had an ego, and a good one. When it looked like he no longer had any value, I think that weighed on him more than anything else."

TIM WHITE: "I was still on the road, so we'd keep in touch every few days or whatever. That last time I saw him, I happened to be out on the road, and the ranch was a

little bit out of the way but I still wanted to stop and see him. When I pulled away from the ranch I was crying like a baby 'cause he looked so bad. He could barely hide his pain. He's stuck on this property with Frenchy, and it's just not a good situation."

His worsening condition didn't keep André from appearing regularly in Japan, where his iconic status far outweighed his now-limited abilities. He toured through December, culminating in a Six Man Tag at Tokyo's Budokan Hall with Giant Baba and Rusher Kimura vs. Haruka Eigen, Masa Fuchi, & Motoshi Okuma.

André returned home for Christmas, with a stop in Mexico for a Six Man Tag match with El Canek & Dos Caras vs. Bam Bam Bigelow, Yokozuna, & Bad News Brown. The match has become something of a legend, though not for its stellar wrestling.

It seems André was tormented that day by a case of Montezuma's revenge. But a little stomachache wasn't enough to keep the Giant out of the ring. About midway through the match, he tossed Brown into the corner, then dropped his always-crowd-pleasing big ass bump.

VINCE McMAHON: "André is sitting on Bad News's chest, holding his arms down. Unfortunately, that's when André's bowels let go, and here's Bad News, he can't move because he's got this five-hundred-pound guy on him, and here comes this river of *ca-ca*. He can smell it, it's coming down all over his chest and wrapping all the way around his neck. He's lying in this pool of *ca-ca*, and there was not a damn thing to do about it. And André's just laughing, 'Ho ho ho.'"

The New Year began with sad news for André—his father was unwell and not likely to last much longer. André flew to France immediately, and on January 15, Boris Rousimoff passed away.

André spent the weeks after his father's death commuting between a Paris hotel and his native Molien, where he spent his days playing cards with his old friends. On January 27, 1993, André returned to his hotel for the night. When no one answered the phone the next morning, André's chauffeur had the hotel staff open the door and found the Giant dead. He had died peacefully, in his sleep, at the age of forty-six. No autopsy was performed, but his death was attributed to congestive heart failure from a buildup of fluid in the body, deriving from his untreated acromegaly.

The death of André the Giant received major news coverage around the world, with Canadian Wire Services reporting that there was huge demand for the story, especially in Europe. The story was page one in Montreal, with CNN and ESPN both devoting portions of their sportscasts for an obituary.

HOWARD FINKEL: "I'll never forget, Vince came over to our department and says, 'I want you guys to know that André passed away.' My heart just dropped. We knew he was ill. Everybody knew it was inevitable. But there will never be another one like him."

TIM WHITE: "I got a call from Frenchy Bernard, in the middle of the night. André's father had passed away, and he wanted Frenchy to let me know that he had already left for Paris to go and bury his father. I'm thinking how hard it was going to be for him to make the trip, because of the way I saw him physically.

"Two, three days later, the phone rings again, and it's Frenchy. I'm thinking, 'What, does André need a ride or something?' He told me André passed away last night and I just was stunned. Stunned. I was devastated. I went numb. I went to my bar, the Friendly Tap, the place was closed, and had a few beers, just staring into space."

All Japan Pro Wrestling paid tribute to André at their January 31 show at Tokyo's Korakuen Hall. The following evening, World Wrestling Federation honored the Giant with a ten-bell salute on its new *Monday Night Raw* show.

"Ladies and gentlemen," announced Howard Finkel over a rambunctious Manhattan Center crowd, "as many of you know, one of the legends, last week, passed away. And I'm referring to André the Giant. André, throughout his World Wrestling Federation career, provided many an exciting moment for both young and old alike, and his unique presence will surely be missed. Ladies and gentlemen, I would like to ask you all to rise in tribute to a man who truly was one of a kind, André the Giant."

Due to André's size, no crematorium in France could accommodate his final wishes to be cremated within forty-eight hours of his death. Instead, he lay in state for nearly a week while a custom coffin was built. Legend has it that the airline flying him home to North Carolina had to adjust its schedule and cargo to be under the weight limit with André's body on board. After cremation, André's ashes were spread over his two-hundred-acre ranch in Ellerbee, North Carolina.

A small memorial was held, attended by a few of André's closest friends. Among the speakers eulogizing André were Darrol Dickenson, who had sold the ranch its longhorn cattle; Dr. P. R. Rankin Jr. of Ellerbee's Rankin Museum of American and Natural History; Terry Todd, who had bonded with André when writing his seminal *Sports Illustrated* feature; and Hulk Hogan.

"A Traveler Coming Home," by the poet Karen Ravn, was printed for the service. The poem stands as a perfect and touching memorial to André the Giant's restless spirit and love of new experiences:

> *He journeyed on from place to place*
> *And gained some value from each one.*

In 1993, World Wrestling Federation created its Hall of Fame, largely to honor André, its first inductee, a towering figure in the wrestling industry for more than two decades. André's Hall of Fame induction honored his astonishing accomplishments and irreplaceable talent.

Today André's visage remains an ever-present aspect of any city, thanks to the work of artist Shepard Fairey. Described by its creator as "an experiment in phenomenology," the "André the Giant Has a Posse" campaign saw Fairey and his cohorts covering streets across America with stickers and posters featuring André's face and the text "ANDRÉ THE GIANT HAS A POSSE 7'4", 520 lbs."

Soon tens of thousands of photocopied and hand-screened stickers adorned with André's mug could be found throughout the world, from Philadelphia and New York City to Atlanta and Austin, as well as such far-flung locales as Greece, London, Mexico, Japan, Florida, and the Caribbean Islands. In 1993, Fairey began using a different image of the wrestler's face, usually with the branding "OBEY GIANT." The guerilla art campaign continues to this day. André's image can be seen peering from phone booths and bus stops, a constant reminder of his lasting impact on the popular consciousness.

In the years since his passing, a number of seven-footers have become featured wrestling attractions, but none has captured the popular imagination quite like André. In the heat of the wrestling wars of the 1990s, Ted Turner's WCW introduced a gigantic new wrestler. Paul Wight—better known today as Big Show—made his debut at the *Bash at the Beach 1995,* interfering in Hulk Hogan's Cage match against Vader. Billed as "The Giant," he claimed to be André's son, come to revenge his "father." Though Big Show has gone on to have a successful career in World Wrestling Entertainment, he'd be among the first to admit that André was unique.

VINCE McMAHON: "André was a very special guy. I don't think you're going to ever find another André again. We had another legitimate giant in Big Show. He also had the same disease, although they caught it earlier. He never knew André. When he debuted in WCW, Hogan introduced him as André's illegitimate son, which of course was bullshit."

STEPHANIE McMAHON: "No one compares to André. It's not only his abilities. There are other giants who can do more than André could do in the ring. But André understood psychology better than any other giants that I have worked with. And that's no disrespect to them, they offer other things. André knew how to be a giant. I think sometimes other giants work so hard not to be giants that they lose sight of the basic psychology. They all have different things to offer. But there's only one André, in terms of his in-ring ability and in terms of his personality. He had an aura."

People everywhere loved André for his gentle manner and formidable ring persona. His contributions helped increase professional wrestling's public profile, leading to its development into a billion-dollar entertainment industry.

When *Pro Wrestling Illustrated* compiled a list of the "Top 500 Singles Wrestlers" of all time, André placed third, behind Hulk Hogan and Ric Flair. This acknowledgment of his extraordinary talents in the ring, his understanding of how the subtlest move could make a crowd pop, would likely have pleased André, for whom wrestling was the highest form of storytelling imaginable.

TED DIBIASE: "André was a sharp guy. He really understood who he was as a character and what it took to make that character work. He was just incredible. Sometimes these muscleheads would come through and go, 'I can't sell for that guy.' I'd say, 'If André the Giant can sell and make people believe it, you can too.' Selling is everything, y'know."

TIM WHITE: "The guy was brilliant. He'd come up with finishers for guys that ended up having careers off those finishes. He was so good at it. How can a guy, seven-foot-four, 520 pounds, make a kid in the top row cry because they think he's getting hurt? How good is that? Is there anyone who can do that now?"

SHANE McMAHON: "His presence was part of why he was a great performer. If you were in the crowd, and he was pissed off, you would've said, 'Holy shit, I'm glad I'm not facing that guy.' And when he smiled, you were like, 'Oh wow, what a gentle giant.' But you always knew that at any second he could take care of business."

VINCE McMAHON: "It was just so much fun working with André. He was such a wonderful man in so many respects. It made you smile to be around him. You knew André was special, and it was a privilege even to be in his presence. It really was a privilege to know somebody like that and for them to trust you as much as they did and to enjoy good times with you."

André the Giant:
May 19, 1946–January 27, 1993.

ACKNOWLEDGMENTS

My endless love and thanks to superagent Dave Dunton at Harvey Klinger Inc., without whom none of this would have been possible. Equal amounts of affection and appreciation must go to my longtime friends and supporters at Pocket Books, the amazingly patient Margaret Clark and Anthony Ziccardi.

As ever, none of this would be possible without the remarkable efforts of Abby Royle, whose hard work and attention to detail prove invaluable every time.

In the "I Couldn't Have Done It Without You" department, thanks must go to my friends and family, all of whom stood by me when the Giant's shadow loomed large and dark: The Krugmans—David, Cynthia, and Michele; the Fitz-Gordons—Jonathan, Caitlyn, Ida, and Reggie; Ken Weinstein; Mike Flaherty; Jason Cohen; Nevin Martell; Andrew Korus; Nikki Van De Car, the Copes—Dorian, Julian, Albany, and Avalon; the Lyles—Keith, Rosh, and Gavin; Robyn Hitchcock; Bob Kaus and Jules Dominguez; Nick Stern; Tracy Zamot; Barbara Mitchell, "El Toro" Kurt B. Reighley, and Steven Trachtenbroit; Sheila Richman and everyone at Atlantic Records; Katie-Jane Bailey; and those swinging cats known as Right on Dynamite—Daniel Murphy, Nicholas Cirillo, Jon Molina.

A special shout-out to two guys whose passion for wrestling inspired me throughout the process: Spencer McGarry and Tony Basile.

Thanks to Fran Antigone, for her creative imagery and support when I needed it most.

Of course, my appreciation to everyone at WWE, especially Vince McMahon, Stephanie McMahon, Shane McMahon, Howard Finkel, and the very gracious and giving Tim White. Also, thanks to those who found the time to share a bit of André's legend with me: Ted DiBiase, George Grey, Stan Hansen, Bobby Heenan, Betty Skaaland, Jack Brisco, Kenneth Johnson, and John Laurinaitis.

Major kudos must go to all those wise, wonderful wrestling experts out there on the Internet, with major gratitude to Graham Cawthon and his invaluable www.thehistoryofwwe.com.

Last, but very definitely not least, big, big love and gratitude to Carrie Hamilton, who retains the World Heavyweight Championship belt of my heart. Her patience, advice, affection, encouragement, and support make it all worthwhile. Hi, Honey!